Internships For Dummies®

BESTSELLING BOOK SERIES

B-60

D1503694

Internship Goals Checklist

Here's a checklist to help you understand and plan for what you want and need from your internship experience.

Stage of career and career goals

Pre-career:

❑ I am at the beginning of my career and need to break into the job market.

❑ I am pre-career and have the option for a regular job with strong learning potential.

❑ I am pre-career but don't have the option of a regular job with strong learning potential.

❑ There are some fields/jobs I would like to try before I get established in a career.

❑ This internship I am considering would likely provide an adequate try-out for the field or fields I am interested in.

❑ This internship would likely provide adequate experience, skills, and contacts to help me launch my career.

In-career:

❑ I already have significant job experience.

❑ To perform better in my present field, I need skills and experience I cannot get from my job.

❑ Classroom education alone would adequately equip me for my present field.

❑ It is likely I will need additional practical experience beyond my present job in order to perform better in my present field.

❑ I really would like to change fields or to try out a different field.

❑ My present employment gives me the option of trying different fields.

❑ To try a different ... ... to consider some form of intern...

❑ To qualify for a different field or career, I will need practical experience.

❑ This internship I am considering would likely provide an adequate try-out for the field or fields to which I may want to switch.

❑ This internship would likely provide adequate experience, skills, and contacts to help make a transition toward a different field or career.

Educational needs

❑ I know enough already to get a good job in the field of my choice.

❑ My classroom education is adequate to get me a job, but I lack practical experience.

❑ I need to augment my classroom learning with practical skills and knowledge.

❑ I need practical skills to make me more valuable and more marketable.

❑ This internship I am considering is likely to equip me with the practical skills I need.

❑ I need a general introduction and socialization into a field new to me.

❑ This internship I am considering is likely to provide adequate socialization into this new field.

❑ I need some form of internship for academic credit to graduate.

❑ No internship is required for graduation, but I can use one for academic credit toward graduation.

❑ Some form of internship is required for licensure or certification in the field or job I am considering.

Internships For Dummies®

Compensation needs

- ❑ I need a certain amount of money (salary, stipend, or whatever) from an internship.
- ❑ I need an internship to cover health, disability, and other benefits.
- ❑ I need my travel, education, or other expenses covered by an internship.
- ❑ It is necessary or highly desirable for an internship to cover all or part of my tuition expenses.
- ❑ A wage or stipend for an internship might affect my student financial aid package.

Geographic flexibility

- ❑ Legitimate factors limit me to considering local internships.
- ❑ Legitimate factors limit me to considering internships within my region.
- ❑ Legitimate factors limit me to considering national internships.
- ❑ I am able to consider international internships.
- ❑ For the field or career I am interested in, some cities or regions are considered centers or proving grounds.
- ❑ I have legitimate reasons for taking an internship far away and at greater expense.

Personal situation

- ❑ Conditions exist in my personal life that need resolving before I can take an internship.
- ❑ I need to consider my personal situation (family, health, and so on) before accepting an internship.

Personal values

- ❑ I have deeply reflected on what values are most important to me.
- ❑ I have discussed my sense of values with other people I respect to clarify and confirm my sense of values.
- ❑ The internship I am considering is likely to challenge and refine my sense of values (healthy).
- ❑ The internship I am considering is likely to violate my sense of values (unhealthy).

Hungry Minds™

For Dummies: Bestselling Book Series for Beginners

Praise for Internships For Dummies

"I am impressed with how comprehensive and helpful this book is. I learned a lot about how to work with interns and advisors as well as how to structure our internships to be more profitable for everyone."

— Mary Hamilton, Executive Director, American Society for Public Administration

Internships For Dummies lays out a beautiful framework for successful interning. Readers will find strategies and tips and the opportunity to learn from the experience of others. Internship supervisors, internship advisers — even professionals who have interns as colleagues — will gain a greater understanding of how to ensure that an internship is a valuable learning experience."

— Michaelann Jundt, Carlson Leadership & Public Service Center

"With meticulous attention to detail, Craig Donovan and Jim Garnett have done a superb job of creating an inspiring guide for achieving a mutually beneficial relationship between an intern and an organization. This is a must read for all those who mistakenly believe that succeeding as an intern or manager of interns is an intuitive process. Don't just read Chapter 7 ("Making the Most of Your First Days") and Chapter 11 ("Political Savvy for Interns"), study them! *Internships For Dummies* is the kind of valuable, hands-on guide that would have really helped me get started as a Presidential Management Intern. In my nearly six years of Federal Government service in Washington, D.C., I've witnessed several disastrous intern experiences. Many of these intern casualties compromised the spirit of collegiality in their quest to develop a functional expertise in the organization. One of the central themes of *Internships For Dummies* is devising a roadmap on how to achieve this delicate balance between collegiality and expertise. Read this guide and you'll be three steps ahead of your peers who believe they are only a leather briefcase and firm handshake away from interning success."

— Steve Kucharski, Systems Modernization Project Manager, United States Small Business Administration

"A valuable resource for both students and advisers — great tone, excellent coverage of relevant materials, genuinely useful."

— Michael Brintnall, National Association of Schools of Public Affairs and Administration

"Internships For Dummies offer sound advice. I have been in the internship business for 25 years, ranging from being an intern, to directing two different programs, to teaching internship seminars, and I find this book's insights very impressive and useful. Everything the authors write is practical and should be helpful to anyone involved with internships. They cover all the bases."

— Ken Oldfield, University of Illinois at Springfield

"As an international student, I have to say this book was a lot of help because in other countries, there is very little information about internship programs. *Internships For Dummies* is a must for anyone interested in doing an internship program."

— Josep Bañón Kelley, Madrid, Spain

 TM

References for the Rest of Us!™

BESTSELLING BOOK SERIES

Do you find that traditional reference books are overloaded with technical details and advice you'll never use? Do you postpone important life decisions because you just don't want to deal with them? Then our *For Dummies*® business and general reference book series is for you.

For Dummies business and general reference books are written for those frustrated and hard-working souls who know they aren't dumb, but find that the myriad of personal and business issues and the accompanying horror stories make them feel helpless. *For Dummies* books use a lighthearted approach, a down-to-earth style, and even cartoons and humorous icons to dispel fears and build confidence. Lighthearted but not lightweight, these books are perfect survival guides to solve your everyday personal and business problems.

"More than a publishing phenomenon, 'Dummies' is a sign of the times."

— The New York Times

"A world of detailed and authoritative information is packed into them..."

— U.S. News and World Report

"...you won't go wrong buying them."

— Walter Mossberg, Wall Street Journal, on For Dummies books

Already, millions of satisfied readers agree. They have made For Dummies the #1 introductory level computer book series and a best-selling business book series. They have written asking for more. So, if you're looking for the best and easiest way to learn about business and other general reference topics, look to For Dummies to give you a helping hand.

Hungry Minds™

6/01

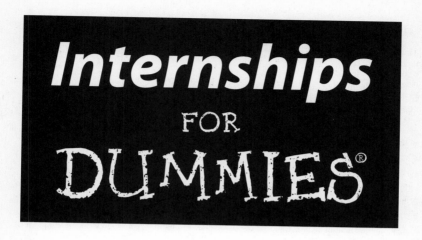

Internships FOR DUMMIES®

by Craig P. Donovan and Jim Garnett

Foreword by Marshall Loeb

Hungry Minds™

Best-Selling Books • Digital Downloads • e-Books • Answer Networks • e-Newsletters • Branded Web Sites • e-Learning

New York, NY ◆ Cleveland, OH ◆ Indianapolis, IN

Internships For Dummies®

Published by:
Hungry Minds, Inc.
909 Third Avenue
New York, NY 10022
www.hungryminds.com
www.dummies.com

Library of Congress Control Number: 2001091997

ISBN: 0-7645-5367-4

Printed in the United States of America

10 9 8 7 6 5 4 3 2 1

1B/RQ/QY/QR/IN

Distributed in the United States by Hungry Minds, Inc.

Distributed by CDG Books Canada Inc. for Canada; by Transworld Publishers Limited in the United Kingdom; by IDG Norge Books for Norway; by IDG Sweden Books for Sweden; by IDG Books Australia Publishing Corporation Pty. Ltd. for Australia and New Zealand; by TransQuest Publishers Pte Ltd. for Singapore, Malaysia, Thailand, Indonesia, and Hong Kong; by Gotop Information Inc. for Taiwan; by ICG Muse, Inc. for Japan; by Intersoft for South Africa; by Eyrolles for France; by International Thomson Publishing for Germany, Austria and Switzerland; by Distribuidora Cuspide for Argentina; by LR International for Brazil; by Galileo Libros for Chile; by Ediciones ZETA S.C.R. Ltda. for Peru; by WS Computer Publishing Corporation, Inc., for the Philippines; by Contemporanea de Ediciones for Venezuela; by Express Computer Distributors for the Caribbean and West Indies; by Micronesia Media Distributor, Inc. for Micronesia; by Chips Computadoras S.A. de C.V. for Mexico; by Editorial Norma de Panama S.A. for Panama; by American Bookshops for Finland.

For general information on Hungry Minds' products and services please contact our Customer Care department; within the U.S. at 800-762-2974, outside the U.S. at 317-572-3993 or fax 317-572-4002.

For sales inquiries and resellers information, including discounts, premium and bulk quantity sales and foreign language translations please contact our Customer Care department at 800-434-3422, fax 317-572-4002 or write to Hungry Minds, Inc., Attn: Customer Care department, 10475 Crosspoint Boulevard, Indianapolis, IN 46256.

For information on licensing foreign or domestic rights, please contact our Sub-Rights Customer Care department at 212-884-5000.

For information on using Hungry Minds' products and services in the classroom or for ordering examination copies, please contact our Educational Sales department at 800-434-2086 or fax 317-572-4005.

Please contact our Public Relations department at 212-884-5163 for press review copies or 212-884-5000 for author interviews and other publicity information or fax 212-884-5400.

For authorization to photocopy items for corporate, personal, or educational use, please contact Copyright Clearance Center, 222 Rosewood Drive, Danvers, MA 01923, or fax 978-750-4470.

Library of Congress Cataloging-in-Publication Data

Hungry Minds is a trademark of Hungry Minds, Inc.

About the Authors

Dr. Craig Donovan is a Professor and faculty member at Kean University in the School of Business, Government, and Technology where he directs the BA/MPA Honors Program. For the past twenty years, Dr. Donovan has served as a college professor, an officer for state and county government, a business owner and corporate consultant, and an advisor and consultant on public productivity, urban/economic development, and management and leadership in California, Oregon, Washington, the District of Columbia, and New Jersey. Dr. Donovan is a noted author and researcher and serves as the Deputy Director for Research and Policy for the Public Policy Center of New Jersey.

Prior to coming to New Jersey in 1994, Dr. Donovan was at the University of Washington where he earned his dual doctorate in both Public Affairs and Business Administration He earned an M.A. degree from San Francisco State University along with a graduate certificate in College Administration and Teaching, and his Baccalaureate degrees were earned at the University of California at Irvine. Dr. Donovan can be reached by phone at 732-901-1200 or by e-mail at cpdonova@kean.edu.

Dr. Jim Garnett is a Professor of Public Policy and Administration at Rutgers University's campus at Camden where he teaches courses in leadership, management, and communication to students of public administration, business administration, health management, law, and social work. Dr. Garnett has also been Intern Coordinator for Public Administration students at Rutgers-Camden. He has also taught at The American University, West Virginia College of Graduate Studies, and Syracuse University and overseas in Germany, Spain, and Australia. In his 24 years of teaching, Jim has drawn upon his experience in government and consulting.

Dr. Garnett has served as consultant in New York, New Jersey, South Carolina, Virginia, West Virginia, Florida, the District of Columbia, Germany, Spain, and Australia. In his consulting, Dr. Garnett has helped businesses, hospitals, and national, state, and local government organizations improve their internal and external communication, reorganize themselves, or strengthen their leadership and management. He has written several other books on communication, management, and reorganization and holds a B.A. in Government from Carleton College (1967) and a Master of Public Administration (1971) and Ph.D. in Public Administration (1978) from the Maxwell School, Syracuse University. Dr. Garnett can be reached by e-mail at garnett@camden.rutgers.edu or by phone at 856-854-8028.

Both Drs. Donovan and Garnett have extensive backgrounds and experience in working with interns, faculty advisors, and employer supervisors. They have helped establish and strengthen academic programs for both academic and employer organizations around the country and the world.

Dedication

This book is dedicated to Hugh Pearce and to Cy Ulberg, who never failed to inspire and prove that nice guys finish first, and to interns past, present, and future. You are the hope for our world.

Authors' Acknowledgments

Many people contributed to making this book a reality, not least of which were the numerous interns, advisors, and supervisors who shared their ideas and experiences with us. We are especially grateful for sound advice from Cole Brash, Jennifer Brinkerhoff, Michael Brintnall, Mary Hamilton, Marc Holzer, Harriet Katz, Joseph McMaster, Ken Oldfield, and Ann Phelps. Erin Garnett and Shelli Koffman helped spot errors and add a student perspective to the editorial process. Thanks to Lacey Clark, Catherine Dean, Elyssa Folk, Anthony Franze, Erin Garnett, Stacy Hill, and Janine Tobias whose true stories add richness to our book and inspiration for interns everywhere. Jim Schmincke helped keep our e-mail flowing and our project on track.

At Hungry Minds, it was Karen Hansen Doran who saw the promise in our project in the beginning and Tim Gallan who conscientiously and competently saw it through to the end. It has been a pleasure working with them and their able colleagues at Hungry Minds

On the personal side, we would each like to heartfelt a word of thanks to our families, friends, and colleagues. From Craig: "My thanks to Debi, Colin, Megan, Josh, Laetitia, Shy, Popcorn, Caesar, and Suzette who tolerated my moods and encouraged and supported my Sisyphus-like efforts. My gratitude to Gladys, Hugh, Edna, Maxine, Charlie, Irene, Cheri, and John who made my presence on this title possible. A tip of the hat to Jim Christian and Dick Axen who still inspire so many to accomplish so much. A final 'Fare thee well' to Justyna Sak who is interning now in a far, far better place. And special gratitude to Jim Garnett who made this partnership fun." From Jim: " My deepest thanks to Petra who put up with my preoccupations, Erin, my favorite "intern," and Sienna who was always there for me. Thanks also to Craig whose enthusiasm and energy are infectious."

We Want to Hear from You!

As we work to improve *Internships For Dummies* for future editions, we want to hear from you, whether you are an intern, advisor, supervisor, employer, educator. We want to hear your thoughts about our book and how we can make it more useful to you and to others like you. What did you find helpful? What wasn't so helpful? What do you think should be added?. Do you have true accounts, handbooks, manuals, reading lists, forms, and learning aids that we should see? We very much want to hear about your experiences in the ever-dynamic world of internships. Who knows, you may be listed in the Acknowledgments for the next edition. E-mail us at cpdonova@kean.edu or at garnett@camden.rutgers.edu. You can send regular mail to us at these addresses:

Craig P. Donovan
School of Business, Government, and Technology
Kean University
1000 Morris Avenue
Union, NJ 07083-7133

Jim Garnett
Department of Public Policy and Administration
Rutgers University at Camden
Camden, NJ 08102

Publisher's Acknowledgments

We're proud of this book; please send us your comments through our Online Registration Form located at www.hungryminds.com.

Some of the people who helped bring this book to market include the following:

Acquisitions, Editorial, and Media Development

Senior Project Editor: Tim Gallan

Senior Acquisitions Editor: Mark Butler

Copy Editors: Tina Sims, Tere Drenth

Technical Editor: Michealann Jundt

Editorial Manager: Pamela Mourouzis

Editorial Assistant: Carol Strickland

Cover Photo: © FPG / Michael Malyszko

Production

Project Coordinators: Maridee Ennis, Regina Synder

Layout and Graphics: Jackie Nicholas, Jacque Schneider, Julie Trippetti, Jeremey Unger

Proofreaders: John Greenough, Charles Spencer, TECHBOOKS Production Services

Indexer: TECHBOOKS Production Services

General and Administrative

Hungry Minds, Inc.: John Kilcullen, CEO; Bill Barry, President and COO; John Ball, Executive VP, Operations & Administration; John Harris, CFO

Hungry Minds Consumer Reference Group

Business: Kathleen Nebenhaus, Vice President and Publisher; Kevin Thornton, Acquisitions Manager

Cooking/Gardening: Jennifer Feldman, Associate Vice President and Publisher; Anne Ficklen, Executive Editor; Kristi Hart, Managing Editor

Education/Reference: Diane Graves Steele, Vice President and Publisher

Lifestyles: Kathleen Nebenhaus, Vice President and Publisher; Tracy Boggier, Managing Editor

Pets: Dominique De Vito, Associate Vice President and Publisher; Tracy Boggier, Managing Editor

Travel: Michael Spring, Vice President and Publisher; Brice Gosnell, Publishing Director; Suzanne Jannetta, Editorial Director

Hungry Minds Consumer Editorial Services: Kathleen Nebenhaus, Vice President and Publisher; Kristin A. Cocks, Editorial Director; Cindy Kitchel, Editorial Director

Hungry Minds Consumer Production: Debbie Stailey, Production Director

◆

The publisher would like to give special thanks to Patrick J. McGovern, without whom this book would not have been possible.

◆

Contents at a Glance

Cartoons at a Glance

By Rich Tennant

page 115

page 39

page 7

page 287

page 77

page 243

page 197

Cartoon Information:
Fax: 978-546-7747
E-Mail: richtennant@the5thwave.com
World Wide Web: www.the5thwave.com

Table of Contents

Foreword

. . . .

*A*s a lifelong journalist, I was fortunate enough to be present at the creation of one of America's most successful internship programs.

Back in 1977, while I was a Senior Editor at the newsweekly *TIME*, I conducted a semester-long seminar at Yale University on the subject of The American Magazine. In very short order, I was blown away by the high quality of the students. What an intelligent, inquisitive, insightful, imaginative group! Many of them, I quickly concluded, could make excellent journalists. (Indeed, several of them went on to do just that.)

One day, back in my office in New York, I just picked up the phone and dialed the Editor-in-Chief of TIME Incorporated and all of its magazines, the formidable Hedley Donovan.

"Hedley," I said, "I'm teaching a seminar at Yale, I think there are some terrific students there, and I suggest that TIME Inc. start an internship program next summer, drawing students from many universities." I added a few words of elaboration, but not much more than that.

"Good idea," responded Hedley. "Take six students."

And that was that — except that we actually started with seven interns because there were so many superlative applicants that my fellow editors and I found it impossible to narrow the list to six. Since then, the TIME Inc. internship has grown and grown. Many of the interns have gone on to full-time jobs in the nation's largest magazine publishing empire.

In the summer of 2001, fully 210 students — almost all of them just entering their senior year at college — served as summer interns at TIME Inc. About 60 of them worked on the editorial side of magazines as diverse as *Fortune, In Style, TIME, People, Sports Illustrated, Money,* as well as many others. And around 150 worked in production, advertising, circulation, and other parts of the magazine company.

Almost all of those interns, I am confident, had rewarding, enriching experiences, which will help them get full-time jobs and build rich careers in the future.

An internship program is a wonderful arrangement for everyone involved, as this highly readable, eminently useful book explains. For young, promising people, an internship it provides a chance to explore various fields, to be exposed to the world of work, to serve alongside professionals whom they respect and hope to emulate. For those professionals and other full-timers, the intern often brings a fresh perspective and enables them to serve as mentors.

The program works best when the intern is given real work to do and is constantly challenged and stretched. The intern should be able to go home each day having learned something new about the field he or she is exploring or simply about the way people interact in the workplace. The intern's manager should always be thinking about worthwhile assignments for the younger person.

And that is why I assigned my current intern, Elyssa Folk, who is entering her junior year at university, to gather material for this foreword and to write the draft, which I then edited. Turning this job over to an intern made my working life easier; it gave Elyssa a challenging assignment; and I think it produced a better piece of work. That, of course, is what internships are all about.

Marshall Loeb, the Senior Correspondent of CBS MarketWatch, *was formerly Managing Editor of* Fortune, *Managing Editor of* Money, *Senior Editor of* TIME, *and Editor of the* Columbia Journalism Review. *Intern Elyssa Folk contributed to this foreword.*

Introduction

Internships, externships, practica, and other forms of experience-based or service-based learning have become key links to a professional career. These days, in fact, internships are, for many students, the only way to get the experience and contacts necessary to break out of hourly jobs and into a professional career. For people already in a career but one they dislike, internships can provide a transition into another career. Data and hard-knocks experience show that internships often lead to a permanent job and even to a life-long career. Internships help students try out different professions and help socialize them into management, law, counseling, or other professions. Internships often lead to finding a mentor, someone who can aid professional development and boost career opportunities.

Realizing the tremendous value of an internship puts you on the right track to a better future, but as Will Rogers said, "Even if you're on the right track, you'll get run over if you just sit there." The keys to a successful internship do include finding a good internship, but that won't do you much good if you don't know what to do before your internship starts, while your internship is going on, and after your internship is over.

That's why we wrote *Internships For Dummies*. We know that you can buy books or go online today and find thousands of internship opportunities. In some of these books, mainly internship directories, you can also find some advice on interviewing or on other bits and pieces related to an internship. But that info is just the tip of the iceberg of what you need to know. What must you do (or avoid doing) during the first crucial days on the job? What are the key tasks you are likely to have as an intern, and how do you do them? What are your legal rights and obligations as an intern? How do you find and work with a mentor? What crucial actions should you take to make your internship a true link to a career and not just a way to put in time? What after-internship follow-through is essential to make your hard work pay off? In *Internships For Dummies,* we draw from our 40 years of collective experience working with internships to guide you through the entire internship process from start to finish — from assessing your objectives for an internship to making the transition to a career. Internships require a tremendous investment of your time and energy. *Internships For Dummies* helps you protect that investment!

Throughout *Internships For Dummies,* we advocate an *active* rather than passive approach to interning. Successful interns take the initiative for finding a good internship, orienting themselves to the workplace, learning how to do the work, assessing their progress, making contacts, and ultimately linking to a job or career. We guide you in *active* interning through each step of the internship process.

Who Needs This Book

Internships today start as early as high school and proceed throughout your undergraduate and graduate education. In addition to the 6 million-plus high school students engaged in some form of experiential learning, roughly 16 million students are working on their undergraduate degree in any given year. As many as 81 percent of college seniors, about 3.2 million people (give or take), report completing *at least one* internship experience, and 66 percent report completing two or more internships (2.6 million). That's a lot of people completing a lot of internships. By buying and reading *Internships For Dummies*, you've already proven that you're one of the best and brightest applicants. After all, wisdom begins with learning what it is you need to know *before* starting a new task.

Internships For Dummies is written for the following people:

- Undergraduate students using an internship to get job experience before graduation and to make a successful entry into the job market

- Undergraduate students engaged in some form of voluntary service as part of their educational experience

- Graduate students making the transition into a first profession or the transition from one profession to another

- Serious high school students involved in mentorships, cooperative programs, or other forms of experience learning

- Students at any level who contemplate an internship in another country and culture

- People not in school who find that they need an internship to make themselves employable or who seek a transition from a dead-end job into a career, or a passage from one career field to another

- Parents who want to understand the internship process from A to Z so that they can be as supportive as possible of their offspring's preparations, experiences, and opportunities

- Employers, who too often suddenly find themselves in the position of creating and managing an internship program, interviewing and hiring student interns, and/or being an internship supervisor without the benefit of preparation or training in how to best manage a student intern

- Academic advisors, who also find themselves suddenly responsible for advising and overseeing both the student interns (and their employers) even though neither role was part of their teacher training

On first glance it would seem that his book is *not* for the most widely-known type of interns, medical interns, who have a highly specialized form of internship experience, but it is! The typical duties of medical interns are substantially different (more clinical and less managerial) from other types of interns, but both medical interns and interns in similar situations and fields need to know how to assess the culture of the place they work, how to understand political dynamics, how to choose mentors, and most of the other lessons covered in *Internships For Dummies*.

How to Use This Book

Individuals can use *Internships For Dummies* as a how-to manual, as a textbook for internship or service-learning courses, or as a reference for looking up key advice as the need arises. The book is designed so that you can pick it up and read only the information that you need to know. Simply use the detailed table of contents or the index to look up a topic that interests you. But if you want to understand the full internship experience, you certainly can read the book from cover to cover. By reading or skimming the entire book, you gain an overall idea of the internship experience and a sense of what is included in each part and each chapter, in case you need specific guidance quickly.

How This Book Is Organized

Internships For Dummies is organized into seven parts, each of which is divided into chapters covering specific topics. Each chapter is a self-contained font of wisdom. Sprinkled throughout are examples of relevant materials, such as sample cover letters, sample contracts and agreements, and sample evaluation forms. We also include sidebars that highlight the experience of interns, advisors, and employers who have survived and even thrived in their intern experiences.

Part I: Understanding Internships

Just what is an internship? Why do they exist? Where did they come from? What are the different types of internships? How do they differ from service learning? What am I getting myself into? What are the key players in the internship game, and what roles do they play? What do I need to know about internships in general? What are my specific goals for an internship? These are just some of the questions we answer as we help you to see the big picture. Part I also introduces the concept of active interning.

Part II: Deciding Where You Want to Go

Any road is the right road if you don't care where you're going. But how do you tell just which sector (public, business, or nonprofit) let alone which organization or which internship is right for you? Part II compares the different employment sectors and provides criteria for deciding which internship is best for you. Part II also explores the different types of international internships, where to find them, and how to prepare for them.

Part III: Getting Where You Want to Go

You know what you're getting into (sort of). You know just what kind of experience you do, and don't, want. How do you go about getting that all-important, just-right-for-you internship? This part covers locating internships and what it takes to get hired, namely resumes, references, and successful interviewing.

Part IV: The Nuts and Bolts of Working as an Intern

The information in this part of the book divides the winners from the also-rans. Most people think that they have already won the race if they get the position. It's what you do with your internship opportunity after you start that leads to your real success. Here, we talk about getting off to a good start, making a good impression, fitting in, and performing the typical administrative, research, and other tasks you may be assigned. Part IV also guides you through the landmines of some potential problems for interns: sexual harassment, racism, confidentiality violations, and other important issues. Finally, we cover some key communication, political, and organizational skills that can help you to be a successful intern.

Part V: Making the Transition to a Job or Career

Ending an internship successfully is even more crucial than beginning it on the right foot. Here, we cover how you and your performance will be evaluated. Because mentors can play such a crucial role to your success, mentors and mentoring get attention here. Part V concludes with advice on how to make your internship a bridge to a successful job or career.

Part VI: For Advisors, Supervisors, and Employers

Interns aren't the only key players. College or university intern advisors, on-the-job intern supervisors, and employers play key parts in this adventure. In Part VI, we offer advice on how to handle these roles. We also cover some of the key issues and tasks these players need to address. Although each chapter targets a different role in the internship process, each player — intern, advisor, and employer — benefits from learning about the challenges and responsibilities of the other players they have to cooperate with.

Part VII: The Part of Tens

Here, in a couple short chapters, you can find some of our most valuable points. Read about the ten habits that shape and define a successful intern. We also point out ten mistakes to avoid as an intern. If you can avoid these mistakes and follow our advice throughout this book, you're well on your way to internship success!

Icons Used in This Book

To flag particularly important or special information, we use little pictures, called *icons,* throughout the book. Here's what they mean:

This icon appears when we want to indicate important advice about maximizing your effectiveness.

When you see this icon, you find words of wisdom to be cherished and passed down to your descendants along with the family silver.

This icon points out anecdotes from our experiences, actual intern diaries, and experiences of others who have braved the internship world before you.

If you ignore the sage advice next to these icons, you risk potential disaster. Remember the captain on board the Titanic and the warnings about those pesky icebergs?

Part I
Understanding Internships

The 5th Wave   By Rich Tennant

"We don't care where you see yourself in five years, as long as you can see where our clients will be."

In this part . . .

We tell you just what an internship is. We explain the different types of internships and how they differ from service learning. We tell you what you need to know about internships in general, and we help you set specific goals for an internship. Part I also introduces the concept of active interning.

Chapter 1

Internships: The Nature of the Beast

In This Chapter

▶ Explaining the importance of internships

▶ Defining internships

▶ Exploring different types of internships

*H*istorically, people learned a profession or trade by apprenticing with a master architect, carpenter, painter, violinist, or other kind of expert. (Picture Michelangelo trying to teach ceiling painting to an apprentice afraid of heights.) These "masters" passed on their expertise and helped socialize the apprentice into the values, customs, and norms of their profession or trade. Before schools were established, learning a craft or profession occurred this way to provide formal training in business, government, education, law, medicine, architecture, music, and other specialized fields. These apprenticeships still exist in a number of trades and professions and are even required for becoming licensed to practice those trades or professions. Today, internships fulfill the historic role of master-apprentice learning, and some of these apprenticeships are even generally called internships in fields such as medicine, business, and government. This chapter explains why internships have become so important to career building today, defines key terms used throughout the book, and describes the different types of internships.

If you're reading this book, you're either about to start hunting for an internship or are already knee-deep in one and want to know how to make the best of it. If you're considering or starting the hunt, you need to know the different kinds and the nature of the beasts you're hunting, the rules and parameters of the hunt, and your goals and motivations for embarking on this hunt. If you start hunting without this basic foundation, you risk losing your game, or even shooting yourself in the foot. Even if you're already in an internship, you need to understand these basics to know why you're there, to know what you can expect, and, yes, to avoid shooting yourself in the foot (figuratively, of course!). Part I of this book prepares you for the hunt and for knowing what to do after you've cornered your internship.

Why Internships Are So Important

As we begin a new decade, a new century, and a new millennium, internships have increasingly become a crucial route to professional success. Sometimes they're required for a license to practice, such as in medicine, social work, and educational administration, and in some cases, internships are simply highly advisable, in areas such as business, government, and law, for example. The increasing reality is that employers want to hire people with experience.

Launching a career

For many students and a growing number of people already in a career, internships are the best way — and in many cases, the only way — to gain that experience. Interns who impress their employers (in part by applying the knowledge gained from this book) have an advantage when competing for permanent jobs because they and their capabilities are already known. Even where employers are willing to hire someone without hands-on experience, they often put those hires through their own in-house internship training program. And even when an intern has to go somewhere else for a job, the experience and references from the internship are often crucial in getting hired. If you're just starting out as a trade school, high school, or college student, jobs as a baby-sitter, fry cook, or car wash attendant provide you with spending money for such expenses as cars, dates, and clothes. They also give you an orientation about certain aspects of the working world, such as being on time and dealing with customers and bosses. There is a limit, though, to how much you can learn from such jobs if you intend to go into management, politics, accounting, environmental policy, or many other professional fields. An internship with a state legislature, accounting firm, environmental advocacy group, or other business will give you more direct experience and training in specific fields, even if you get less or no pay. The added experience and learning are likely to pay off in higher salaries in future jobs.

During a tight job market, internships are often the only way of breaking into the labor force, especially with highly desirable employers who can be selective in the little hiring that occurs. Even in the boom economy of the past several years, the growing importance of cooperative education and other forms of on-the-job-training has increased. Employers are still looking for someone with experience and a proven track record of accomplishment. Also, jobs are becoming so much more complicated and technical (and not just in the high-tech industries) that some form of apprenticeship is necessary to learn enough of the basics to get hired.

Using an internship to reinforce learning and to launch a career

Catherine Dean, from Grinnell College in Iowa, aims for a career in museum artifact restoration. Catherine really enjoys restoring costumes and other museum pieces so they are faithful to their original condition. To do this right involves using what she has learned about art, history, anthropology, and other subjects. Catherine followed the trend by interning in more than one organization when she was an undergraduate intern at both the Cranbrook Institute of Science (Birmingham, Michigan) and the State Historical Society of Iowa.

Catherine's duties in both of these internships primarily involved practical day-to-day maintenance and organization of the museum collections. For both internships, she did a lot of storing and displaying of artifacts and inventory. In the first internship, she focused on completely reorganizing and rehousing the jewelry collection as well as working with several other collections (textiles, basketry, pottery, and so on). In the second internship, Catherine worked with the product packaging and medical collections, devising different solutions for storing and displaying artifacts and doing research on the medical implement collection. Her exploring involved looking in old catalogs to identify the names and purposes of the various medical implements, some of which looked more like torture devices than medical tools. Because Catherine showed she could handle responsibility, her supervisors mostly showed her what needed to be done and left her to it.

Both of Catherine's internships are closely linked to her educational and career plans. Her understanding of the Museum field is that you need a graduate degree to get very far. And if you want to get into a graduate program in Museum Studies, practical experience as a volunteer or intern is absolutely essential. Catherine claims that her internships helped her get admitted into the George Washinton University's Museum Studies program. Also, working behind the scenes in a museum really helped her understand what the jobs are and what they involve. This helped Catherine to know that museum work is really what she wants to do. So her internships provided the means to apply and test what she learned in school as well as providing both experience for furthering her career and verification that it was the right career for her.

Making transitions between jobs or careers

If you've already launched your career, what can an internship do for you? If you're typical, you'll change careers in your lifetime several times. You'll also change individual jobs many more times than that. How do you make the transition from one career to another? You may be fortunate enough to convince an employer that you can manage a rock band as well as you have taught elementary school. Chances are, however, that you would need either educational credentials in music management and/or some experience in the field. That's where the internship comes in, to provide that kind of transition experience, either in combination with extra education or by itself. An

Changing careers with the help of an internship

Anthony Franze is a retired attorney who is changing direction in his life by working to help communities overseas through the Peace Corps or other international organizations. After 33 years of helping U.S. pharmaceutical firms obtain international patents, Anthony wants to help people in developing countries improve their standard of living. Preparing for that challenge, Anthony is interning with the Rutgers-Camden (New Jersey) Public Law Clinic as part of his graduate program in public administration. With his internship experience, Anthony is using his legal experience to establish a program that provides free legal help to local small businesses and community organizations in Camden, a city where people are trying hard to improve living conditions but where extra help is needed. The knowledge that Anthony is gaining during his internship equips him for helping microenterprises and community organizations in his host country overseas. He savors the thought of making his legal services free to small businesses that need help. Anthony is among the growing number of people who use internships as a transition into a different career and an entirely different lifestyle.

increasing number of people with job experience are getting a graduate or professional degree to help them advance in their present field or to switch fields. An internship experience is typically part of that education. In one such program, two-thirds of the graduates of the Rutgers University at Camden Master of Public Administration program where Jim teaches say that an internship led directly or indirectly to a full-time job. These results are fairly typical. Internships *do* give you an advantage over those without the experience, knowledge, skill, and contacts gained from an internship. They are the next best thing to full-time job experience and in some cases better because interns may be singled out for special seminars, fast-tracking, mentoring by top people, and other special treatment.

Socializing interns into work or a career

If you're in a new job or a new profession, you need to learn more than how to perform the job-related tasks. You also need to learn proper behavior in that work setting, how to dress, the key issues and challenges of that profession, and many other things related to the job. In other words, you need to be socialized into the profession, whether it's management, law, teaching, counseling, travel advising, or any other field. Internships help socialize you into the world of work (if you're just starting) and also to a particular profession or career. If you're beyond entry stage, your socialization will concentrate on learning what it means to be a professional in that field. Internships also typically have an advantage in the socialization department because they often provide accompanying orientation, training, conferences, and mentors that accelerate your socialization into a profession. For example, interns at

Andersen (formerly known as Arthur Andersen corporation) get extensive training in accounting and management consulting through the Center for Professional Education, are assigned mentors to guide their progress, and perform demanding work along with professionals in the field. Many of the top internship programs are similar to Andersen's. Such learning in regular jobs can be hit or miss — usually more miss than hit unless you happen to be working for an exceptional boss in an enlightened atmosphere. A warning, however: Not all internships provide this extra learning, and many don't even give much help with learning the actual duties required. Learning value is one of the key criteria for selecting an internship, as discussed in Chapter 2.

Broadening career knowledge through an internship

Janine Tobias chose her first assignment in the Presidential Management Intern program in the United States Department of the Interior's Minerals Management Service. Janine chose this assignment in large part because of her interest in environmental issues, having earned a bachelor of science degree in environmental policy before earning a master of public administration (MPA) degree and law degree. While working on environmental matters, Janine got involved in a wide range of other issues ranging from conflict resolution to aviation safety to teaching seminars in places like Alaska, California, and Nevada. In addition to her official duties, Janine finds time to volunteer at an elementary school, play volleyball, and have a social life.

As a Presidential Management intern, Janine is among a select group of recent graduate and professional students from across the country chosen to work in varied professional positions in government, mostly federal. As a Presidential Management intern, Janine is starting a professional career in government with opportunities to work in various agencies and fields. The Presidential Management Intern Program also provides Janine continuing education in the form of seminars, conferences, and meetings with top officials in the executive branch and Congress. Because of the program, Janine is given freedom to experience many different aspects of the federal government without fear of losing her position or pay during her rotations, rotations that might send her to other bureaus within the Department of the Interior, other states, or other branches of government.

The Presidential Management Internship is just the most recent of her internships. Along the way, Janine served as a student intern in a U.S. senator's office, helping constituents with immigration and other issues. In another internship with the City of Camden, Janine helped track grants for City services. Later she completed a summer internship through the New Jersey Housing Scholars program with the Trenton YWCA, where she helped manage people and money to get low-cost housing built. She also completed a school-year internship with the Camden County administrator's office, where she worked to disseminate information to the public and to increase awareness of the Americans with Disabilities Act. In each of these internships, Janine gained experience, knowledge, skill, and confidence. And each of these internships helped to socialize Janine into a career of public service by acquainting her with the issues and norms of conduct common to government. Realizing internships are a key part of her education, Janine has parlayed them into a promising, fulfilling career.

What Does Internship Mean?

Internships come in different shapes and sizes and even with different names. Whether called internship, externship, practicum, experiential learning, service learning, cooperative placement, or something else, they have several features in common:

✔ The placements typically involve three primary players: the intern, the employer (such as a corporation, government agency, or public service organization), and the educational institution (such as a college, university, high school, trade school, or union) that emphasizes the learning role of internships.

We use the term "employer" rather than "host organization" or other term to underscore that internships are real employment and need to be treated that way. Internships have the essential qualities of employment. Both entail handling a workload, following instructions, behaving according to expectations, and receiving some sort of compensation. Sometimes internships provide no monetary compensation but produce other forms of compensation: experience, skills, and contacts. Treating an internship as real employment and taking it seriously increase the odds that it will lead to regular employment. On the other hand, acting as if an internship is a "pretend" job or "pre" job is one of the biggest mistakes an intern can make.

✔ Each player has particular goals. Interns aim to acquire knowledge and skills that will make them more productive and more employable. Employers aim to gain extra help and to prepare interns for potential permanent, or at least longer-range, employment. Educational institutions want to enhance student learning through internships that provide the hands-on, practical experience that is difficult or impossible to provide in the classroom. For internships to work most effectively, all these goals must be met, and each actor in the process must understand and support the goals of the other actors. Chapter 2 covers these roles and goals in more detail.

✔ Internships, by whatever name, last a finite period of time: the length of a school term, the length specified by union contract, the amount specified by law, or some other fixed period. In other cases, internships last until the intern is hired on a permanent basis. Whatever the length, internships have different stages: the initial feeling-out stage, the main work-learning stage, and the end/transition stage. This book addresses what you need to know to succeed at each stage. Because experience-based, real-world learning has so much in common no matter what it is called, we use the term "internship" to represent practicum, externship, cooperative placement, work study, and so on rather than risk confusing you (and us) with so many different names.

Jargon Alert: Key Terms Used in This Book

Internship: In this book, we define internship to mean "placement with an organization primarily to gain work experience, learn about the nature of that work, acquire skill and knowledge in doing that work, and acquire contacts that can assist in getting a job and building a career."

Externship: Same as internship but used to emphasize the fact that the placement is outside (external to) the student's academic program. Law schools, for example, often use this term. The term "internship" emphasizes being on the inside of the *employing* organization.

Practicum: A specialized type of internship usually done as part of an academic program, such as some programs in social work, nursing, educational administration, or health administration. Often a practicum is a requirement for a specific course.

Experiential learning: Applies generally to any learning by actual experience, typically in an applied setting such as the workplace.

Service learning: Typically involves learning by serving people as a volunteer. This service can be through a community group or organization, social services agency, recreation league, or other outlet.

Cooperative placement, cooperative education, or just co-op: Usually refers to placements in business or industry that are part of an academic program in a high school, college, or trade school. Sometimes the co-op placement alternates with terms in the classroom. Sometimes, as is typically the case in high school, co-op placements are intermingled with classroom study, for example, several hours a day.

Field work or field study: Another name for a placement experience done as part of an academic program.

Work-study: Applies to the Federal Work-Study program that provides financial aid to undergraduate and graduate students with financial need. Students can learn and get paid for working in offices around campus or in organizations (for example, community service agencies or governments) off-campus. You can find out more about this topic in Chapter 5.

Intern: You or someone else getting experience and learning through an internship.

Employer: The organization — company, agency, theater company, laboratory, or business — in which the intern is employed. Often we just use the generic term *organization* instead of continually repeating specific types of organizations such as companies, hospitals, government or nonprofit agencies, and the like. Usually we mean "employing organization," but it can also have a more general meaning.

Intern supervisor: The person in the organization where an intern is employed who is officially responsible for supervising the intern's work.

Educational institution: The college, trade school, graduate school, professional school, trade union, or other organization primarily responsible for ensuring that interns learn during their placement.

Academic advisor (or just *advisor*): The teacher, professor, intern coordinator, or other person responsible for advising interns and guiding and overseeing their learning.

Mentor: Your guru and confessor, the one who most guides, enables, and influences your career. Your mentor may be your academic advisor or intern supervisor but may also be someone else, either inside or outside your employing organization. Some placements are called *mentorships.* This typically means you will follow a mentor through his daily schedule, learning from the master. This assigned mentor may or may not become your real career mentor.

No general agreement exists in the use of these terms. Not all law placements are called externships, not all business placements are called internships, and not all psychology placements are called fieldwork. To avoid confusion in *Internships For Dummies,* we use the general term *internship* unless we're pointing out a difference in a specialized form of internship.

Types of Internships: All Shapes and Sizes

Internships come in as many sizes and shapes as names. A staggering range of internships exists. All major trades and professions use them. Despite the diversity, internships come in several types:

- **Paid internships:** These internships offer a salary and possibly other benefits in addition to job experience. Andersen pays on average about $3,000 per week for undergraduate interns majoring in accounting, finance, or economics during its summer and winter internships. Most placements don't pay that much, but many offer a salary or stipend and expenses. Microsoft, for example, provides interns round-trip airfare and subsidized housing at its Redmond, Washington, headquarters.

- ✔ **Unpaid internships:** These internships offer experience and learning and possibly academic credit (as can paid internships). The White House Internship Program provides no pay, but the experience and contacts gained can pay off in jump-starting a career in government.

- ✔ **Formal/institutionalized internships:** These internships have defined contracts, procedures, levels of compensation, and so forth. Examples include the Presidential Management Intern Program, Microsoft Intern Program, the American Heart Association, and MTV.

- ✔ **Informal internships:** These internships tend to lack contracts, written procedures, and formal listings, relying more on personal contact.

- ✔ **Professional internships:** These internships are intended to help prepare interns for what is generally recognized as a profession: management, accounting, law, social work, medicine, counseling, and so forth. These can also include internships in newer professions such as information technology and consulting.

- ✔ **Internships in the trades:** Often called *cooperative education,* these internships can be in vocational areas such as auto mechanics, cooking, and computer repair. Internships in the trades often occur through a co-op program that pays students to work in business or industry.

Internships also differ on whether academic credit is offered. Students take for-credit internships as part of an academic program. Noncredit placements usually occur apart from schools, but some school-based internships may not earn credits.

Internships can also be typed by primary function: administrative, research, clinical, legal, political, teaching, or other. Internships can also differ by the geographic area from which interns are drawn, whether locally, regionally, nationally, or internationally.

Keep these differences in mind when deciding what kind of internship is right for you. Obviously, internships may combine several of these characteristics. For example, the internships offered by the tongue-in-cheek-named Internet firm called GirlGeeks are unpaid, formal, and professional. Keep these characteristics in mind when defining your goals for an internship.

Active Interning Versus Passive Interning: A Critical Choice

Interns can act in a number of different ways before, during, and after their internship. There are two vastly different overall approaches to interning, however: passive interning and active interning. While no intern is totally passive or totally active, interns tend to use essentially one or the other of these two approaches.

Passive interning: Avoid this approach

Interns using the passive approach wait for opportunities to come to them. Passive interns wait until an internship falls into their lap. Then they wait for someone else to orient them to their new workplace. They wait some more until someone shows them how to do the work. They wait until the final evaluation to find out how they are doing. They wait for people to contact them about future opportunities.

Passive interns are less likely to succeed because they leave so much to chance and rely too heavily on other people to make things happen. Passive interns take too little responsibility for their own internship. They tend to coast through the experience waiting to see what happens and reacting to what does happen. Passive interns miss opportunities they could have created by using some initiative. Passive interns are less likely to impress their employers and supervisors because they fail to show initiative with their own work and their own learning, which makes passive interns more difficult to motivate and supervise. The time and effort employers and supervisors spend on passive interns just to get them to do anything could have been spent grooming them for a profession.

Active interning: The only way to go

In contrast, active interning involves taking responsibility for your own internship — for your own work and learning and, ultimately, for your own future. In his highly useful book, *How to Be a Star At Work: 9 Breakthrough Strategies You Need to Succeed,* Robert Kelly reports the results of extensive research on what it takes to be a star performer. Star performers, people who work differently and accomplish far more than other employees, aren't born that way or don't always have more intelligence Kelly concludes. But this research found that star performers follow nine strategies that make them more productive and effective. The top ranking strategy to be a star, according to this research, is initiative, seeing opportunities and pursuing them. Kelly's research reinforces what we have observed in hundreds of interns. Interns who take initiative, those whom we call active interns, are far more likely to succeed in their internship and their career. They actively assess their needs and goals, actively search for internship opportunities that meet their needs and goals, and actively work to get the right internship. On the job, active interns take the initiative to get oriented, to learn their work, and to find out how they stand. Active interns reach out to make contacts who can help them in their work and career. And active interns take the initiative to help make their internship link to other opportunities.

Successful interns operate in what we call *AIM* (Active Intern Mode). Let's be clear that we aren't advising interns to jump in, half-cocked without waiting to size up the situation. Sometimes waiting to be shown what to do is necessary. But we do advocate taking the initiative to show that you are ready to work and to learn — and to take the initiative yourself if the right things aren't done to help you work and learn. Table 1-1 compares how passive and active interns would approach the major internship tasks we cover in this book.

Table 1-1	Comparing Passive and Active Interns	
Skill	*Passive Interns*	*Active Interns*
Assessing needs and goals (Chapters 2, 3)	Only casually think about their needs and goals if they do it all.	Systematically reflect on their needs and goals for an internship.
Searching for internships (Chapters 3, 4, 5)	Wait for opportunities to come their way or only come up with a few leads through the obvious sources.	Explore a range of leads using a range of sources (not just the obvious ones) and compare those leads to their needs and goals.
Getting the internship (Chapter 6)	Submit one or two applications, wait for a response, and take the first offer if they get one.	Submit a number of applications for internships that meet their needs and goals, follow up with prospective employers, don't automatically jump at the first offer, and negotiate terms if feasible.
Orienting yourself to the workplace (Chapter 7)	Wait for a formal orientation and go through the motions during the orientation. If no orientation occurs, passive interns let the opportunity drop.	Take the initiative to get the most out of any organized orientation, but if none is arranged, they actively orient themselves and work to get an organized orientation.
Handling problems (Chapter 8)	Wait until problems occur during the internship and wait for the work supervisor, school intern advisor, or someone else to solve these problems.	Anticipate the kinds of problems that might occur and work to avoid these problems. Actively seek appropriate help before a situation gets out of control.
Doing the work (Chapters 9, 10, 11, 12)	Wait until assigned a task, fail to get essential information for completing that task, and fail to keep supervisors informed of progress (or problems).	Energetically seek assignments, probe to get essential information about them, and actively keep supervisors informed of progress and problems before they get out of hand.

(continued)

Table 1-1 *(continued)*

Skill	Passive Interns	Active Interns
Evaluating your performance (Chapter 13)	Wait until the end-of-internship evaluation to find out what they are doing well and poorly. If no formal evaluation exists, they write off this opportunity for feedback.	Conscientiously (but tactfully) seek informal feedback each week or with each task. They learn what the formal evaluations are and prepare for them.
Networking (Chapters 14, 15)	Wait until co-workers or others contact them. If contact occurs, passive interns let the other person carry the relationship. If contact doesn't happen, they miss these chances to network.	Systematically and conscientiously contact other people to share experiences and to obtain advice about the immediate job and career. Active interns keep up their end of the professional relationship by helping mentors and others where possible.
Linking to a job or career (Chapter 15)	Sit back to see what happens at the end of the internship. If nothing happens, back to square one!	Conscientiously work toward parlaying their internships into full-time jobs or other opportunities by performing well during the internship, building a professional network, and developing knowledge and skills for the next step.

So take AIM! Operate in Active Intern Mode. Being an active intern involves mastering the insights and advice in *Internships For Dummies* and keeping your AIM before, during, and after your internship.

Chapter 2

Before You Start: Understanding Internships and Yourself

In This Chapter
▶ Looking at the participants in an internship
▶ Finding out the specifics
▶ Deciding on your goals

*I*f "the unexamined life is not worth living" (Socrates), then it's also not ready to pursue an internship. You may have many questions about who you are, where you are, where you want to go, and what you're willing to do to arrive there that need to be answered before you begin looking for any specific internship.

This chapter continues to get you ready for the search by adding specifics to the general knowledge conveyed in Chapter 1. In this chapter, we begin with a more specific discussion of the roles played by the key actors introduced in Chapter 1 and continue by introducing key issues about internships that you should keep in mind while you conduct your search and while on the internship itself. Finally, we conclude by helping you formulate *your* goals for *your* internship.

Internship Actors and Their Roles

The successful internship today is really a play with three main actors: intern, supervisor, and advisor. In order for the entire performance to be a success rather than a tragedy for all the actors, you need to know, understand, and respect the roles each plays in the internship process.

The intern

You, the intern, are the key actor in the process. The intern has the dual roles of learner and worker. Ideally, these roles reinforce each other. Solid, practical work experience complements academic learning, and sound academic learning improves work performance. Intern experience also allows you to apply and test classroom knowledge, improving your understanding of that knowledge.

The intern's role as learner

As an intern, you're asked to satisfy academic requirements for your college, university, trade school, or high school. The most common types of school requirements include keeping a log or diary of your internship experience, writing a research paper on some aspect of the internship, or completing a work-related project. Work-related projects tend to be more applied than research term papers and can range from developing a business plan for a new Internet start-up company to looking at housing stock for a church-based housing agency to directing a play for a local theater. Some internship programs require a log, a paper, and a project — or at least two of the three assignments — by the end of the internship. More specifics about how to deliver these specific products come in Part IV.

One tool for helping interns succeed in their educational role is the Learning Contract. Such contracts or agreements specify the intern's learning objectives for the internship and may also list the learning activities for achieving these learning objectives. Figure 2-1 shows an example of a learning contract that many internship programs use to make sure interns, supervisors, and advisors agree what the learning outcomes should be.

Some internship programs also require students to take a class in conjunction with their work placement. Such courses may precede the actual placement, preparing students for their internship — as is done in many undergraduate service-learning programs. Some courses may run at the same time as the placement, allowing interns to discuss in class the issues they're confronting in their internships and to directly integrate school learning and work learning. This arrangement is typical of health services administration programs that require an administrative practicum in a hospital, nursing home, HMO, or other organization as part of an advanced course before graduation. Whatever the academic requirements, you will typically get an academic grade for your internship whether that internship is part of a regular course or is separate. Your grade is generally based on the academic requirements (log, paper, and project) but may also be based on your work performance as reflected in an evaluation by your work supervisor. As important as meeting academic requirements is the learning that comes from applying and testing the knowledge gleaned from school. Internships are ideal for this kind of learning.

Sample Learning Contract

Note: The learning contract is best completed at a meeting of the intern, intern supervisor, and intern advisor either before the internship begins or during the first week.

1. List major learning objectives for intern (e.g., to apply course knowledge of accounting, to learn a new computer application, to explore hospital management as a possible career)**:**

1.

2.

3.

2. Repeat each learning objective and identify for each objective the work and learning activities intended to accomplish that objective and the means for evaluating whether that objective has been met.

Example:

Objective 1: To explore hospital management as a possible career.
Activities aimed at meeting this objective:
* intern in a hospital for 12 weeks under supervision of the Vice President for Operations
* accompany supervisor to meetings and assist with correspondence and other duties
* have weekly discussions with supervisor about the general field of hospital management and the specifics of running that particular hospital.
* attend conferences and meetings of the state hospital association

How objective is to be evaluated: Intern and supervisor assessments of interns overall understanding of the advantages and limitations of hospital management as a career.

Objective 1:
Activities aimed at meeting this objective:
How objective is to be evaluated

Objective 2:
Activities aimed at meeting this objective:
How objective is to be evaluated

Objective 3:
Activities aimed at meeting this objective:
How objective is to be evaluated

Etc.

Resources committed to interns learning:

Employer commits (e.g., sending to conferences, intern orientation and workshops, providing library access):
School commits (e.g., access to computer system, library, intern seminar, career center support):

Figure 2-1:
A sample
Learning
Contract.

The intern's role as worker

As an intern, you must satisfy obligations to your employer as well as to your school. An internship contract that you sign with an employer typically specifies the number of hours per week you will work and may give further details about what is expected in terms of conduct, performance, or other conditions. Some schools also set a minimum and maximum number of work hours per week — enough to fulfill a genuine work requirement but not enough to detract from schoolwork. As an intern, you fulfill your working role by arriving on time prepared to work, doing competently those tasks you're assigned, and not doing schoolwork or other tasks during working hours. Working on anything except your assigned work during working hours makes you, your academic advisor, and your school look bad. Part IV of *Internships For Dummies* gives practical guidance on doing some of the more common work-related tasks.

The supervisor: The intern's contact at work

Interns are usually assigned to a supervisor before or after they report for their internship placement. Highly organized internship programs may have an internship coordinator who assign interns to a supervisor within the company or agency. In other cases, this assignment may be made by a top-level manager. In some smaller programs, the internship coordinator may serve as supervisor for all the interns. At any rate, your supervisor is your primary point of contact at work. Your supervisor generally assigns and evaluates your work. Most of your relationships with other permanent employees will likely be through your supervisor. Good, interested supervisors also play the role of mentor (more in Chapter 14) by introducing you to other people and guiding your work and career. Their role may include sticking up for you when you're being treated unfairly by other employees or interns.

Unfortunately, not all supervisors offer constructive help. In some internship programs, intern supervisors are assigned because they're the boss of the unit in which you're placed; they may not even want interns in their department. Intern supervisors may also be assigned because they're the only ones who aren't productively busy. These kinds of intern supervisors are to be avoided whenever possible because they're likely to be indifferent, unsupportive, and even hostile to interns.

The academic advisor: The link to school

In this book, *academic advisor* refers to the person who guides the intern's learning role, not necessarily the advisor for the intern's academic major. (One person can play both roles, however.) Academic intern advising involves helping the student assess his goals and interests, guiding research about internships, monitoring the student's progress during the placement, possibly visiting the student at the job site, developing a learning contract with the intern and work supervisor, and assigning a grade for the internship, possibly after consulting with the supervisor at work. The academic advisor may also be the one teaching the course that accompanies an internship and also be your instructor. The overall role of academic intern advisor, therefore, is to ensure that valid learning takes place during your internship by helping develop your learning contract, helping you see the relevance of your studies to work and work to your studies, and guiding you with additional learning needed for your internship. Your work supervisor may also care about your learning, but doing so is not the supervisor's primary role. If you think you aren't learning enough in your internship, you should talk this over with both your intern advisor and your work supervisor. If you still aren't getting a worthwhile learning experience in your placement, you may need to ask your intern advisor to intercede with your supervisor or the employer organization.

The academic advisor for your internship may be someone such as the director of field learning at your school, head of your academic department, instructor for a course that has a work experience component, or an advanced student with some practical experience. Advisors, like internships, come in all shapes and sizes and levels of ability and interest. Some advisors are highly able and dedicated, while others have little interest, time, or preparation for their role and may even need your guidance. (Part VI is written specifically for intern advisors and supervisors.) It would certainly pay for interns to know about the roles their advisors and supervisors play so that they can know what to expect and how to do their part.

What You Need to Know about Specific Internships

Understanding the key roles of interns, supervisors, and advisors gives you a good start in knowing what to look for in an internship. Some other issues to consider include the duration and timing of internships, whether credits are awarded, whether application deadlines are rolling or fixed, your qualifications for the position, the kind of training and preparation you can expect, and your rights and obligations as an intern.

Duration and timing

You need to decide when you want to do your internship and how long you want it to last. Internships can last from a few weeks to six months or more.

Most internships follow a schedule built around the academic calendar. That is, they generally run during the fall, the spring, or the summer, or some combination thereof.

In making your decision, you need to think about what else is going on in your life at the same time. Trying to do an internship while taking a full load of difficult courses is asking for trouble. Something — your internship, your classwork, or both — is very likely to suffer.

If you're doing an internship primarily to get a feel for a type of work (to see what it's like and whether it's for you), then a shorter internship period will suit you best, perhaps six to eight weeks done early in the academic year. On the other hand, if you're doing an internship to give an employer a chance to see what a great worker you are (and why the employer should keep you on permanently), then a longer period makes sense. You may even try to arrange an internship that ends near graduation, when you're ready to accept a full-time position.

Fixed or rolling deadlines

For most internships (except ones with your Aunt Martha's consulting firm or Uncle Harry's radio station), you need to apply for the position, just as you would for a job, which is what an internship is. Some application deadlines are fixed, meaning that they occur only once or a few times a year. If you want a summer internship with the prestigious *Wall Street Journal,* you must apply by Thanksgiving of the year before. Thinking about this at the end of spring term is too late, but you still could apply to the Center for Investigative Reporting, which has a May 1 deadline.

Other internships have rolling deadlines, meaning that you can apply for them at any time. Sometimes rolling deadlines reflect the fact that the employer's internship program runs year-round or will accept qualified applicants whenever they can enter. Deadlines for Gensler and Associates architecture firm are rolling for fall and spring intern placements, which are flexible in length. In other cases, the deadlines may be rolling, but dates for starting and ending the actual internship are fixed. Intern placements at Intel corporation generally fit this pattern.

Whether deadlines are fixed or rolling, our best advice is this: For those internships that strike your fancy, find out the deadlines as soon as possible and work toward applying in time. Chapter 5 guides you in planning and carrying out your search, and Chapter 6 helps you get your application together and interview for internships.

Matching the qualifications of the interns to the requirements of the internships

Carefully review the internship requirements. It won't help you to meet a rush application deadline if you discover that the program was for engineering majors only — and you're a communication major. Some internship programs are for certain levels of education. NASA and MTV have internships for high school students. Hundreds of internships exist for undergraduate students, some specifying junior or senior level. Other programs, such as The Carter Center and Robert Mondavi Winery, accept recent college graduates. Still other internships take graduate students — Ford Motor Company and the United Nations Association of the United States of America, for example. Some accept graduate students only, and some (Presidential Management Internship, for example) take only graduates of graduate or professional programs.

Intern employers may also require specific majors. For example, NASA's Space Life Sciences Training Program requires applicants to be majoring in the life sciences. Other employers may require particular experience in a given field or give extra duties or pay to those with experience. Many intern employers require some kind of relevant sample of your work, such as a research report, demonstration video, or design portfolio. Many intern employers in public affairs, journalism, and publishing want evidence of writing ability and may ask for a writing sample along with your application packet.

Our best advice here is to quickly weed out the opportunities for which you don't meet any specific minimum qualifications, such as age, degree, major, or grade point average. Then you can focus on whether you meet the more flexible qualifications in the remaining positions, such as acting ability and research skill.

Academic credit

If you're a student, you most likely will receive academic credit for your internship. Many employers (MTV, for example) require you to be receiving academic credit in order to be an intern. Some programs allow you to take an internship for a varying amount of credit, typically from one to six quarter or semester credits. The amount of credit you receive is a function of how many hours you intern and/or how many weeks your internship lasts. Some schools, on the other hand, only give three credits, for example, for internships and hence can accommodate only students working a fixed number of hours per week or weeks in total. Make sure that what you want, what the employer offers, and what the school permits are all a match.

Training and preparation

What do you expect to learn from your internship experience? Some employers look upon an intern as cheap labor that provides the intern with valuable on-the-job experience for a resume. In such cases, the employer generally expects the intern to have all the necessary skills and abilities when she reports to work. At the other end of the spectrum, some employers see an internship experience as a time to provide an intern with some very specific skills and abilities; in other words, they expect to train you for the work you'll be doing.

Both of these types of internships, along with all those in between, are perfectly fine and normal. The key is that you and the employer should agree on what you can offer to and expect from each other.

Duties

Think of an internship experience as a give-give situation: You give your labor to the employer, and the employer gives you training and experience. The best way to tell whether this exchange is what you're each looking for is to learn as much as possible about your duties.

Read all that you can about any internship experience you are investigating and ask as many questions as necessary to get a clear picture of what you'll be doing. Remember that there is no right or wrong answer about an internship, per se. The important thing is that all parties get what they want and need.

Think of a spectrum. On one extreme, an internship may consist of a lot of busywork in a position in which the employer primarily sees you as a reliable go-for. Although you may not have the chance to do significant or highly meaningful work, you *are* getting a chance to experience the working world, and that can be critical in getting your first real job.

At the other end of the spectrum, an employer may provide you with the training needed to work on the front lines, side by side with regular employees, and with an opportunity to become a full-time employee after the internship. Most internship experiences are somewhere in between these two extremes. The amount of responsibility and meaningful work you're given depends on both the field in which you work and the specific employer.

Rights and liabilities

Whenever you're doing an internship, and especially when doing so as part of an academic program, you need to be clear on your rights and liabilities. Most labor laws are designed around the notion of "employees" (either full-time or part-time). In some respects, interns are treated as employees, but in other respects, they're not. This ambiguity raises some sticky questions.

For example, if you're injured on the job, what coverage do you have? Will you be protected under Workers' Compensation? Are you actually working for the employer or for the academic institution. What if you accidentally injure someone else? Are you protected under the employer's liability, or the school's, or are you on your own?

Your academic advisor should be both knowledgeable and inquisitive in the areas of rights and liabilities to make sure that you (and the employer and the school) are all on the same page and that all legal and other types of issues are clear *before* the internship begins. Asking about these kinds of issues may be especially difficult when you're already anxious about getting or starting an internship with a desired employer. But don't enter an internship if you think you may find yourself unprotected if you happen to be an injured or an injuring party in an accident. Organized internship programs usually cover liability and other legal issues in the internship agreement. Read the fine print of the internship agreement that acts as the contract for you, your school, and the employer. Figure 2-2 shows an example of an Internship Agreement that addresses many of the issues we've just discussed.

Your internship or theirs?

Most people think of an internship opportunity as a mold that needs to be filled. In many cases, that's how internships work. The employer has a very clear picture of the "shape" that the internship should take and then simply looks for someone who fits the mold. And you just may be the intern applicant that's the right size and shape, figuratively speaking, for the job.

But maybe what you want to do as an intern is to create a new mold, one that the employer hasn't yet developed. Thus, you may be able to create an internship opportunity where none exists or to modify an existing opportunity to be more of what you want.

The steps in creating a new opportunity or modifying an existing one are very similar to those you would use in applying for any internship. The difference in tailoring your own internship is that you must take the initiative to research the employer organization in order to understand their existing structure and positions and what you can offer by serving as an intern. Even within the boundaries of an existing internship, you may be able to negotiate your duties and assignments in order to make this *your* internship experience, one that matches your needs and interests as closely as possible.

Sample Internship Agreement

Personal Data

Name of Intern:
Address:
Work phone number:
Home phone number:
E-mail address:

Internship Information

Name of organization employing intern:
Organizations: address:

Intern supervisors name:
Intern supervisors title:
Intern supervisors phone number:
Intern supervisors e-mail address:

Description of Intern Position/Assignment

Summary of the intern position including major projects and assignments:

Specific products or deliverables intern contracts to complete:

Monitoring and Evaluation of Intern Performance

Types of evaluation (evaluation by supervisor, by others, self-evaluation):

Date(s) of school intern advisors site visit:

Terms of Internship

Start date: End date: Number of weeks: Hours per week:

Salary pay: Tuition benefits: Expenses covered:

Other benefits:

Legal Conditions

Clause(s) relating to how liability will be covered and any other legal matters involving the internship:

Signatures

Signature of Intern:_____ Date:
Signature of Intern Supervisor:_____ Date:
Signature of School Intern Advisor:_____ Date:

Copies to: intern, intern supervisor, school intern advisor, personnel, intern coordinator

Adapted from: *Internship Handbook,* Lewiston-Auburn College, University of Southern Maine.

Figure 2-2:
A Sample
Internship
Agreement

So whom do you contact initially? If you're dealing with an organization that has a large and well-defined internship program, your best bet is to contact the head of the internship operation. This person, often called the Internship Coordinator or similar title, is in the best position to see what possibilities can arise and how to make the most of them. In those organizations where internships are more of a department by department affair, the head of the unit in which you would like to intern is the person you have to contact.

Defining Your Goals for an Internship

Before even considering specific internship opportunities, you need to identify your own needs and goals. Otherwise, you have no way to compare internship opportunities intelligently and may end up taking the first one or the wrong one. You need to consider several issues, which are detailed in the following sections.

Goals for pre-career and just-getting-started readers

If you're at the pre-career point (still in school or just graduated and without significant work experience), you need the kind of internship that will get you the most valuable experience for choosing a career and launching a career. You should ask yourself whether an internship will give you a good look at a field you're considering for a career. If you're interested in business management as a career and the assignment predominantly involves compiling news releases for a nonprofit agency, the internship is unlikely to give you a true sense of whether business is for you. This assignment may be unwise even if it pays better than other placements. The amount of pay should be a secondary consideration at this stage. Instead, look for an internship with a high-performing company or agency and the chance to work with a skilled, respected mentor. Such a position will likely result in higher pay in the long run because it will accelerate your learning curve, enhance your network of personal and professional contacts in the career field of your choice, and thus it also improves your ultimate employability.

If you're at the pre-career stage, you also need to be flexible in your choices of career. If you've been a finance major but find you prefer marketing, you should look for internships that give you experience and exposure in both of those fields. At this point in your life, you want to look for internships that give you broad experience in and exposure to a number of different fields and that allow you to make more informed choices about the careers best for you. You don't have to decide on a career during the first internship (and probably shouldn't). Remember that you'll probably change careers several times during your lifetime if you're typical of other people. (Whew! Knowing that fact should take some of the pressure off, shouldn't it?) Although you should make careful, thoughtful decisions about your internships, you may find your first internship is a dud and fails to provide valuable experience or exposure. In that case, you can ask to get reassigned or you can figure out ways to transform your assignment into a beneficial one. Find out more about these strategies in Part IV.

Internships with built-in rotations to a range of fields generally provide broader exposure than internships with one placement. The Presidential Management Intern Program run by the U.S. government typically provides three rotations. Some of these can be with other federal agencies, state or local government, or even nonprofit organizations. Even if there is no built-in rotation, you can negotiate a rotation or put together one. You can find out more about this strategy in Chapter 7.

Goals for in-career readers

If you already have job experience and are into your career, you may want an internship that provides specialized knowledge to help you in that career or to make a transition into another career. As with pre-career interns, you need an internship that provides valuable learning and exposure to the field — and good contacts. If your aim is to specialize further within an existing career or acquire a skill or body of knowledge that complements your existing field, you will likely need a more specific assignment rather than broad exposure. If a transition into another field or career is your goal, however, an internship with broad exposure has more advantages. Such an internship gives you a better idea of whether this new field is right for you and provides a broader base of knowledge and skills. The later in life that you make a transition between careers, the more crucial your choice of internship becomes. You don't have as much time to waste on an unproductive placement, so you should put more effort into choosing an internship and be quicker to request reassignment. Fortunately, your experience, knowledge, and skills should give you more leverage in making this change.

Your educational needs

Remember that an internship is both give and take, on both sides. In an ideal internship, you meet your employer's needs for an able, enthusiastic worker and you have some of your educational needs met in return. Part of your educational needs probably include learning the hands-on skills and abilities that will make you successful in finishing your education and ultimately in your chosen occupation The learning facet of your internship involves three sets of needs:

- ✔ What you think you need to learn to become more valuable as a student and worker
- ✔ What your school thinks you must learn to graduate
- ✔ What a professional licensing body requires for you to get licensed or certified

Make sure that you know whether you need a specific type of internship to complete an undergraduate and graduate degree or qualify for a certain kind of license or certification. Some law schools require internships to graduate. Others don't. If you need academic credit to graduate or to earn a license or certification, be sure that the internships you consider would qualify. Certification for school principal in most states requires an extensive placement supervised by an already certified principal. If these standards aren't met, the internship won't lead to principalship. Some colleges, universities, or trade schools don't allow students to intern with their own employer or at least not doing the same job they currently perform. Other schools may allow this. Find out the precise requirements of your educational program as well as any professional standards you must meet. Chapter 3 deals with such specifics. You may need the experience and contacts more than academic credits or any kind of formal qualification. In that case, an informal, learning-packed internship may be more valuable to your skill level and career than a formal internship for credit.

Types of compensation you need

You may need to earn something from an internship to keep your financial head above water. In that case, you may have to hold out for one that pays instead of an experience-only placement. As with job searching, you may have to lower your sights and go for lower pay or no pay if a fully paid internship is not in the cards. If your living expenses are covered by other employment or by someone else (aren't parents and spouses wonderful?), you may have the luxury of choosing a placement based entirely on the value of what you learn and how it will help your career. Formal, institutionalized intern programs typically spell out the terms of compensation: wages, health insurance and other benefits, tuition or travel expenses, academic credit, and so forth. Informal, improvised programs may not offer more than experience, but you may be able to negotiate for travel expenses, tuition, or the like. How hard you negotiate depends on how badly the employer wants you, how many others have applied, the employer's budget, and other factors.

Your geographic flexibility

You may need a local internship if school, job, residence, public transportation, or the age of your car limits how far you can travel. Some internships provide transportation to and from the site, but such a benefit is rare. If you're tied to an area for legitimate reasons (and not just because you feel more comfortable where you live now), you need to be more inventive in finding or "making" an internship (unless you happen to already live in New York City, Washington, D.C., or some other internship mecca).

When restricted geographically, you may need to augment your list of official internships by turning to neighbors, partners, parents, or others for ideas and contacts.

On the other hand, the purpose of your internship may be to get you away from home, school, and familiar routine. If the arts are your passion, you may want to head for New York, Boston, London, or some other center for the arts. If you're interested in politics or government, many internship programs exist in Washington, D.C., Philadelphia, Denver, or other government centers. If your interest lies in the travel and recreation industry or you just like to work in beautiful places, programs like Resort Intern Connections has sites in the United States, the Caribbean, and other resort areas. If an international experience is a priority, hundreds of opportunities exist overseas. Part II covers the issue of internship location.

Your personal situation

Personal factors also play a role in choosing an internship. A spouse, children, ill parent, or financial situation can restrict options if they require you to be at home more often or earning money, regardless of the learning value. Physical challenges (for example, blindness, deafness, lack of mobility, health problems, and age) can also rule out certain opportunities. Internships at Sony Music, for example, typically require good hearing. The U.S. Peace Corps requires volunteers to be healthy enough to reduce the risk of medical problems in the countries where they're sent. You get the idea. But don't overlook the opportunities that may come your way *because* of your personal situation. For example, caring for a chronically ill child may lead you to intern in an organization focused on treating or preventing that type of illness. Youthfully-challenged interns may find the American Association of Retired Persons or a similar organization a rewarding and accepting place. Likewise, younger interns (who are at least 18) may be better suited to placements with the Student Conservation Association, which works in wilderness areas and frequently requires strenuous activity.

One key trick to finding a suitable internship is to be sure that you aren't unnecessarily ruling out valuable internships because of your personal situation — or ignoring opportunities that your situation presents.

Your personal values

Managing Your Career For Dummies, by Max Messmer (Hungry Minds, Inc.), rightfully emphasizes that you should do some soul-searching about your own personal values before deciding on a career or important job. Because internships have become crucial entries into a career and key transitions between careers, the same advice applies. What do you value most? Making money? Helping people? Doing interesting work? Being your own boss? Your reflection on these values shapes your decision about whether you need an internship and your choice of internship. Would an internship force you to do something against your values? This may be something unethical (as addressed in Chap-ter 8) or simply something that goes against your personal values. People who strongly oppose artificially restricting animals shouldn't intern in zoos, for example, or at least not some zoos. People whose primary value is economic security may gravitate toward internships in business rather than in human service organizations such as halfway houses, counseling centers, and the like.

The Internship Goals Checklist

Here's a checklist to help you start to understand and plan for what you want and need from your internship experience. Read each sentence and check all that apply. When you're done, review the lines you checked to get a clearer picture of just what direction your internship should follow. When you are finished with your checklist we advise you to discuss the results with your campus internship coordinator, intern advisor, career counselor, or some other professional in the campus career center.

Stage of career and career goals:

Pre-career:

- ✔ I am at the beginning of my career and need to break into the job market.
- ✔ I am pre-career and have the option for a regular job with strong learning potential.
- ✔ I am pre-career but don't have the option of a regular job with strong learning potential.

✔ There are some fields/jobs I would like to try before I get established in a career.

✔ This internship I am considering would likely provide an adequate try-out for the field or fields I am interested in.

✔ This internship would likely provide adequate experience, skills, and contacts to help me launch my career.

In-career:

✔ I already have significant job experience.

✔ To perform better in my present field, I need skills and experience I cannot get from my job.

✔ Classroom education alone would adequately equip me for my present field.

✔ It is likely I will need additional practical experience beyond my present job in order to perform better in my present field.

✔ I really would like to change fields or to try out a different field.

✔ My present employment gives me the option of trying different fields.

✔ To try a different field, I will need to consider some form of internship.

✔ To qualify for a different field or career, I will need practical experience.

✔ This internship I am considering would likely provide an adequate try-out for the field or fields to which I may want to switch.

✔ This internship would likely provide adequate experience, skills, and contacts to help make a transition toward a different field or career.

Educational needs:

✔ I know enough already to get a good job in the field of my choice.

✔ My classroom education is adequate to get me a job, but I lack practical experience.

✔ I need to augment my classroom learning with practical skills and knowledge.

✔ I need practical skills to make me more valuable and more marketable.

✔ This internship I am considering is likely to equip me with the practical skills I need.

✔ I need a general introduction and socialization into a field new to me.

✔ This internship I am considering is likely to provide adequate socialization into this new field.

✔ I need some form of internship for academic credit to graduate.

✔ No internship is required for graduation, but I can use one for academic credit toward graduation.

✔ Some form of internship is required for licensure or certification in the field or job I am considering.

Compensation needs:

✔ I need a certain amount of money (salary, stipend, or whatever) from an internship.

✔ I need an internship to cover health, disability, and other benefits.

✔ I need my travel, education, or other expenses covered by an internship.

✔ It is necessary or highly desirable for an internship to cover all or part of my tuition expenses.

✔ A wage or stipend for an internship might affect my student financial aid package.

✔ I don't need any economic compensation (wages, expenses, or benefits).

Geographic flexibility:

✔ Legitimate factors limit me to considering local internships.

✔ Legitimate factors limit me to considering internships within my region.

✔ Legitimate factors limit me to considering national internships.

✔ I am able to consider international internships.

✔ For the field or career I am interested in, some cities or regions are considered centers or proving grounds — for example, Silicon Valley for computers, New York City for the arts, Washington, D.C., for government, Las Vegas for gambling. Note that these are not the only centers for these fields. In virtually all cases you have a choice.

✔ I have legitimate reasons for taking an internship far away and at greater expense. For example, maybe you need to fight burnout or to increase your understanding of the world. But if the internship is really a glorified vacation that comes with considerable expense (yours or someone else's) and offers few long-range benefits, think hard before leaping.

Personal situation:

✔ Conditions exist in my personal life that need resolving before I can take an internship.

✔ I need to consider my personal situation (family, health, and so on) before accepting an internship.

Personal values:

- ✔ I have deeply reflected on what values are most important to me.
- ✔ I have discussed my sense of values with other people I respect to clarify and confirm my sense of values.
- ✔ The internship I am considering is likely to challenge and refine my sense of values (healthy).
- ✔ The internship I am considering is likely to violate my sense of values (unhealthy).

Part II
Deciding Where You Want to Go

The 5th Wave   By Rich Tennant

"I don't take 'no' for an answer. Nor do I take 'whatever', 'as if', or 'duh'."

In this part . . .

We compare the different employment sectors and provide criteria for deciding which internship is best for you. We also explore the different types of international internships, where to find them, and how to prepare for them.

Chapter 3

Finding Internships by Sector: Business, Government, and Not-for-Profit

● ●

In This Chapter

▶ Understanding why choosing a sector is important

▶ Assessing your preferences for choosing a sector

▶ Checking out internship opportunities by economic sector

● ●

*T*his chapter explores some of the choices you have in choosing internships in the various *sectors*, or areas, of the economy: business, government, and not-for-profit.

Interns tend to choose a sector on the basis of their overall priorities: to make money through business, to serve the public through government, or to serve humanity through not-for-profit, volunteer-oriented organizations. However, traditional differences among these sectors are becoming increasingly blurred as the methods and technologies used by these three sectors become shared across the sectors:

✔ Many businesses now sell more than goods to customers. They also sell services, such as tax preparation, research on family or company history, and even some of the services traditionally offered by government, such as managing prisons or delivering packages.

✔ Many governments now sell products as aggressively as their business counterparts. Go into any post office and observe all the merchandise for sale: stationery, key chains, address books, and the like. In fact, post offices are run by the U.S. Postal Service, an organization that is part public and part private. Other government agencies sell computer programs, scientific information, and other so-called products.

✔ Traditional not-for-profit organizations, like the Audubon Society, now sell books, calendars, and even clocks and watches to raise revenue for their cause.

Does this mean that it doesn't make any difference which sector you choose for your internship because they are carbon copies of each other? No. As with many stereotypes, some truth exits about the differences among these sectors. While incomes in government and not-for-profits have risen considerably in the past several decades, if your major concern is what you'll earn, the big money is still to be found primarily in business. While governments and not-for-profits are acting more businesslike in terms of their management and services, a strong motive exists in these sectors to help people, even if those people can't pay for this help. Consider, therefore, some important general tendencies among sectors when assessing your goals for an internship and deciding which sector may be the most appropriate for you. Keep in mind that just as people increasingly change sectors during their careers, interns frequently work in more than one sector.

Because of this blurring of sectors, however, concentrate on comparing differences among sectors rather than assuming that all businesses are alike, all government agencies are alike, and all not-for-profit organizations are alike. Such assumptions can be faulty and lead to decisions by stereotype. If you think that because a not-for-profit agency's mission is humanitarian, it will automatically be humanitarian in its treatment of interns, employees, and others, you may be sadly mistaken. Some of the most competitive, cutthroat tactics we have encountered have been by community service agencies who felt their survival was threatened. Some government agencies are highly bureaucratic; others are as entrepreneurial as most businesses. Some businesses have a highly competitive, survival-of-the-fittest atmosphere, while other businesses are relaxed and supportive. When comparing internships, analyze, don't generalize! Look beneath the stereotypes about sectors.

Choosing a Sector Based on Your Work Preferences and Goals

Go through the Internship Goals Checklist in Chapter 2 before choosing a sector or a particular internship. That checklist helps you frame your overall needs and wants; however, some additional soul-searching can be helpful in the process of choosing an internship, so we've included a Work Preferences Checklist in this section.

Spend an hour or two working through this checklist. After you have finished indicating which statements ring true for you, spend another hour or so writing a profile of your situation, your needs, and your preferences based on this checklist. Compare your results to your profile based on the Internship Goals Checklist in Chapter 2. How do they compare? Do they reinforce each other or do they lead you in different directions? If, for example, you indicate in one checklist that money isn't important to you, and in the next you indicate that it is, you need to reconcile your position on this.

Use the following Work Preferences Checklist to determine which of these best describe you. This checklist can be helpful in exploring your work preferences so that you can better identify appropriate internships. It may be the case, especially if you haven't had much job experiences yet, that you aren't sure what you kinds of work you prefer. That may be the very reason you are pursuing an internship, to discover your preferences about work. So if you don't know the answer to all these checklist items, don't panic but do note that you may need to find this out about yourself through future internship/work experience.

The Work Preferences Checklist:

- ✔ **I thrive on competition and always want to know how I rate compared to others.**
- ✔ **I prefer a less competitive, more cooperative working atmosphere.**

    Business tends to be the most competitive of the sectors. The convenient measuring rod of money attracts people who want to know how they compare with other people in terms of income, amount of sales, dollars saved through accounting practices, and the like. Government and not-for-profit sectors are increasingly driven by financial constraints these days and can be competitive as well, especially in the larger organizations and at higher levels.

    Still, in general, government and not-for-profit agencies tend to be more supportive and less competitive. This may particularly be the case with smaller agencies, but you still need to steer clear of a small agency run by a driven workaholic who lives and breathes his crusade and expects you to do the same. Business tends to attract competitive types, but politicians, government managers, and not-for-profit agency heads can be highly competitive, too, and may create this kind of atmosphere around them. While many people prefer cooperating on a team, others feel less comfortable cooperating and would rather complete tasks on their own and get the full credit for it.

- ✔ **I work best under pressure.**
- ✔ **I don't work well under pressure and need a relaxed work pace.**

    Organizations whose work revolves around fixed deadlines often put considerable pressure on interns and other workers. This is true whether the deadline is tax time for private tax accountants or the government's Internal Revenue Service. Legislature interns can be under substantial pressure while the legislature is in session, but too often idle when the session is in recess. The same holds true for political party interns during the campaign compared to the campaign's end. Interns in publishing houses or for magazines are likely to have frequent deadlines. Find out beforehand what the pace of work is like and whether the place is clock-driven and deadline-driven. Is the workload fairly even and predictable or does it vary drastically depending on cycles or other conditions?

✔ **I need to make a great deal of money.**

✔ **I need to make enough to support myself and my family.**

✔ **Money is no object as long as I can survive.**

Internships in the public and not-for-profit sectors are unlikely to match the pay of top private accounting firms, computer and high-tech companies, law firms, and the like, although the most desirable government internships, such as the Presidential Management Internship, are equivalent to full-time jobs in pay and responsibility. Many of the internships in not-for-profit advocacy or public interest organizations don't pay at all, but some do — and well. Teaching interns may not expect to get rich, but at the Choate summer teaching program (www.choate.com), college student interns can earn almost $2,000 plus room and board assisting master teachers for a summer.

✔ **I prefer working with numbers and ideas instead of people.**

✔ **I prefer working directly with people to keep me pumped up.**

This is another case where it is misleading to generalize by sector. Internships in research and data analysis tend to be more idea-oriented. If a research internship involves heavy door-to-door interviewing, however, it may become more people-oriented. An internship at *People* magazine may deal more with layouts and words than with people. Here, too, you need to know yourself, whether you thrive working with other people or gravitate to ideas. A number of psychological surveys can help you discover whether you're an extravert who gains energy from contact with people or an introvert who needs to be alone more of the time. One such diagnostic can be accessed via www.keirsey.com.

Before taking on an internship, remember to find out what types of duties are involved, as prescribed in Chapter 2.

✔ **Having independence and sense of control over my work is necessary.**

✔ **I prefer assignments that are highly structured and for which I don't have to use much discretion.**

A tendency exists for large bureaucracies to limit independence and feelings of control over your work environment. This would likely be the case whether the bureaucracy is the Social Security Administration or Aetna, Inc., a large, private insurance company. A large organization invariably has regulations and procedures that are in place to help coordinate the efforts of so many people. Interns who prefer the security of structured duties and methods may find that environment in actuarial work or other highly structured work for either the Social Security Administration or Aetna. But if you prefer to take initiative and exert more independence in your internship, you can probably find it in these two organizations, as well. The Social Security Administration has made some dramatic changes recently in how it does its work. Interns in the Social Security Administration have, therefore, been exposed to some of this revolution and helped shape it, learning in the process. Likewise, on the business side, big doesn't necessarily mean bureaucratic and stodgy. Some large consulting firms like Andersen expect a lot from top level interns and give them considerable responsibility.

✔ **I prefer a work routine with a small number of predictable, well-defined tasks.**

✔ **Routine bores me. I prefer significant variety and unexpected tasks in my workday.**

All other things being equal, you're more likely to find routine in large organizations that are highly specialized and find variety in small organizations that don't have a separate person to handle each unique task or function. Paid staff members, and even interns, in most small, not-for-profit agencies, for example, have to tackle a variety of tasks from office work to fundraising, and even sometimes talking with the news media. Likewise, small, new entrepreneurial businesses tend to operate more like a team, with each member doing a variety of jobs. The CEO may well get her turn making copies right along with interns and others.

The amount of variety or routine also depends on the nature of the work involved. Insurance tends to be more predictable and routine, while telecommunications is more varied and unpredictable. This assessment will likely hold true whether in large or small organizations. Even large bureaucracies can provide variety if interns are rotated through various positions or deliberately assigned a range of responsibilities. In her Presidential Management Internship with the U.S. Department of the Interior, Janine Tobias handles a variety of issues, from resolving conflicts to promoting the federal government's charity campaign. Look for the possibility of rotations when choosing an internship and remember that if no structured rotation exists, you may be able to arrange your own job rotation.

✔ **I prefer being an identifiable and important person in a small organization (a big fish in a small pond).**

✔ **I prefer being one of many people who contribute within a large, important organization (a little fish in a big pond).**

If you're like most people, you tend to thrive better in either a big pond or a little pond. If you are a pre-career intern just starting out, you may not yet know your preference. We recommend taking different internships in large and small organizations to help you discover your preferences. Some interns want to make a mark and be an important member of the team, and this is more likely to happen in a small organization, although separate offices or work units in large companies and agencies can sometimes have a family atmosphere. For other interns, being part of a major effort or cause is more important than standing out. Such interns may prefer Microsoft to a small, start-up software development company.

Size isn't the only variable to consider. Another factor to look for is age: How old is the organization? Organizations just starting operations, regardless of sector, tend to provide more opportunity for interns to make their mark in important ways. They may not have much of a staff yet. The interns may be the staff, or most of it, anyway. Regulations and procedures are not likely to have been developed yet, so greater flexibility and variety are also likely to occur. Find out as much as you can about the leaders of a new organization and their plans for the future. The new venture may just be an ego trip for the founder, who has no intention of using you for anything but errands. On the other hand, the founder may be looking for a protégé to mentor. See Chapter 14 for a fuller discussion of the protégé-mentor relationship.

Now that you have examined your own druthers about work using the Work Preferences Checklist, using Tables 3-1 and 3-2, you're able to compare these results with what you found out about yourself using the Internship Goals Checklist in Chapter 2. Making this comparison allows you to check your responses for consistency and gives you additional insight because it makes you summarize your overall needs, goals, and preferences.

Table 3-1	My Profile Based on the Internship Goals Checklist
Stage of career:	
Educational needs:	
Compensation needs:	
Geographic flexibility:	
Personal situation:	
Personal values:	

Table 3-2	My Profile Based on the Work Preferences Checklist
How do I feel about competition?	
How do I feel about cooperation?	
Do I work better under pressure or without pressure?	
What are my values and goals toward making money?	
Do I prefer working with ideas or people, or am I comfortable with both?	

Do I prefer taking initiative and exerting independence or prefer to be told what to do?
Do I prefer predictable, well-defined tasks or unpredictable variety?
Do I function better as a big fish in a little pond or a little fish in a big pond? Or don't I know yet?

Looking at your total assessment of your internship goals and interests, consider the following:

Agreement: What are the points of agreement between your results on the checklists in Tables 3-1 and 3-2?

Disagreement: What are the points of disagreement between your results on the checklists in Tables 3-1 and 3-2?

Musts: What must you have: salary, job rotation, housing, specific sector, and so on?

Wants: What elements would you like but aren't absolutely essential?

After you have your needs and preferences in mind, you can review some of the options available for internships in the United States, covered in the following section. See Chapter 4 to explore your international options.

Sketching Your Options for Internships

This section gives you a lay of the land in terms of internships in the business, government, and not-for-profit sectors. Even though no clear-cut boundaries exist among these three sectors in terms of actual differences on the job, these categories make a useful framework for mapping out internship possibilities.

The Economic Census divides businesses, governments, and not-for-profits into standard classifications. This information from the United State Bureau of the Census (www.census.gov) is useful to know. You can find out, for example, where jobs are by type of industry. Knowing where the jobs are helps you in your overall career planning and, even though no official listing of internships exists, gives you an idea of where internships are likely to be: They will be in industries where the jobs are. In the following sections, we list the standard classifications along with a description of the types of employers in each category and how many employers there are (based on the most recent 1997 census data).

Because so much diversity exists among the three sectors, and because they are growing more alike than different, avoid dismissing or discounting any of the sectors out of hand. You may find your ideal internship in any of the sectors if you look hard enough and in the right ways. Remember that you are hunting for and choosing an internship within an organization, not within a general sector. You can find organizations that meet your internship goals and interests in any sector.

Business sector

Business has long been a ripe sector for learning by experience, whether they call them internships, cooperative education, traineeships, or something else. And the business (or *private*) sector has become increasingly diverse. You can still pursue traditional businesses, such as banking, insurance, retailing, and manufacturing, but many newer businesses now exist, and the diversity will grow in the years ahead. Internet companies (the *dot-coms*) are proliferating, and they provide opportunities to get in on this wave. Of course these firm's lifespan may not be too long, but then neither is your internship. Different forms of consulting and advising now exist. Businesses are increasingly providing services that used to be the sole domain of government: delivering mail and packages, running prisons, collecting trash, and so on. Private enterprise also has moved into health and human services in a big way. Businesses now provide home health care, addiction treatment and counseling, and similar services, as do government and not-for-profit organizations. Even if you're a stalwart humanitarian, you can probably find a business internship that serves people in a caring, effective way.

Don't overlook the number of smaller, regional, or local manufacturers that need interns. Going after smaller companies will likely mean less competition for internships. In addition, you may have more knowledge of these smaller businesses and may have connections to help you land the internship. Some smaller companies may not have a formal internship program but could be persuaded to take you on in a learning capacity, especially if you're willing to work for free or for expenses only. This same advice applies to smaller employers in the other sectors, as well.

The following aren't the only categories of employers in the business sector. But these are the ones with the most number of employers and largest number of potential jobs (otherwise known as "life after interning").

- ✔ **Manufacturing** (363,753 employers): Manufacturing includes the production or assembly of products.

- ✔ **Retail trade** (1,118,447 employers): Retail trade includes establishments that sell products directly to consumers.

- ✔ **Finance and insurance** (395,203 employers): This category includes banks, investment firms, insurance companies, and loan and financing companies. Examples of internships in finance and insurance include those with Citibank, Paine Webber, J.P. Morgan & Co., and Lehman Brothers.

- **Information** (114,475 employers): The information category includes publishing, motion picture and recording industries, broadcasting and telecommunications, and information services such as news services and data processing companies. Examples of internships in this sector include Walt Disney studios, National Public Radio, *The Washington Post*, Random House, Loews Cineplex Entertainment, Sony Music Entertainment, and MTV.

- **Accommodation and food services** (545,068 employers): Examples of internships in this category are found with Hyatt Hotels and Resorts, Walt Disney World (in accommodations).

- **Professional, scientific, and technical services** (615,305 employers): This classification includes employers who provide a service of some kind for individuals, governments, or other businesses and includes legal services, accounting services, management consulting, engineering, architecture, advertising, public relations, and so on. Examples of internships in this category include PriceWaterhouseCoopers and Andersen (consulting), law firms, Ruder-Finn (public relations), and Liggett-Stashower, Inc. (advertising). Legal internships, sometimes called *externships* or *clerkships,* may be with law firms or with businesses or governments needing legal services.

- **Arts, entertainment, and recreation** (79,636 employers): Examples of private sector arts, entertainment, and recreation internships include those with Walt Disney World, SeaWorld, U.S. Olympic Committee, Comedy Central, National Basketball Association, and for-profit museums, orchestras, and theater companies.

- **Health care and social assistance** (532,069 employers): This large and growing industry has two parts. Health care includes hospitals, nursing homes, clinics, doctors' offices, and so on.

- **Educational services** (33,783 employers): Included in this category are many trade schools; vocational business schools teaching office skills, merchandising, and so on; schools for the arts; sports camps; and more.

Government sector

The government no longer fits the stereotype of being dominated by stodgy bureaucrats or green-visored bean counters; in fact, it is so vast that it can accommodate different interests. You can be a high-tech specialist, a product entrepreneur, or a humanitarian and still work in the government sector. In fact, it's possible to combine all three of these interests. Another advantage of government as a source of internships is that every part of the country has some government organizations in the vicinity, even if it's a village office, township government, or rural agency. In our experience, small government agencies are more likely to take interns than are small businesses, which are often too focused on cutting costs or growing the business to supervise interns. (Of course, exceptions to this tendency certainly exist!)

The government sector contains thousands of internships for people of varying levels of education, specialization, and motivation. Government internships can be found by *level of government* (federal, state, regional, or local), by *function* (for example, environmental protection, transportation, or health), or by *professional specialization* (finance, management, engineering, or computers).

Federal government internships

The U.S. government, commonly called the *federal government,* contains hundreds of agencies, almost all of which have internships of some type. The best known federal government internships are with the White House, the Presidential Management Internship Program (multiple agencies), the Supreme Court, and Congress. Each has well-established programs and offers substantial opportunity to move within the circle of movers and shakers. Opportunities don't end there, however. Practically every federal agency of any size (virtually all of them) has internships of its own. You can find internships in the Environmental Protection Agency, Department of State, National Aeronautics and Space Administration (NASA), Central Intelligence Agency, Federal Bureau of Investigation, Library of Congress, Department of Health and Human Services, Treasury Department, and many more places.

Interning in private sector publishing

Internships should not be seen as a one-time thing. Many people have found that a variety of internships can provide a wide range of exciting and powerful learning opportunities. One such person is Elyssa Folk. Now a junior at Yale, Ms. Folk completed her first internship during her summer break as a junior in high school and has interned every summer since. Currently a political science major, she wants to combine her love for journalism with her passion for business and government. To date, she has interned at *Modern Bride* and *New York Magazine* and now is working in a paid internship as the personal assistant to a senior editor and correspondent in New York City.

"This has been a terrific opportunity for me," say Ms. Folk, "I have been given a lot of responsibility and oversight and have really learned a lot. My major pieces of advice to other interns are: Don't be lazy or coast. It's your life, your internship opportunity, and ultimately it is what you make of it. And don't be shy to try your hand. Speak up. Don't be discouraged if things don't always go your way but never quit trying."

Elyssa expects to complete an internship in the summer after her junior year as well. "I want to make the most of my time and opportunities through internships right up until I graduate and start my first full-time job."

In fact, internships exist in all of the major functions of federal government: administration and financial administration, judicial and legal, police, corrections (prisons), transportation, public welfare (social assistance), health, social insurance (Social Security Administration), parks and recreation, housing and community development, natural resources, national defense, international relations, postal service, space research and technology, education, and libraries. Virtually all federal internships are paid, and many offer other benefits. A range of majors are relevant for internships in federal service. Majors from anthropology to zoology are appropriate for some federal internships.

Even if you're ultimately aiming for a career in the business or not-for-profit sector, having an internship with a federal or other government agency can boost your career. Some examples: Experience with the Internal Revenue Service (IRS) is probably the best preparation for tax accountants, because interns can learn the rules directly from the source. Interning with the National Endowment for the Arts (NEA) is useful in making contacts in the arts community because the NEA is the friend of so many arts organizations that get money from them. Few better ways to "win friends and influence people" exist than to be associated with the outfit that gives out money.

State government internships

All 50 state governments have internships of some form, and most states offer a large variety. Some of the best known are the California Governor's and Legislative Internships, New York State Administrative Intern program, Alfred E. Smith Legislative Fellows (New York), Georgia Governor's Intern Program, Illinois (multiple programs), Rhode Island State Government Intern Program, and Maine State Government Internship Program. Other states have good opportunities, too. Internships exist in all state government functions, including financial administration, central administration, judicial and legal, police, corrections, transportation, public welfare, health, social insurance, parks and recreation, natural resources, and libraries. State opportunities extend to water supply, electric power, elementary and secondary education, and higher education. In addition, organizations primarily concerned with state government also train interns. These organizations include the National Governors' Association, National Conference of State Legislators, and Council of State Governments.

Local government internships

Internship opportunities abound in local governments across the United States. The most recent count shows 3,043 county governments, 19,372 municipal governments (cities primarily), 16,629 township governments, 13,726 local school districts, and 34,683 special districts (water districts, transportation districts, sewer districts, and so on). Whew! Even though not all of these local governments have internships, enough do to keep you searching and comparing for a long time. Some of the best known are those with the cities of Phoenix,

New York City, Chicago, Dallas, Seattle, Washington, D.C., and Los Angeles. Yet these are hardly the only local governments with internships. Other cities and a number of counties (for example, Montgomery County, Maryland; Camden County, New Jersey) have programs for interns, as do many towns, villages, school districts, and special districts, so if you aren't in a large metropolitan area, don't despair. Many internships are available in these smaller governments, and the competition may be less intense. Local government internships come in just about every major or specialty. Also, most of the government functions that you can find on the state level are also available in local government, along with some extra ones, like gas, electric, water supply, and solid waste treatment.

If a local government or school district in your community doesn't have an organized internship program, you may be able to negotiate a position. Use your contacts or your parents' or academic advisor's connections. Make sure the agency and position are approved by your school so that you get academic credit for the internship you propose. If you don't depend on academic credit, you'll likely have even more flexibility in negotiating your placement.

A great government internship

Lacey Clark has always been interested in politics, both the national and international varieties. As a political science undergraduate at Mississippi State University, she was extremely active in campus organizations. Her participation in these groups put her in contact with people such as the Chief of Staff for Congressman Gene Taylor in Washington, D.C. That spring, Lacey applied for and was awarded an internship with Congressman Taylor. During her internship, Lacey was asked to perform several tasks, from maintaining a database to handling constituent complaints on issues such as military spending and tobacco regulation. As an added perk, she sat in on committee meetings where Congressmen and women were making legislation right before her eyes! She even got to meet some movers and shakers like Senator Ted Kennedy and Bob Dole, who was a Senator at the time. The work Lacey performed for the Congressional office was important, but it was the whole Washington, D.C. experience that really got into her blood. Someday, she knew she would return to the nation's capital.

Lacey's internship the next summer whetted her love of international politics. The United Nations Association of the United States of America serves as a research and advocacy group for the United Nations in the U.S. The organization, housed in New York City, has several different arms. Lacey worked for the Model U.N. and Education branch. At UNA-USA, Lacey was handed the task of writing the background guide for a high school simulation. Over 200 high school students from New York used her background guide as a foundation for their debates during the conference held later that summer. In addition to writing and researching, she had access to the United Nations building and library. While neither of Lacey's experiences led directly to employment, Lacey learned something valuable from both internships and she continues to keep in touch with the contacts she made during those internships.

Not-for-profit sector

Before getting into the jobs in this sector, consider some terminology about not-for-profit organizations. The term *community organization* typically means not-for-profit. Not-for-profit organizations can be *faith-based* (for example, Catholic Charities or United Jewish Appeal) or *secular* (like the American Civil Liberties Union or Common Cause). Not-for-profits can also be *service* organizations, whose mission is to provide needed services to people (think of the American Red Cross or YMCA), or *advocacy* organizations, whose mission is to help people by influencing the actions of governments, businesses, or other institutions (for example, the Environmental Defense Fund or Human Rights Watch). Many not-for-profits can fit into more than one category. The Christian Coalition, for example, is a faith-based advocacy organization. The National Council of La Raza and the Association for the Help of Retarded Children are secular organizations that combine services with advocacy.

The not-for-profit sector has grown substantially in recent years and has become more professionalized. Where not-for-profits used to be run on a shoestring by their founders and a few others, today managers, attorneys, accountants, engineers, scientists, educators, counselors, and other professionals can find a fulfilling career in the not-for-profit sector in one of the following categories:

- **Professional, scientific, and technical services** (5,824 not-for-profit employers): While you won't find as many consulting and professional services employers here as in the for-profit sector, you still have literally thousands of internship sources from which to choose. Some of these employers are tax exempt because they offer public services, such as Legal Aid societies that provide free legal advice to indigent people are of this type.

  Research labs and think tanks engaged in not-for-profit research are another type, whether the research is in the natural sciences (biology, chemistry, or physics), social sciences (economics, sociology, political science, or anthropology), behavioral sciences (psychology, social psychology, and so on), or humanities (history, languages, or philosophy). Examples of internships in these kinds of organizations include Crow Canyon Archeological Center, the Brookings Institution (policy research), Aspen Center for Environmental Studies, Southern Poverty Law Center (ClanWatch and monitoring of other hate crimes), Center for Strategic and International Studies, and the Wetlands Institute (marine science research). Internships in this category can allow you to use your professional or pre-professional knowledge and skills in law, natural sciences, social sciences, engineering, and so on while pursuing noble causes. Some of these internships pay, but because of the invaluable experience they provide, most pay off handsomely in the future.

✔ **Arts, entertainment, and recreation** (19,463 not-for-profit employers): This grouping covers internships with not-for-profit community theaters, orchestras, museums, sports teams, parks, and so on. The great thing about this part of the not-for-profit sector is that almost every community of any size has some of these arts or recreation organizations that are desperate for help — especially eager, lower-paid or unpaid help. Almost certainly, communities large enough to have a college will have some of these organizations. Remember that even if they have no formal, advertised internship program, many of these organizations are eager to get good help. And because they tend to have a lean staff, you often get considerable responsibility and a range of duties. Examples of internships in not-for-profit arts, entertainment, and recreation include Mystic Seaport Museum, Minneapolis Art Institute, and the Dance Theatre of Harlem.

Another bonus is that many of these community arts or recreation organizations have one or more godfathers or godmothers who started the organization, nurtured it, and take pride in mentoring others in their work. This often results in a superior learning experience for interns, but be wary of the founding director who won't let go of the reins enough for others to get really involved.

✔ **Health care and social assistance** (114,784 not-for-profit employers): Hospitals, nursing homes, home health agencies, counseling services, and other health and social assistance employers have their counterparts in the not-for-profit and public sectors. This increases your number and range of internship choices in the growing health and social services field. While you can certainly scratch your altruistic itch to serve people in this sector, you should understand that the "businessization" of the health industry means that many not-for-profit hospitals, nursing homes, and so on are just as driven by financial necessity as their business counterparts. Some people swear by this change in medicine and health while others swear at it! This change does mean, however, that you need to check out each prospective employer more than ever to see what the working environment and conditions are really like.

✔ **Educational services** (7,153 not-for-profit employers): Over 7,000 employers exist among not-for-profit business schools, computer training schools, trade schools, and so on. This doesn't include public school districts and colleges and universities that are counted in the government sector. Whether you're interested in teaching, administration, counseling, computer systems, or another field, thousands of internship opportunities are available in the educational field. Examples of such internships include those at Summerbridge National and Choate Rosemary Hall (teaching internships) and Columbia University (internships for prospective elementary teachers, college teachers, and for educational specialists in school psychology, speech and hearing problems, and so on).

Not-for-profit internship

Stacy Hill has always been interested in what makes people tick — understanding human behavior and helping people learn and behave more effectively. She built on her psychology major at West Virginia University with a practicum in behavioral psychology at Children's Seashore House in Philadelphia. During her three-month internship practicum, Stacy worked with children who were diagnosed with autism and attention deficit hyperactivity disorder. She also helped professionals evaluate and treat autistic and hyperactive children by using behavioral and drug therapies.

Just as one good turn deserves another, in Stacy's case, one good internship deserved another, so she followed this practicum with a one-year paid internship at Seashore House, helping children with severe behavioral disorders, such as severe aggression or self-injurious behavior. After showing what she could do during her one-year internship, Stacy was offered a permanent position with Seashore House as a clinical specialist in bio-behavior. Four years after her second internship, Stacy is now an administrator for a highly specialized brain injury rehabilitation program at the New Jersey shore. As program director, Stacy supervises the work of a staff of 100 and is ultimately responsible for the quality of care for about 50 people being rehabilitated after brain injuries. Her aim is to continue in health care administration, especially building on her experience with behavioral and neurological disorders.

Internships in not-for-profit organizations can also be found in other job categories, but those listed in this section are the categories with the most employment prospects.

Chapter 4

International Internships: How Far Can You Go?

***

In This Chapter

▶ Understanding why interning internationally may be right for you

▶ Taking a look at the different types of international adventure

▶ Coping with planning and logistical problems

▶ Landing internships in the U.S. (for international visitors)

***

Maybe your idea of a dream internship expands beyond national borders. Picture yourself working for a Japanese multinational corporation in Tokyo, doing environmental research at the Australian Great Barrier Reef, cataloguing art in an Italian museum, caring for children in a Russian orphanage, helping rebuild a school in Brazil, helping manage a hotel on a Caribbean island, or planting crops on an organic farm in Norway. Perhaps you picture yourself in a different country doing different tasks. Fortunately for you, the range of potential countries and opportunities is expanding rapidly.

This chapter explores the international breed of internships. We start by examining your motives in pursuing such an internship. We then compare different types of international experience, offer advice in planning and logistics, and give some leads for further information on the topic. Because international internships are a more specialized form of internship, we give specific leads in this chapter for finding international opportunities rather than mixing these leads in with the sources for domestic internships included in Chapter 5.

Assessing Your Motives for Interning Internationally

Before checking internship postings or airline bookings, examine your motives for considering an overseas placement. Review how you responded on your Internship Goals Checklist (see Chapter 2). Do your goals reflect any of the following motives for taking an international internship?

Seeing the world and broadening your horizons

Many people — especially students or recent graduates — want to "see the world." This is certainly understandable. For many, the grind through college and possibly graduate school has been grueling, and attention has been focused on studies. A stint abroad that varies the setting and the pace can be appealing and beneficial. Because our world is becoming increasingly global, broadening your horizons by exposing yourself to the different cultures, languages, and lifestyles of fellow global villagers is becoming more important and expected. An international experience can broaden your aspirations or possibly change them. Every returned Peace Corps Volunteer we've ever known said their experience significantly changed their values and thinking. But some other work placements abroad provide only a superficial and temporary exposure to different cultures.

For a growing number of recent graduates, internships or work-abroad placements allow them to decompress (after years of intensive study), broaden their horizons, and make the transition into the world of work. These three aims can all be achieved if you pursue your international internship correctly, which means doing some planning and initiative that turns mere bumming around Europe (or Asia, Africa, Australia, North America, or South America) into an experience through which you learn and grow, as well as have fun. Having fun and decompressing from college or graduate school are worthwhile aims, but the price can be high if you're doing it overseas. Why not piggyback some extra benefit from your experience to justify the cost?

Increasing your odds of getting into graduate or professional school

Another legitimate motive is to use international work experience as a credential for getting into graduate or professional school. This certainly doesn't hurt if you're aiming for a field that has an international thrust. Relevant international experience probably helps your case if you're considering advanced study in international business, international relations (foreign affairs), anthropology, international law or human rights law, international development, or another internationally oriented field. And the more relevant the experience, the better: Listing a month-long job in a London pub doesn't show as much preparation for international business as working for an exporter of British beers. Working in fast-food restaurants can help support your travel habit, but it doesn't show as much commitment to or preparation for graduate study in international human rights law as does volunteering to work in a refugee camp.

International experience can pay off even when the advanced study isn't obviously international. The explosion of knowledge comes from so many places that working and learning in some of those different places can be a huge asset. An internship with a company like Philips in the Netherlands that has pioneered the CD-ROM and CD writer would be a definite plus for getting into engineering graduate school. Working on an organic farm in Norway to learn different farming techniques, for example, could help you get into a graduate program in environmental studies or agriculture. An international experience can also show initiative and responsibility that can help you stand out in the competitive admissions process. Using your international experience to help you get into and complete a graduate program that isn't primarily international in content requires more creativity and initiative, but it can also be worth the effort.

Preparing for an international career

You may have heard that the world is getting more connected because of advances in communication technology, transportation, and so on. More than any previous generation, you have the option of pursuing an international career. Some obvious areas like business, banking, and communication are becoming more internationally focused, but so are entertainment, education, law, health, and other fields.

For some of these fields, international experience is a requirement — or at least a strong asset. If you're preparing for a career in international development (helping people abroad develop and build their countries), experience in the Peace Corps, CARE, or other international organizations is a tremendous asset. You can't really understand the issues or conditions until you've been there yourself. The same goes for a career in diplomacy. You wouldn't be considered legitimate until you've served in one or more assignments in different countries to learn the ropes. Having prior international experience is a huge advantage in getting a longer-term business job overseas, especially if that experience is in the same (or similar) country to where you would be assigned. Down the line, you'll have so many details and tasks to learn that already knowing something about the language, customs, and geography, gives you an advantage in a new job in a different country.

Preparing for a career at home (but one where international experience is an asset)

As international trade expands, you may be one of the growing number of employees who are working in their home countries for companies, not-for-profit organizations, or government agencies that do business (and may even have offices or operations) overseas. If so, you may spend all or most of your

Ten bad reasons for wanting to intern abroad

International interning isn't for everyone. Consider the following faulty reasons for interning internationally:

- You can't think of anything else to do with your life, so you want to convert as many foreigners as possible to your way of thinking.

- You've just broken up with your significant other and want desperately to get far away.

- You've just had a spat with your family and want desperately to get away.

- Someone told you that the grass really *is* greener in Greenland.

- You get anxiety attacks where you live and think this will be less of a problem in a foreign country.

- You're so bummed after a long course of study that you'll do anything to get away — even if you have to pay for it over the next five years.

- You hear that girls (or guys) go for guys (or girls) who know some French (or Spanish, Swahili, or Chinese).

- You've had no success landing a good job or internship in your country but think the task may be easier abroad.

- You're feeling sorry for yourself and want to see people who live in far worse conditions than you do.

- You've just seen a warning that the world is coming to an end, and you want to see as much of it as possible before it does.

This may be humorous — at least we hope so — but we are also serious in emphasizing bad reasons for wanting to work overseas. If your motives are to run away from someone or a problem, to foist your values on others without learning about theirs, or to gloat over other people's living conditions, an international experience may not be right for you at this time. After clearing up the problems and making an attitude adjustment, the time may be right.

time in the U.S. or wherever else you live, yet still have to deal with the international dimension. You may have international partners, customers, suppliers, or regulators that you need to know about. Having international internship experience gives you a greater understanding of the problems and opportunities that exist when different cultures, currencies, legal systems, and political systems are involved and can help you "think outside the box" by bringing insights from other cultures and ways of doing things.

Keep in mind that you can accomplish some of these goals without leaving the U.S. (or whatever country you live in). Because international organizations are located in Washington D.C., New York, London, Beijing, Tokyo, Sydney, Rio de Janeiro, and most major cities of the world, you can get experience working for an international business or agency without traveling across the border. Granted, a stay-at-home internship may not be as exotic or culture-expanding as working for an international organization overseas, but it does give you the experience of working on international issues and problems and working with people who have different languages and cultures.

And it may be less expensive and fit better with your plans to work internationally but live domestically. For example, you may be able to intern with an international organization while pursuing your degree at your own school. This could save you time and credits that may be lost if you had to delay your studies or had problems transferring credits from overseas.

Not all placements overseas or at home provide a rich international experience. Some placements offer substantial professional experience in a multicultural setting. Others employ you in minimum wage jobs that just pay for living and travel expenses — if you're lucky. The following section describes the different kinds of international placements available.

Comparing the Types of International Internships

Many different international placements are available, but they fall into five main types: organized internship programs, negotiated internships, work abroad programs, help/humanitarian projects, and teaching.

Organized internship programs

Organized international internship programs come in the same sectors (business, government, and not-for-profit) as domestic internships, but far fewer of them are available. Organized programs tend to offer more of a complete package of work and learning; while the learning part may be missing from some of the other types of overseas placement, unless you make it happen yourself. Organized programs also tend to provide more logistical support in arranging visas, transportation, housing, and so on than do the other types of placements. Organized international internship programs come in several of the following varieties:

 ✔ **University-based internships:** For organized internships abroad, look first at your college or university. Most organized international programs have university sponsorship. If your university has no such program, hundreds of other schools do. Most of these programs accept students or graduates from other schools as space permits. University-based programs may include academic classes or may include just the work experience without formal classes. For example, American University combines study abroad with internships in a number of countries including Russia, Spain, China, Chile, and Italy. Likewise, Boston University has study/internship programs in Australia, Ecuador, England, and other places. Syracuse University provides a range of internships and field placements in such fields as communications, business, law, social services, and drama through its study centers in Europe, Asia, and Africa. Students can take internships with or without classes. Ohio State University offers business internships in Japan. These are just the tip of the iceberg. Most major universities and many colleges offer international placements.

Some sources of university-based internships include Council on International Education (`www.cie.uci.edu/iop/internsh.html`), Colorado College Career Center (`www.cc.colorado.edu/CareerCenter/SummerJobsAndInternships/Intern.html`), and Studyabroad.com (`www.studyabroad.com`). Studyabroad.com lets you search for educational programs, including experiential education like internships, by country (`www.studyabroad.com/exp.html`), and just about every possible country is included. Most of the programs shown are university-based, but some are from other kinds of organizations.

Check out programs directly to find out what services they do and don't provide, and consult your own school's study abroad office before signing up. This is good advice for any international placement.

- **Intern placement programs:** A number of placement programs that aren't university-based also sponsor organized internships abroad. Two of the most useful ones are The International Cooperative Education Program (ICE) (`www.icemenlo.com`) and CDS (`www.cdsintl.org/cds`). ICE has placed more than 15,000 American students in work/internship positions in Germany, Switzerland, Belgium, Luxembourg, Finland, Japan, and Singapore. Students work 30 to 40 hours a week and are paid! (This is one of the few international internship programs that pay. It isn't much, but it helps pay bills.) Local host families or employers provide accommodations. CDS helps place interns both leaving the U.S. and coming to the U.S. and has a number of scholarships.

- **Specialized internship exchange programs:** Some internship programs exist for specialized fields. The AIESEC (`www.aiesec.org`) is a student-run exchange organization that operates in over 80 countries and at over 700 universities. AIESEC arranges paid internships/work exchanges in business, economics, computer science, education, engineering, and development among its member countries. The more than 25,000 companies that use AIESEC interns include AT&T, IBM, Ford, and Price-WaterhouseCooper. AIESEC also has a program for not-for-profit development. AIESEC handles the logistics of getting visas, work permits, accommodations, and so on.

One business finance major went on an AIESEC internship to Colombia. Her "traineeship" focused on identifying investors in North America willing to invest in a Colombian company. Even though this intern knew no Spanish before moving to Colombia, her Spanish improved dramatically and she was able to find and arrange numerous investments in her Colombian firm. Besides her learning payoff, her stipend was enough to cover basic living costs plus enough to cover personal travel throughout Colombia.

In addition, the Fascell Fellowship Program specializes in international affairs, languages, and area studies in Romania, Hungary, Poland, Russia, Kazakhstan, Czech Republic, and other countries in that region. Finally, IAESTE, the International Association for the Exchange of Students for Technical Experience {www.iaeste.org) operates an intern/trainee exchange program for engineering and technical students in over 70 nations.

✔ **Formal programs directly with international organizations:** Some of the best international placements can be found by directly contacting the organizations providing the internships. No schools or matchmaking services need to be involved. It helps to think of these in the same categories as in Chapter 3: the business, not-for-profit, and government sectors.

- **Business sector:** Multinational corporations such as Coca Cola, 3M, General Electric, Intel, Boston Consulting Group, Samsung, JP Morgan, CNN, and others have formal internship programs overseas. These can be scoped out via their Web pages and company information. *The Directory of International Internships,* 4th Edition, available from Michigan State University (www.isp.msu.edu/Internationalinternships/order.htm), has numerous business and other listings, as do some of the general internship directories described in Chapter 5.

- **Not-for-profit sector:** A wide range of humanitarian, educational, and other not-for-profit organizations offer international intern placements. These include International Red Cross, CARE, Make-Peace International, Habitat for Humanity International, and the Academy for Educational Development. Some of these show up in general internship directories, but *The Directory of International Internships,* 4th Edition, is a more promising place to check.

- **Government/public sector:** In this category, you can choose from among your own government's agencies abroad or government organizations of other countries. The former group is easier to uncover and probably gives you the better chance of getting an internship. U.S. Departments with international placements include the State Department and the Agency for International Development. On an even broader scale, check out internships with the World Bank, United Nations, European Community, and other organizations. Some programs allow interns from other countries to be placed in government settings. For example, interns can work in the British government through the Hansard Scholars Programme, Educational Programs Abroad, and other programs. *The Directory of International Internships,* 4th Edition, and World Wide Web searches (explained in Chapter 5) are good places to start.

Negotiated internships

Not all the best internships come in organized programs. This especially holds true in Asia, Africa, Australia, Europe, and South America, where the practice of internships has not taken root so strongly. Many companies, not-for-profits, and government agencies can provide terrific experience, but they have to be discovered. Another option, therefore, to packaged, formal intern programs is to negotiate your own.

You have to shift to or stay in AIM (active intern mode) to actively seek internships that can't be found in general directories or through two-click World Wide Web searches. This kind of searching takes more initiative, but is often worth the effort. You can seek these internships before traveling to a country and while you're staying there, but be sure to research the requirements to work legally in that country. (Keep in mind that in many countries, the only way you can get a work permit or special work visa is through a formal internship program.)

While in a country, do your homework on prospective intern employers. Being in the vicinity allows you to personally visit organizations to see whether they could use someone with your knowledge and skills. By showing initiative (and the necessary language and job skills), you can often convince an employer to take you on, especially if you're willing to work primarily for the experience and perhaps some expenses. Don't forget to negotiate for learning benefits, as well as other benefits. Consider asking for work rotation to vary your experience. A mentor who can help you navigate problems at work may also be particularly important in a country where you don't know the language or the customs as well as at home.

Don't cast your net too narrowly. If your heart is set on getting a placement involving production, and you restrict your search to typical manufacturing firms, you may miss a small baking company that can provide valuable experience on manufacturing processes. On the other hand, know your limitations in terms of speaking the necessary language or languages and being able to function in the situation you're considering. Being way in over your head — linguistically and perhaps legally — will likely produce more frustration and trouble than bona fide work experience and learning.

Because most countries require a work permit to work legally, even for an internship or part-time job, some of the work abroad options covered in the following section can help you get overseas.

Work abroad

Not so long ago, unless you were well-established in your profession, work abroad meant either being an au pair taking care of an overseas family's kids or bussing dishes in a resort. These opportunities still exist, but the range of options has expanded.

Work abroad, whether arranged before you travel or found on the spot, typically is just that — work. You can learn on the job but you probably don't have access to classes, training, or other structured learning unless you negotiate this or initiate it. These jobs are paid but are mostly short-term (typically up to six months depending on labor and immigration laws of the host country). They can be ideal in supporting your travel habit and in giving a relatively brief but real dose of work overseas.

Sound like what you want but aren't sure how to get the necessary work permits and job leads? The following organizations do just that for you:

✔ The Council on International Education Exchange (CIEE) Work Abroad Program helps students and recent grads obtain work permits in the following countries: Australia, Canada, Costa Rica, France, Germany, and Ireland. The Council also has programs for teaching English in China, for providing internships in the U.S. for students from other countries, for volunteer abroad experiences, and for high school student exchanges. The Council also can help arrange transportation, international identity cards, and other matters. A participant handbook and lists of employers and potential accommodations provide some information. Many times, however, students find a job or place to live via other students in the program. Most of the jobs involve waiting tables, office temping, bartending, and store clerking, but some more career-oriented jobs and internships are available in Canada, France, Germany, and Ireland. Contact CIEE via the Web at www.ciee.org; via mail at 205 East 42nd Street, New York, NY 10017-5706; or by telephone at 888-268-6245.

To decompress after college graduation and to broaden her work experience and horizons, Erin Garnett went on a work abroad program to Australia and New Zealand through the Council on International Education Exchange. CIEE helped with the paperwork, travel arrangements, and provided information on jobs and housing. In her six months down under, Erin worked in a variety of settings ranging from computer work in an Auckland office to picking vegetables in the Australian countryside. On weekends and in between jobs, Erin and her other work abroad "mates" would explore the region, trying activities like scuba diving, glacier trekking, and blackwater rafting.

✔ British Universities North America Club (BUNAC) provides the same kind of help as CIEE in getting work permits for Britain, Australia, and New Zealand. Contact BUNAC USA through the Internet at www.bunac.org; by mail at P.O. Box 430, Southbury, CT, 06488; or by phone at 888-GO-BUNAC.

These are not placement programs as such. They help you get your work permit, provide useful information about where and how to find jobs, and point you in the right direction. The rest is largely up to you. You can get minimum wage jobs fairly easily on site, after they know you have a valid work permit. To get career-oriented jobs and internships typically requires writing to prospective employers several months ahead and sending your resume along with a cover letter explaining when and how long you will be in their country and what work skills you have. See Chapter 6 for help on cover letters and resumes.

Help projects

Do you have the desire to help improve someone else's quality of life? A wide range of humanitarian *help projects* gives you the chance. Volunteers from all over the world join hands and minds to help build schools and houses, make drinking water safe, help prevent the spread of diseases like AIDS, plant crops and forests, build communities, and help in other ways.

The bonus from help projects comes from the fact that as a volunteer, you benefit just as much. Many students we know of who participated in a help project consider their experiences to be one of the highlights of their lives. Through volunteering, you get to broaden your horizons by meeting people with different backgrounds, cultures, and values. Many projects, including work camps, form work teams from as many different countries as possible. You get to interact with co-workers and with the people you help in ways that simply being a tourist never allows. You also get to test and expand your own capabilities, learning to do things you never thought you could. Many students even discover they want to continue helping people through their careers.

Volunteer opportunities range from two years (in, for example, the Peace Corps) to the two to four weeks in work camps. Many projects, especially work camps, are scheduled to coincide with summer vacations or university winter and spring breaks. Many provide food and lodging on the work site. Lodging is often in tents, churches, public buildings, or people's homes. A few of the longer, more official volunteer opportunities provide transportation, but most don't, and some, especially those offering academic credit, may cost you more than transportation. Longer international volunteer opportunities can be found through the Peace Corps, CARE, and the United Nations. The UN Volunteers Programme (www.unv.org/unvols/index.htm) takes volunteers at least 25 years old who have professional skills in agriculture, public health, computer systems, and the like. The Peace Corps (www.peacecorps.gov) increasingly prefers such skills but is still willing to take volunteers with more general qualities.

A staggering and growing number of not-for-profit organizations around the world sponsor volunteer opportunities. One of the best ways to find out about these opportunities is through Action Without Borders (www.idealist.org). This database allows you to search for volunteer opportunities in Africa, Asia, Australia, Latin America and the Caribbean, and North America. These opportunities cover a wide range of fields including art, children, disaster relief, fundraising, race and ethnicity, voting and democracy, women's issues, and many more. You can also search by what skills are needed and whether the placement is paid or unpaid. CharityGuide.org (www.charityguide.org) is another useful Web site, especially for volunteer vacations. CharityGuide.org links to causes all over the world you can help from your own computer at home or on campus, allowing you to become a "virtual volunteer."

Even with humanitarian organizations, check the conditions of your contract carefully.

Teaching

Teaching English used to be the most common way American students could work abroad, although today, many other kinds of opportunities exist. Teaching opportunities come in different forms: teaching a language, an academic subject like math or science, a particular trade like carpentry, or a profession like law or administration. Teaching can also be a form of volunteering, as with teaching English to villagers in China. Teaching can also come via a paid internship or job abroad as with teaching in schools run by the U.S. government, multinational corporations, or other international organizations. Even if the teaching assignment doesn't pay a salary and is more volunteer teaching, you receive other benefits. Because of the nature of teaching, you tend to form close, lasting relationships and have a built-in support group with students and other teachers. Most teaching assignments also either assist with food and lodging or provide it outright.

Even though the U.S. State Department doesn't employ teachers abroad, its Web site on Teaching Overseas (state.gov/www/about_state/schools/oteachdirectory.htm) links dozens of employers or agencies recruiting teachers overseas. This is a great place to start your search. The International Educator (TIE) offers a newspaper and interactive Web site (www.tieonline.com) that lists hundreds of overseas teaching positions and allows you to post your resume and teaching interests. TIE charges a small fee for these services. The site at teachingenglish.com lists useful books and directories on teaching overseas, especially for teaching English.

Understanding the benefits and costs of international opportunities

Although the preceding sections provide a sense of the range of overseas opportunities open to you, as well as some of the strengths and shortcomings of each type, we summarize these advantages and disadvantages in Table 4-1. Keep in mind that the advantages and disadvantages don't automatically apply to every internship in that category: Exceptions exist. Some volunteer opportunities are paid; some organized internships don't provide good training. But Table 4-1 gives you a good sense of the overall strengths and weaknesses of each type of placement.

Table 4-1	Advantages and Disadvantages of International Internships	
International Opportunity	*Advantages*	*Disadvantages*
Organized internships	Usually has a learning component, especially if university-based. Typically provides the best ammunition for your resume. Lodging is often provided or arranged.	Comparatively few international internships pay salary or wages. Often have to pay tuition or placement fees. May require a longer-term commitment.
Negotiated internships	Can be tailored to your needs. Not as likely to be as competitive because placements aren't advertised.	Harder to find. May not have as many features (job rotation, training, and so on) as formally organized internships. Employers may be inexperienced working with interns and may not know the legal requirements.
Work abroad	Usually paid, although often at minimum wage. Can provide learning if you negotiate well. Short-term, temp-type jobs offer flexibility for traveling around or moving on.	Most work abroad jobs lack structured learning. Need to pay work permit costs and other expenses.
Help projects	Gives satisfaction of helping others. Offers growth in self-awareness and self-confidence. Often covers room and board. Can help on resume and application to grad school, especially if related to academic program (for example, international law).	Usually aren't paid wages and many actually cost volunteers. Type of volunteering (for example, disaster relief) may not be career-oriented.
Teaching	Offers the same satisfactions and personal growth as with help projects. Improves your knowledge of a subject by having to teach it.	Teaching English usually requires a bachelor's degree. Teaching for Department of Defense schools requires certification. Most teaching posts don't pay a salary.

Mastering the Planning and Logistics of International Internships

Regardless of what type of placement abroad you may choose, you need to handle some key logistical matters. These include financing your placement, arranging travel, clearing legal hurdles, getting permission to work, arranging lodging, and other matters.

Planning and preparing ahead is doubly important for international internships. Not only are more hurdles involved (for example, passports and visas), but the process often takes longer because of distance and differences in language and procedures. Six months to a year is not too early to start identifying the best placements for you and following up on them. Most organized intern exchanges or placement programs usually require three months lead time. Be sure to get the specifics for the placements that interest you. You also need advance time to figure out how to pay for your experience abroad.

Financing your adventure abroad

As terrific as an adventure abroad can be, your time overseas will feel even better if you know you won't still be paying for it five years after you get back. Some of the ways to pay for your internship are as follows:

- **Employer-paid transportation and housing expenses:** For a few rare placements, the employer pays transportation and lodging expenses or covers these in the salary. This is most likely to occur with organized, longer-term placements: Volunteering via the Peace Corps and teaching for the U.S. Department of Defense Educational System are examples.

- **Employer-covered room and board:** A much larger number of intern employers overseas cover all or part of room and board, leaving interns to pay transportation to and from the host country. Many of the employers in all four types of placement cover these expenses either directly or indirectly. Volunteer programs tend to provide room and board directly on site while work abroad programs tend to pay wages that can be applied toward room and board.

- **Grants and scholarships:** A limited number of scholarships are available to help support student travel and interning abroad. Some of the best scholarships are based on volunteer service. The Target All-Around Scholarship program offers five $10,000 scholarships and 1,900 $1,000 scholarships based on a student's community and volunteer service. Each store gives two $1,000 scholarships, and most stores are conveniently located throughout the U.S. These scholarships can be applied toward tuition and fees for a university-based international program — perhaps to do even more service. The Bonner Scholars Program supports as many as 1500 students with four-year scholarships up to $4,000 per year. Recipients are expected to provide community service in return. Information on these and other service-oriented scholarships can be found through www.charityguide.org/scholarships. The CDS International internship program (cdsintl.org) offers scholarships to U.S. students who intern overseas. Rotary Clubs and other service organizations also sponsor overseas travel. In addition to doing your own search, consult your school's international center, career center, or financial aid office for other leads.

✔ **Fundraising:** Some interns raise money to travel abroad via fundraising — soliciting sponsors, selling pizzas, or whatever. This tends to work better for volunteer, help projects because people are more likely to contribute to humanitarian causes. However, your relatives and friends may help sponsor you even if the internship isn't a service project.

✔ **Payment by prior or future earnings:** Another method of financing your experience abroad is to *pre-pay* or *post-pay* it. Translation: Earn or acquire the money ahead of time to finance your trip or afterward to pay off loans or credit card bills that you run up while abroad. We support pre-paying your experience because having your international adventure to look forward to can motivate you to earn and reward your hard work. We discourage the post-pay option because having sizable bills to pay off can put a damper on an otherwise terrific experience — and put you in the hole for years to come.

No matter how you finance your adventure, most countries require you to have enough money with you to show you won't get stranded or be a deadbeat in their country. Some programs require proof of resources up front, such as $1,000 in savings.

Making travel arrangements

Some of the organized internship programs and work abroad exchanges help you arrange flights and other forms of travel. The Council on International Education Exchange (CIEE) has its own travel service, Council Travel, that finds student air and rail discounts and books your transportation for you. Other programs may refer you to regular carriers; with still others, you may be on your own. If you're arranging your own travel, consider some of the many discount travel companies and Web sites. A few of the most common include www.travelocity.com, www.onetravel.com, www.priceline.com, and www.airtech.com. Whether booking your own transportation or working through a placement or exchange organization, check the terms carefully. If the bargain sounds to good to be true, it may be. For further advice, get *Travel Planning Online For Dummies,* 2nd Edition, by Noah Vadnai and Julian Smith (Hungry Minds, Inc.).

Passports: Getting out of your country and into another

If you don't already have one, apply for your passport several months ahead of time. You can get forms and information online (`state.gov/ passport_services.html`), at a federal building that has a U.S. Passport Office, and at some post offices near you. Other government offices, such as county clerk offices, libraries, and other offices also may process passport applications. The passport Web site lets you search for where you can apply nearest where you live.

Getting a passport takes time, but you can obtain one within a few days if you're willing to pay an extra $35 (on top of the $60 fee) and go through more effort. You're also required to show proof that you're already scheduled to travel. Our advice: Apply for your passport early (before the summer travel rush) and avoid the hassle.

Before leaving, make three copies of your passport's identification page. That's the page with your gorgeous photo and the official information on it. Leave one copy with your family or trusted friend before leaving and take the two copies with you. Keep one copy with you at most times; keep the other in a safe place. Leave the official passport in as safe a place as possible; you don't usually need the official passport for cashing checks or for identification within a country. You will need to show your official passport and visa/work permit when accepting a position, however.

Visas: They're not just credit cards

You need a work visa or work permit to work legally in most countries. Having a passport is good enough for a tourist, but because you seek a longer-term and more meaningful relationships, a visa is also required. That applies to interning and volunteering. Different countries have different policies about visas, so do some research to find what the countries you're aiming for require. Some work abroad exchanges help with the visa-application process.

Housing: Where will you stay when not working or traveling

Housing varies depending on the place you go and the type of international placement you have. Volunteering in work camps usually means tents or dorms, but you rarely have to hunt for housing. You're simply told which tent is yours. Peace Corps volunteers typically live in homes or apartments because they stay longer, and Peace Corps helps arrange these accommodations.

Some of the organized business, government, or other internships either provide lodging or help you find it. Work abroad exchanges give you lists of potential housing (usually housing that previous students have had), but you have to follow up on your own.

Good resources on international internships

While we give you a solid start in this chapter, a topic as intricate as international opportunities — with all the legal, political, and cultural nuances — deserves follow up on your part. Some other useful sources include the following:

Several online articles by William Nolting, Director of International Opportunities for the University of Michigan, are excellent and well worth your attention:

- ✔ "Work Abroad: International Internships" (www.umich.edu/~icenter/over-seas/work/internships1.html)

- ✔ "Work Abroad: Work Abroad Overview and Calendar" (www.umich.edu/~icenter/overseas/work/waoverweb.html)

- ✔ "Work Abroad: Short-Term Paid Work Abroad" (www.umich.edu/~icenter/overseas/work/shortterm.html)

GoAbroad (www.goabroad.com) has a wealth of information on international opportunities for interning and studying. It also has useful legal information.

Intern Abroad (www.internabroad.com) is a link from GoAbroad and describes a number of different kinds of internships in multiple countries.

Transitions Abroad Online, the Online Magazine of International Travel and Life (www.transitionsabroad.com), offers a range of international opportunities as well as information on travel, work, study, and living overseas.

The U.S. Department of State does more than negotiate peace treaties and issue passports. The State Department regularly issues several kinds of announcements that every traveler should consult before going abroad. Interns from other countries should use the announcements, as well, before going into a different country.

- ✔ **Travel warnings** tell you to avoid certain countries because of war, disease epidemic, or other prolonged conditions.

- ✔ **Public announcements** tell you about terrorist threats, short-term coups, bomb threats to airlines, and other relatively short-term risks to American (and other) travelers.

- ✔ **Consular information sheets** are written and updated regularly on every country in the world. They are a font of good information including a description of country, entry requirements (and where to inquire about visas), medical care and medical insurance, other health information, crime, aviation safety oversight, customs regulations, drug penalties, location of U.S. embassies and consulates, and more.

Taking advantage of this information via (www.state.gov/travel_warnings.html) is like having your own multi-million-dollar research unit checking out all the countries you may possibly visit.

Checking with other students working at the same site or students just leaving that site may be one of your best bets if you haven't lined up housing in advance. You can often share a house or apartment with other students or take over the space of someone just leaving. Word to the wise: Some intern program Web sites' links to apartment finders may not be connected with that program. In all cases, consider the terms of any rental contract carefully. You may be getting work experience but may be getting worked over on rent at the same time.

Taking care of other important logistical issues

A few other issues, such as insurance and references, deserve your attention.

✔ **Be sure you're insured and that the insurance is accepted in the country where you will work.** More than one internship overseas has been ruined by an accident or illness to an uninsured intern who had to come home early. While abroad, you need to be covered with health and accident insurance. In some cases, you can get this coverage through your program, especially if it is an organized university-based program. You may be covered through a family policy, but don't depend on it because not all insurance is accepted in every country. Check with your intern program or overseas employer to be sure your insurance is valid in that country.

✔ **Know the money requirements of your host country and comply.** Countries typically require visiting interns to have enough to support themselves for several months, if necessary. Some programs require you to show proof that you will have at least $1,000. Countries also have limits on the amount of their currency that can be taken out of the country, but those limits are less likely to concern interns. In all cases, check the requirements of your host country.

✔ **Have multiple sources of ready cash.** Having different sources of cash — credit card, debit card, traveler's checks, and a checking account in local country — gives you more flexibility in case one supply is cut off. If you lose your credit card or a merchant won't take your check, you have a backup. Also, make arrangements in advance with a banker, parent, or broker to send you money if you need it. Setting up these arrangements in advance avoids hassles and stress.

✔ **Have written references with you.** Most countries are bigger on references than the U.S. You may need a reference to do the following:

- Set up an account at a local bank (reference from your banker or current statement)

- Rent an apartment or house (reference from a landlord at school or creditor whom you have paid faithfully)

- Give to a prospective employer (references from prior jobs)

- Apply to schools overseas (your current transcripts and any recommendations from your teachers)

Obtaining an Internship as an International Student

International interning is such a good thing that it isn't just Americans who want to intern abroad. A growing number of internationals come to the U.S. each year for business internships, volunteer projects, work exchanges, seasonal jobs, and other types of experiences. And, like American students and others, they also want to intern in other countries in Europe, Asia, Africa, North America, South America, and Australia.

Most of the advice and leads we give in this chapter apply to interns coming from other countries as well as those coming from the U.S. You need to figure out your motives for interning abroad, sort out the different kinds of experiences available, and choose the best for you. You also need to know the visa requirements of your host country and handle the same logistical issues. But some advice applies principally for you as an international reader, especially if you want to intern in the U.S.

Getting a U.S. work visa

International students needing information about obtaining visas for temporary work or work exchanges in the U.S. should check out `travel.state.gov/visa_services.html`. That site tells you about the different kinds of U.S. visas, the different kinds of work visas, and how you can obtain these. Most students coming to the U.S. for internships and other forms of on-the-job training need the "J" form of visa for exchange visitors.

Finding leads on internships in the U.S.

Some of the exchanges or placement organizations discussed in the "Work abroad" section of this chapter also help visiting interns come to the U.S. The following, however, are additional resources:

- ✔ **For business internships and traineeships in the U.S.:** AIESEC U.S. (`www.us.aiesec.org`) is good for U.S. internships. Remember that AIESEC also places interns and trainees in over 80 countries and handles most of the logistical arrangements.

- ✔ **For engineering and technical internships and traineeships:** IAESTE (`www.iaeste.org`) offers technical placements in the U.S. and other countries. Make sure you first contact the IAESTE committee in your home country. Links and contact information are on the Web site.

✔ **For placements in the U.S. (and other countries) in business, technical, engineering, and hotel administration:** CDS (www.cdsintl.com) offers several different U.S.-based programs as different levels of preparation and in different fields.

✔ **For internships and work programs in the U.S. in a number of fields:** The Council on International Education Exchange (CIEE at www.ciee.org) not only operates work abroad and volunteer programs in a number of countries, it also helps place students in U.S. jobs.

✔ **For placements in volunteer help projects:**

- Idealist.com (www.idealist.org) is a terrific source, allowing you to search for humanitarian jobs or volunteer opportunities by country. You can also submit your employment or volunteer profile and get e-mails about jobs or volunteer opportunities that fit your profile.

- CharityGuide.org (www.charityguide.org) gives leads on volunteer vacations and longer-term internships.

✔ **For a variety of listings:** Internships for America (internship4america.com) has mostly business listings (some international) but primarily handles international students who want internships or jobs in the United States. Three-quarters of their interns are international.

Part III
Getting Where You Want to Go

The 5th Wave   By Rich Tennant

@RICHTENNANT

YEAR 1 - GET RESCUED
YEAR 2 - GET RESCUED!
YEAR 3 - GET RESCUED!! NOW!!
(FOCUS MORE)
YEAR 4 - GET RESCUED
(SCREAM LOUDER!)
YEAR 5 - BUILD GOLF
RESORT

"My thinking has changed a little this year."

In this part . . .

We show you how to go about getting that all-important, just-right-for-you internship. We help you locate internships, and we cover what it takes to get hired, namely resumes, references, and successful interviewing.

Chapter 5

Locating Successful Internships

• •

In This Chapter
▶ Developing a time frame for finding your internship
▶ Researching internships and organizations
▶ Staying on track in spite of distractions

• •

*A*fter you discover what you're looking for in an internship (see Chapters 2 and 3) and what sectors of the employment world you're interested in (see Chapters 3 and 4), you can begin the search for successful internships: those that match your goals, needs, interests, and preferences. The key to this entire hunting process is research and more research.

You'll find various sources for leads on prospective internships, and you want to use them all: your academic institution and advisor, traditional printed sources, CD-ROMs, the Internet, and your diverse personal contacts. Depending on your situation, some of these sources will be more valuable to you than others.

College, university, trade school, and high school libraries and career centers are useful to students and recent graduates, although graduates already in their careers can also consult their alma maters' career centers. Many schools also provide career services for graduates; in fact, most of the Internet databases and the popular annual directories of internships aim for college students or recent grads. If you're substantially into your career, you have to be more inventive — and more persevering. Probably more valuable to you than those directories and databases are annual reports and other information directly from employers and networking. Pre-career students who also use these other sources will have an advantage over students who limit their searches to the easiest sources: internship directories and online databases.

Look through all your sources and come up with a preliminary list of 15 or 20 internships that seem most promising. From there, use your preliminary research to help you narrow this list down to the eight or ten finalists on which you can concentrate. Then begin the process of actually getting the internship you want (see Chapter 6).

Understanding the Time Frame for Internship Searching

You can never begin searching for your internship too early. A good rule is to begin searching for the internships you may apply to at least six months or a semester or two (depending on how long your school terms last) before you want your internship to begin. For example, if you plan to begin an internship in January, begin your preliminary searching during the summer (and certainly no later than September).

Why begin so soon? Mostly because getting a good internship isn't an easy thing to do. All the steps required take time. You don't want to be in a situation of having to rush either yourself or the organizations you will be contacting. In addition, many internships have annual or fixed deadlines that require advance planning (see Chapter 2). Even internships with rolling applications require some lead time for you to get your act together, make contact, research the organization, prepare your application, and prepare for interviews.

In addition to giving yourself plenty of time for all you need to do, starting early helps you begin creating your image as a person with initiative and foresight with your academic institution, advisor, and the organizations considering you. You want to be seen as someone with maturity and forethought, not someone who is haphazard, rushed, and unprepared.

Don't wait until the last minute to begin. Get out a year-long calendar and start filling in some dates, working backward. Begin with the day you want your internship to start. Suppose you want your internship to start in the summer semester after classes end on June 5. That, plus a couple of weeks to recuperate from exams, means you begin with June 15 as your red-letter day — the day you want your internship to begin. Now, work backward figuring at least six months from the time you start working on getting an internship till the time you actually start an internship.

All the final details of your internship with the organization should be worked out at least four weeks before your internship starts, so go back a month and mark May 15 as the latest date the internship agreement and all the details related to it should be finalized. In between the two, you make plans about your life while an intern. For example, if you're going to be working around the corner while living at home, little is going to change for you. On the other hand, if you're going to be working across the country (or in another country all together; see Chapter 4), you may well need to make a lot of plans for moving, finding a place to live, obtaining a work visa, and so on. So, giving yourself at least two months to get these details settled, mark April 15 as the date by which you need to have all your permits, licenses, moving plans, and so forth in order.

To get that internship offer means, in reverse order, interviewing and sending applications (both covered in Chapter 6), selecting organizations to apply to, researching and selecting the various possibilities (see Chapter 5), deciding on your geographical preferences (Chapters 2 and 4), understanding what sector or sectors of the workforce you're interested in (Chapter 3), and understanding yourself and what you want from your internship (Chapter 2).

You probably need about two months to get your applications out and to interact with the various organizations before you can get an offer. So mark March 15 as the last date to get the applications sent off. Because you may need to take a month or so to do the research and prepare the applications, mark January 15 as the last date to start researching your list. You need a month to do your preliminary research and to analyze your own interests, needs, and wants, so mark December 15 as the latest date to start the process of finding and starting your successful internship. Finally, remembering that anything that can go wrong will go wrong, give yourself some extra time and mark November 15 as the date to start your internship hunt.

The following is a sample timeline worktable:

Start date	*June 15th*	
All last minute details completed	May 15th	One month prior to starting
Finalize all living plans, obtain work permits, visas, credits, and so on	April 15th	Two months prior to starting
Have and accept offer	March 15th	Three months prior to starting
Begin sending out applications	January 15th	Five months prior to starting
Begin researching opportunities	December 15th	Six months prior to starting
Get an early start	November 15th	Seven months prior to starting

Researching, Researching, Researching: The Search Begins

Unless you have a rich parent who will be dropping you into the family business, your ability to find and land an internship is critical in your internship success. Thus, in this section, we help you understand the process and obtain the tools you need.

Matchmaker, matchmaker, make me a match!

Applying to an organization you know little about is like going out on a blind date. You may have a wonderful experience or a nightmare. Too many people who know little more about an organization than its name and address apply for internships (and for jobs, too). Here are examples of the type of information you need:

- Do you know how financially secure the organization is?

- Is it in a growth or a contraction mode?

- Does it have a reputation for producing high quality goods or services?

- What kinds of opportunities do they offer for growth and advancement?

- Do most employees think it is a good place to be or do low morale and high turnover exist?

As emphasized in Chapter 3, many organizations contain a wide range of jobs and professions. You don't have to intern in a law firm to practice law or a business to apply business skills. An active search considers various types of organizations that offer the kinds of training and experience you are interested in.

You have a lot to discover before deciding whether to apply to a given firm. Equally important, if you find that an organization will work well for you, you can use this same information to draft resumes and cover letters that are specifically tailored to that particular position and organization.

Have you ever known someone who sent out a resume to tens or even hundreds of employers? What about the high school student who applies to colleges without knowing much more about them than where they are located? What are the chances that even if their applications get into the right hands exactly when openings occur, students will find this job or school a perfect match? Slim to none!

For this reason, we strongly recommend you take a different path. Reach out to discover who has internship opportunities you can apply for and also which employers sound really wonderful but don't seem to use interns. Then, as you find out more about these organizations, you can begin to see which ones sound like a possible good fit for you. If the fit looks weak, save yourself the time, energy, and cost of applying to that organization. If it does look like a good match, the information you've gathered will help you to write a cover letter and resume that closely matches what the organization is looking for. You'll also be prepared to wow them during an interview (see Chapter 6).

Knowing what questions to ask in your scouting report

In scouting out prospective internships, remember to use the Internship Goals Checklist from Chapter 2 and the Work Preferences Checklist from Chapter 3. These help you assess each prospective internship in terms of your needs, interests, values, work preferences, and other characteristics. In addition to this baseline information, research other characteristics about potential employers. Trying to find information about a not-for-profit, business, or governmental organization can often be a case of feast or famine. Either you find very little or you find so much information that you're hard-pressed to say what is and isn't useful.

From the published sources (internship directories, organization annual reports, brochures, and so on), try to answer the following questions:

- What is the organization's structure (consider divisions, subsidiaries, location, and so on)?

- What services or products are produced by each portion of the company and where?

- What is the mission or vision of the organization according to official statements?

- What is the organization's size and scope, including the size of budget, number of employees, number of interns, revenue, and profits?

- How does the organization compare to and fit in to its industry and how does it shape up against its competitors?

- What does the future look like? Growth, little change, layoffs, or shrinkage?

By calling your personal contacts, you can focus on trying to discover what you can about the internal dynamics of the organization overall and about the part of the organization you'll be working for. Here are some examples:

- What kind of reputation does the organization have; are people drawn to the organization or fleeing from it?

- What do present (and former) employees and interns have to say about the place?

- What do outside people have to say? Is having worked or been an intern there a good thing for your reputation?

Finding Sources of Information

This section discusses three major sources of information about possible internships: linear, two-dimensional search vehicles; non-linear, electronic search vehicles; and interactive, interpersonal search vehicles. Don't rely on any of these too highly or too exclusively, but use each to the fullest extent possible.

Linear, two-dimensional search vehicles (books and articles)

You can use this fancy term to impress your family and friends as in, "I've been utilizing the latest in linear, two-dimensional search vehicles to research my internship possibilities." What this means is that you've been looking through recent books and other sources that are *linear* (read from front to back) and are *flat* (two-dimensional as opposed to being a solid three-dimensional object like yourself).

While this book is a reference to consult on a regular basis, you can find a number of other print sources to access but not necessarily own. For example, a number of good books and other print sources share information on what internship opportunities exist. While you can buy many of these sources for yourself, your public or college library or career center is a good source for much of this.

Your library or other databases can help you research the following:

- ✔ Internship opportunities found in annual internship "directories" or "guides"

- ✔ Articles and books about specific fields and organizations that you may want to apply to

- ✔ Information about various organizations that may have internship opportunities

- ✔ InfoTrac, Lexus-Nexus, and other such CD-ROM and electronic databases that let you search past and present newspapers, magazines, professional journals, government publications, and so on

General internship directories

Three big annual internship directories are released each fall. Be sure to use the latest edition; for example, in fall of 2002, be sure you're using the (upcoming) year's 2003 annual edition.

- ✔ *The Internship Bible,* **200X Edition.** This annual edition from Princeton Review comes out each fall and includes thumbnail sketches of information on over 100,000 internships across the country.

- ✔ *The Yale Daily News Guide to Internships,* **200X Edition.** Another annual collection from *Yale Daily News* and Kaplan Books that also provides thousands of thumbnail sketches and helpful tips.

- ✔ *Internships 200X.* Peterson's annual fall collection of thousands of internships from around the country.

- ✔ *America's Top Internships.* This annual guide from Princeton Review Publishing (written by Mark Oldman and Samer Hamadeh) describes their top-rated internships at over 100 organizations that employ thousands of interns. It also indexes internships by type of organization, application date, pay, and location.

Specialized directories and books

You can find internship directories for specific career fields, such as the following:

- ✔ *Gardner's Guide to Internships in New Media: Computer Graphics, Animation and Multimedia* (published by Gardner Inc.).

- ✔ *Criminal Justice Internships: Theory into Practice* by Gary Gordon and Bruce McBride, 1995.

- ✔ *Jumpstarting Your Career: An Internship Guide for Criminal Justice* by Dorothy Taylor, 1998.

- ✔ *The Internship, Practicum, and Field Placement Handbook: A Guide for the Helping Professions* by Brain Baird, 1998.

- ✔ *Megaree's Guide to Obtaining a Psychology Internship* by Edwin Megaree and Sansford Pederson, 1997.

- ✔ *Directory of Internships in Youth Development,* 1994.

You can also find internship directories for specific geographical areas, such as the following:

- ✔ *Miami Job Source: The Only Source you Need to Land the Internship, Entry-Level, or Middle Management Job of Your Choice in the Miami Metro Area* by Mary McMahon, 1997.

- ✔ *Pittsburgh Job Source: Everything You Need to Know to Land the Internship, Entry-Level, or Middle Management Job of Your Choice in the Pittsburgh Metro Area and Western Pennsylvania* by Mary McMahon, 1997.

Sources on associations

Another set of rich leads comes from general information about organizations themselves. This set includes general directories such as the *Encyclopedia of Associations,* annual reports, and other information about specific organizations. Using these more general sources may be a bit more indirect and time-consuming than consulting directories or books specifically about internships, but this approach can often be well worth the effort for several reasons: Many of the best (and especially newest) internships aren't listed in directories or books about internships. In addition, by searching off the beaten path, you won't have to compete with so many other prospective interns for the leads you do uncover. Finally, using these broader sources helps educate you about the organizations in which you are interested — and helps prepare you for interviews (see Chapter 6).

Sources on specific companies

To try and track down information on most private and public firms, begin with the following, many of which are standard in most library reference sections:

- ✔ *The Almanac of American Employers*
- ✔ *America's Fastest Growing Employers*
- ✔ *Hoover's Guide to Computer Companies*
- ✔ *Hoover's Guide to Private Companies*
- ✔ *Hoover's Handbook of Emerging Companies*
- ✔ *The Million Dollar Directory*
- ✔ *Standard & Poor's Corporate Directory*
- ✔ *Ward's Business Directory of U.S. Private and Public Firms*

Non-linear, electronic search vehicles

Essentially, *non-linear* is a show-off term to describe the various *search engines* (as they like to be called) that help you surf the Internet for information.

You can enter a specific term like "internship" and get a few thousand responses (or hits), but by being more precise and using "internships, radio stations, New York" you may get some very specific leads to follow.

Listing specifics in this field is tricky. Not only do things like Internet addresses change literally overnight, many dot.coms come and go with great fanfare and rapidity. Six months from now (or perhaps six weeks from now), referring to some of these sites may seem as quaint as showing Pan-Am as the space-going airline in *2001: A Space Odyssey* (filmed in the mid '60s) seems today.

That said, today's most well-known search engines include the following:

- ✔ AltaVista (www.altavista.com)
- ✔ Direct Hit (www.directhit.com)

- Iwon (www.iwon.com)
- Go To (www.goto.com)
- Google (www.google.com)
- Find What (www.findwhat.com)
- LookSmart (www.looksmart.com)
- Lycos (www.lycos.com)
- Excite (www.excite.com)
- Yahoo (www.yahoo.com)

Some engines are really meta-searchers; that is, they let you search multiple engines at one time. For a good example, check out DogPile at www.dogpile.com or CNET at www.search.com.

For a thorough overview of smart Interneting, get yourself a copy of *The Internet For Dummies,* 7th Edition, by John R. Levine, Carol Baroudi, and Margaret Levine Young (Hungry Minds, Inc.).

Useful Web sites for internships

Many Web sites exist specifically on internships, while there are literally thousands that touch upon it. Some are goldmines, while others are empty claims. Although you have to spend time and effort to find the sites that are most beneficial to you, this process still is far faster and easier than making all those calls or trips to libraries.

As with anything on the World Wide Web, be careful how you use these and other internship Web sites. The Web changes so quickly that these sites may no longer exist or may have changed content. In addition, while the ones we list don't require a fee, some others do. When using the Web, always be careful about what information and how much information you supply. Never include your social security number or bank account information. Employers don't need such information until they hire you.

- **Internship Resources on the Web, Colorado College Career Center** (www.cc.colorado.edu/CareerCenter/SummerJobsAndInternships/Intern.html): This site contains dozens of useful links to general internship databases and to internship sites for the following categories: international internships; art, entertainment, communications and design; computer, technical, and engineering; seasonal internships; not-for-profit, education, counseling; health, sciences, and environmental; and law, government, and public service. It also links other college and university Web sites about internships that, in turn, link to other sites. A highly useful bonus is the raft of online publications available at this site covering topics such as cover letters, interviewing skills, job search strategies, and medical school. Link to Publications at the bottom of the home page.

✔ **Career Related Links, University of Florida Career Resources Center** (www.crc.ufl.edu/Internship.html): The University of Florida Career Resources Center has a valuable online *Internship Handbook* that gives a lot of useful information. This site also links to major internship sites, including international internships, Walt Disney World, and others.

✔ **JOBTRAK.com, a service of Monster.com** (www.jobtrak.com): This is a major online database where employers list job opportunities, including internships. In addition, students and alumni can register and post their resumes and find considerable job-related information. Anyone can access some of the general information, but to do a search or register your resume, you need to be affiliated with a participating school. Most major colleges and universities participate, and you can contact the career services office for your school's password.

From the homepage, click on Students and Alumni, and then click on Find a Job. Select your school from the scroll-down list and enter its password. From your school's JOBTRAK site, you can select Jobs & Internships, Registration (to enter your user profile and resume), Online Career Fair, Jobtalk (which allows you to post messages to employers and receive messages from them), and Job Search Tips. If doing a search for internships, click on Jobs and Internships, and then type in your search criteria (type of work, industry, location, and so on). This mostly shows job opportunities. To get internships, type **internship** into the key words search. You can search for on-campus or off-campus opportunities.

✔ **FutureCollegeGrads.com** (www.futurecollegegrads.com): This site allows you to search by keyword for internships or entry-level jobs with the option to specify any state. Students can register free and receive a newsletter about opportunities.

✔ **InternJobs.com** (www.internjobs.com): This national database for college graduates and recent graduates allows for registration, placement of resumes, and search by keyword. It also lists a wide range of placements from business, government, and not-for-profit sectors.

✔ **Internships for America** (www.internship4america.com): This site has mostly business listings, with some international. It primarily handles international students who want internships or jobs in the United States.

For internships in Washington, D.C., check out the following:

✔ **The Washington Center** (www.twc.edu): The Washington Center is an independent not-for-profit organization that provides internship programs and seminars to college students. The Center is affiliated with over 800 colleges and universities in the U.S. and works with 2,000 to 3,000 interns placed in the Washington area in the business, government, and not-for-profit sectors. The Center charges a fee for being in one of its programs. For that fee, however, the Center assists with the logistics involved in finding and pursuing an internship in D.C.

✔ **Washington Intern Foundation** (www.interns.org): This not-for-profit foundation is organized to help individuals find internships in the Washington, D.C. area. Most internships are in government (including some for members of Congress) and not-for-profit advocacy and public service organizations. The site allows registration and search.

The following sites offer special value to some groups:

✔ **Graduate Assistantships Data Base** (www.GradAsst.com): Allows a search for graduate assistantships, one form of internship for those who want to stick around campus or go into a career in university teaching or administration.

✔ **Federal Work-Study Program** (www.ed.gov/prog_info/SFA/StudentGuide/2000-1/fws.html): This site explains in simple terms the Federal Work-Study Program, which provides jobs for undergraduate and graduate students with financial need. These jobs can be on-campus or off with not-for-profit and government organizations that serve the public interest. Ideally, these jobs relate to the student's course of study. This program can help pay for undergraduate or graduate coursework while providing valuable part-time work experience. Check with your school's financial aid office to find out more.

✔ **INROADS National Career Training** (www.inroadsinc.org): INROADS, Inc. provides intensive leadership and career preparedness training for minority college students interested in business and industry. According to INROADS, over 7,000 students from 36 states and Canada participate in its Leadership Development Institute. Participating students are current interns with over 1,000 corporations. They receive coaching in communication skills, self-management, business sophistication, management skills, and other areas.

✔ **Guide to Internships for the Deaf** (www.deafness.about.com/library/weekly/aa062899.htm): This useful site is for specialized kinds of internships for deaf people. Readers with other physical challenges may want to directly contact any national, state, or regional society that specializes in helping people with that challenge.

✔ **Entry Point!** (www.entrypoint.org): Entry Point! is a program created by the American Association for the Advancement of Science and offers summer internships in science, engineering, mathematics, and computer science to students with disabilities. Placements include those with IBM, NASA, Lucent Technologies, Texas Instruments, and others.

✔ **American Association of Retired Persons (AARP)** (www.aarp.org): AARP is a large organization serving people over 50, not just those who are retired. It provides a wide range of services, including advice on careers, career changing and options, volunteer opportunities, and so on. This site is a good source for readers seeking internship-type opportunities or career changes well into their career.

And finally, the following general sites are worth checking out:

- ✔ Monster Board Direct (`campus.monster.com`)
- ✔ Policy.com (`www.policy.com`)
- ✔ Rising Stars (`www.rsinternships.com`)
- ✔ National Internships Online (`www.internships.com`)
- ✔ Roll Call (`www.rollcall.org`)
- ✔ Idealist (`www.idealist.org`)
- ✔ Internship Programs (`www.internshipprograms.com`)
- ✔ U.S. Office of Personnel Management (`www.opm.gov/interns`)

Interactive, interpersonal searching (networking)

The new buzzword for this type of searching is a simple one: networking. *Networking* means making and using your connections with other people (that is, conducting an interactive, interpersonal search) and by extension, with all the other people they know, to help you in your search for the successful internship opportunity.

People say it isn't what you know but who you know. In one sense, this is true. The people you know (and who know you or know of you) create a wide net of individuals who can let you know of internship possibilities. Remember though, that while your network may help you find an opportunity, your skills and abilities will help you land and succeed in your internship.

Networking is easy in theory but difficult in practice because most people feel uncomfortable talking about themselves and asking other people for help. While successful networking is a book unto itself, some basic steps can get you started.

1. **Begin by keeping track of your network as it exists now and as you help it grow.**

   Write down the names of all the people you know. Don't censor yourself by listing only the people you can think of who may have an internship position or work in a given field or location; list everyone. Some of the people on your list will be close, longtime friends and relatives. Other people will be recent acquaintances, while still others will be somewhere in between. You may feel comfortable talking to some of the people; others whom you may not know as well may seem more difficult. Some are more likely to have a good connection to an organization or field you're interested in, while others are not. In all cases, for each name, keep track of the following information: name, address, phone number, e-mail address, title, organization, field, how and for how long you've knows this person, how comfortable you are talking to this person about your search, and how and through whom you got this name and number (which becomes important as you start getting names from your first circle of contacts).

2. **Speak with these people to let them know about your search for an internship.**

   What you're asking of them is three-fold. First, you want to know whether they're aware of any opportunities you may investigate. Second, you want to ask them to keep their eyes and ears open for you. Finally, you want to ask them for the names and numbers of anyone they know who may be able to help you.

   What is the worst thing that can happen? Will someone shoot you for asking? Will he run over your dog with his car? No! The worst thing that can happen is that the person will say no when you ask. While no one likes to be told no, that's a small price to pay for the possibility of getting help in finding your internship opportunity.

If you're looking for an internship in a particular field, don't forget to make contact with the local, regional, national, or international professional organizations in that field. This is especially important if you're already in a career and looking for an internship to change careers or if you're seeking a hard-to-find internship (for example, you're looking for an internship in a geographic area where few are listed or you seek a highly specialized placement). Professional associations not only involve people in the profession or trade you're considering entering, but they are also committed to helping train and socialize people into that profession or trade. Eureka! These associations are tailor-made for your internship search. They contain contacts predisposed to helping other people get started, because they probably got similar help at the beginning of their careers.

How do you find these veritable safari parks for internship (and job) hunting? Directories, journals, and the Internet are good places to turn. The *Encyclopedia of Associations* (available through college or public libraries) is especially useful because it indexes professional and trade associations in alphabetical order and by category (government, scientific, education, and so on) and gives, for each association, the names, addresses, phone numbers of members, along with the number of members, publications, leading activities and awards, dates of conferences, and other pertinent information. (And if you need a break from your search, look up all the associations about Sherlock Holmes or *Star Trek*. You may be surprised at how many there are!)

If you're interested in government, for example, the *Encyclopedia of Associations* leads you to a number of associations including the American Society for Public Administration (www.aspanet.org), whose over 10,000 members work in a variety of government settings across the world. This association, like many others, holds conferences where you can make contacts and hunt for opportunities, conducts workshops and training in the profession, and even has a Young Professionals Forum specifically geared to helping young people get started in the management of government and not-for-profit organizations.

By going to meetings and conferences, getting involved in helping operate the association, and even running for office, you increase both the size and strength of your network and increase your professional knowledge and skill. The same principle applies to associations in business, journalism, education, science, accounting, graphic design, and other professions. Find the right association or associations and get involved.

Chapter 6

Getting the Internship

● ●

In This Chapter

▶ Conducting an active search for your internship

▶ Reviewing the applications process

▶ Creating a top-notch cover letter

▶ Polishing your resume

▶ Succeeding in an interview

▶ Considering an offer

● ●

*A*fter having researched and identified a variety of potential internship opportunities, you have the difficult decisions about which ones to pursue. From your pile of potentials, you need to winnow the list to about ten to which you'll apply. You must take in to account not just which ones that sound best to you but which ones make the best fit — for you and for the employer.

This chapter helps you narrow your list, find that best fit, survive the applications process and interview, and choose from among your offers.

Searching Actively

You can conduct your internship (or job) searches in two basic ways — passively and actively. Of course, no search is totally passive, because you would simply sit at home, waiting for employers to call, without your ever having done any research, put out any feelers, or even submitted a resume. But getting only a few names and addresses for an internship and registering with a few online internship databases is still basically a *passive* search. You find a few leads, respond to them, and then wait (and hope) for employers to come after you. While some interns may manage to find an internship with such minimalist effort, they are the rare exceptions. More typically, passive searchers either get no response or they have to take whatever turns up, and that's usually not the perfect match!

The experience of many interns, intern supervisors, and advisors, tells us that an *active,* assertive search strategy leads to success. An active search involves using all (or at least most) of the sources and strategies we describe in Chapter 5 rather than limiting your search to one or two sources.

Applying for the Internships That Fit Best

After you've created a list of finalists, the next step is to make contact, selling yourself as someone employers want to hire — in other words, the perfect intern for them. In this *selection phase,* you continue the careful, step-by-step internship process that began with clarifying your goals and needs (see Chapters 2 and 3) and proceed with locating the "best-fit" internships to which you will apply. Best fit internships are those that do the following:

- ✔ Give you a chance to apply and test your learning from school.
- ✔ Allow you to explore the kinds of jobs or professions you are most interested in.
- ✔ Provide the on-the-job learning you need to pursue those jobs or professions.
- ✔ Meet your needs for compensation.
- ✔ Provide the kind of working environment that meshes with your work preferences (see Chapter 3).
- ✔ Meet your other goals and preferences (see Chapters 2 and 3).

It is in this selection phase that you select opportunities to pursue, and employers select interns to hire. The selection phase begins with the creation of two documents (your cover letter and resume); continues through your written and interpersonal follow-ups with the organizations you contact, the acceptance of interview opportunities, and the interviews themselves; and concludes with considering offers and accepting the best one for you.

Your research should tell you what specific information each employer requires you to submit with the application. In some cases, you may have to submit a form to an online database search. In other cases, you may need to write directly to the organization, sending your cover letter and resume. In still other cases, you may be asked to submit a writing sample or other samples of your work: paintings, architectural designs, Web page designs, and so on.

Choose your work samples carefully. A good rule is to submit samples of your work that most closely resemble the kind of work you will do in that internship. If you're applying for an internship as a policy analyst for an environmental advocacy organization, send your critical analysis of incinerator pollution, not your magnum opus on voting reform (however badly needed). If business plans or legal briefs are what the internship requires (according to your advance scouting), submit those as work samples, not your honors thesis on deregulation of the communications industry.

If you don't have a sample corresponding to the actual internship work, submit the closest thing — as long as it's good work. For example, if you don't have a good environmental analysis (or the ones you have aren't up to your standards), an analysis of another policy area (for example, transportation) that uses the same kinds of skills would probably be appropriate. When in doubt, ask the contact for the internship program.

Carefully plan and execute all your contacts with your potential employers. Remember that the people who review your cover letter, resume, and other written materials will decide whether to pass your application along to the next step in the process or to just pass on you altogether. Your winning personality and keen questioning are useless if you never get the chance to show them off in an interview.

The cover letter

No matter what additional materials may be required with your application, a cover letter will likely be required at some stage.

Purpose of cover letters

The *cover letter* covers your resume, both literally and figuratively. This is the letter that you place on top of your resume (see "The resume" section, later in this chapter) before putting both of them into an envelope. It is the first piece of information seen and read.

The cover letter serves a variety of important purposes, including the following:

- Serves as your introduction to the organization
- Makes a critical first impression of you
- Contains useful and detailed information (both about you and your knowledge of the organization) that can't fit in your resume or doesn't belong there
- Allows you to amplify and/or call attention to certain elements of your resume

Your cover letter, like all your other communications, must appropriately demonstrate your writing skills. It should also, like your resume, be concise. That means no wordiness or padding. Some experts advocate limiting a cover letter and resume to one page each. For students with limited and mostly part-time work experience, one page is probably sufficient. But you may write more, especially in your resume, if you have solid content and aren't padding it with unessential detail. This particularly holds true if you have substantial work experience and are using an internship to switch fields rather than enter a career.

Whatever the length, print your cover letter on high-quality paper, the same paper you use for your resume. In general, we recommend you stick to a high-quality, plain, bright-white paper. Some job hunters resort to unusual paper colors or lengths, hoping to make their applications stand out. And it often does stand out — but rarely favorably. These kinds of tactics make employers wonder why applicants need to resort to gimmicks rather than relying on their records.

Think of your cover letter as a sales document. It must convince the reader to read your resume. The cover letter and resume, acting together, must impress and sell him or her on wanting to offer you an interview or an internship. (Not all internships require interviews, but most do.) Any flaws or weaknesses in your cover letter, resume, application form, and other written materials jeopardize your chances with this organization. If you're sending letters and resumes out to organizations but aren't getting offers for interviews, go back and rework one or both documents. If you're getting the chance to interview but are not getting offers, re-examine your interview style (see the "Surviving an Interview: It's Not the Third Degree" section, later in this chapter) and fix whatever isn't working for you.

Recipe for a successful cover letter: Key ingredients

A persuasive cover letter follows a logical pattern:

- ✔ **The beginning paragraph** explains that you're applying for an internship (giving its title or description) and how you learned about the position.

- ✔ **The middle paragraph** sells/tells about yourself, explains how you're a good fit to what organization's wants and needs (from information you gathered in your organizational research), refers to your resume, and makes any special points about yourself or your background. If any small issues are hanging over you, this is the place to clarify them. Avoid flowery, vague language.

  You want readers to know the following:

  - What you can do for them (be realistic and confident without being boastful)
  - What you expect to get from being the company's intern

  This is also the place to mention details like university credit, financial or other types of support you may be receiving, and so on. Your search should have told you which employers require you to be getting academic credit along with the internship.

- ✔ **The closing paragraph** concludes your letter by reaffirming why you think you're a good match with this organization and its internship and expresses your availability for an interview, if required.

Using standardized forms

A number of internship databases now exist online (see Chapter 5). Many of these allow you to list your credentials with that service either for free or for a fee. Be sure to check for any up-front or hidden costs. Prospective employers of interns can then review the database of intern applicants to see which ones to pursue. These services tend to have a standard form you need to fill out that contains information usually conveyed by your cover letter and resume. In these instances, you have to complete the standard form or submit your general resume to use the service without getting to tailor your "pitch" to specific employers.

You may need to play by these rules if participating employers and the service insist on standardization. If allowed, you may want to make the contact directly, tailoring your letter and resume to specific employers. While placing your information in the database to see if any employers contact you doesn't hurt, don't leave it at that. A passive search (posting your credentials on several databases to see if any organization is interested in you) rarely pays off. To succeed, you want to conduct an active search: taking the initiative to uncover good leads, doing your homework on these leads, and applying directly, tailoring your pitches to how you fit with each employer.

Different types of cover letters

You can use one of two styles of cover letters, depending on your purpose.

✔ **Targeted cover letter:** This letter, along with your resume, is written to apply for a specific position. The cover letter targets that position and employer by including information from the job description itself as well as other specific information that demonstrates how you're a perfect match. You include specific, relevant information about the organization's mission or activity that coincides with your goals, training, or experience.

Here's an example: "Your firm, Abraham Planners and Architects, interests me because you specialize in historic restoration of city buildings. My honors design project (enclosed) focused on the restoration and use of historic train terminals in Cleveland and Philadelphia. My academic emphasis has been on restoration, something I am committed to as an alternative to sprawl. A summer internship with your firm would allow me to apply what I have learned about restoration and expand my competence working with your experienced professionals."

These kinds of points in your letter show the following:

- You've done your homework on the prospective employer.
- Your goals and capabilities fit with the employer's goals and needs.

Note how this is done in Figure 6-1.

✔ **Exploratory cover letter:** The second type of cover letter, an *exploratory cover letter,* aims at organizations that don't have an official internship program. You send it with your resume in order to explore opportunities. Because your cover letter and resume make you sound valuable to them (or potentially valuable with the right training), the company contacts you about any openings they have or to discuss the possibility of creating an internship for you. See Figure 6-2 for a sample exploratory cover letter.

References

Organizations will want to do some research on you, just as you've done on them. Consider individuals who are willing to be called in order to talk about your qualifications as an intern.

Good references may include academic advisor, a former boss (or, potentially, a co-worker) from a current or former job, and perhaps even one of your instructors. Relatives, friends, the clergy and the like, while they can attest to your great character, aren't going to be able to talk about some of the other important issues an organization will want to know about, including your motivation, work ethic, emotional maturity, and so on.

You can mention your reference(s) in a couple of different ways. If your references have a direct connection to either the organization or person you're writing, mention the reference(s) in the body of your cover letter. If you see no particular connection, mention your reference(s) only in your resume.

For more details on cover letters, check out *Cover Letters For Dummies,* 2nd Edition, by Joyce Lain Kennedy (Hungry Minds, Inc.).

The resume

The second part of your sales pitch is your resume, and your resume should be tailored as much as possible to be a good fit for the organization to which it is sent. Consistent with your active search approach, your research should discover what knowledge and skills the employer needs, and your resume should show how well you fit those needs. This doesn't mean that you distort the truth in any way; instead, you're selective about the experiences and skills you include and the areas you emphasize. You want to try as much as possible to select the experiences and descriptions about yourself that are likely to be of interest and value to your target organization.

In each of your resumes, you want to paint not only an overall positive image of yourself but an image that will engage the reader. Because you create each resume, each should reflect the specific blend of information and descriptions that are that make you stand out as a serious, highly qualified applicant but that still convey an accurate picture of your experience and qualifications. Portraying yourself as someone you aren't lessens the likelihood of a "best fit."

Sample Targeted Cover Letter

Joshua Colin Donovan
2200 N. Mayflower Blvd. #24
Home Town, California 98000
555-543-0925
readytogo@whoopee.com

August 9, 200X

Ms. Laetitia DuFour, Human Resources Manager
First Bank of Paris
1 Rue de Times Square
New York, NY 14785

Re: Financial Analyst Internship Program

Dear Ms. DuFour,

It requires little analysis to understand why First Bank of Paris is a leading bank in international trade and development. First Bank has taken many innovative steps to bring international banking into the 21st century including expediting and tracking international money transfers and increasing the services provided to international visitors via automated tellers.

I too am committed to matching tradition to technology in the financial field and I would like to be a part of First Bank's continued growth and success in the years to come. Your Internship Program for International Financial Analysts matches my interests and goals: To support your operations in the northeast with a range of international clients. When it comes to this blending of the old and the new as well as the American and the international, I have to offer:

- A range of financial and accounting skills in international banking
- Expertise in computerized database management and forecasting software
- Experience living and working in a variety of cultures both in the U.S. and abroad
- A track record of success in analysis projects both large and small

The specifics on these and other qualifications are included in my enclosed resume where you will notice that I am currently working for one of the largest international brokerage firms in the world.

I look forward to the opportunity to meeting with you to discuss my background in further detail and how I may be of service to you and the First Bank of Paris as the new century unfolds. I will contact you next week to see what we can arrange.

Sincerely,

Enclosure: Resume

Figure 6-1:
Sample
Targeted
cover letter.

Sample Exploratory Cover Letter

Joshua Colin Donovan
2200 N. Mayflower Blvd. #24
Home Town, California 98000
555-543-0925
readytogo@whoopee.com

June 29, 200X

Ms. Megan Desrosiers
Director of Finance
Bigger Brokerage of Burbank
7 Pittsfield Rd
San Mateo, CA 94321

Re: Broker Analyst

Dear Ms. Desrosiers,

Bigger Brokerage of Burbank claims to provide "some of the best brokerage services to be found anywhere." This is quite a claim. However, when one analyzes not just your profit and loss data, but your customer satisfaction scores and continued growth over the past several years, it becomes apparent your are all that and more.

I too have spent the past several years working hard, working hard to be the best broker analyst possible.

After a tour of duty in the Army in which I was able to develop my interpersonal and team building abilities, I set out to learn all that I could about the brokerage field and to hone my skills as sharply as possible. During this time I . . .

- Graduated second in my class overall (trailing first place by .004 grade points)
- Gained expertise in computerized database management and forecasting software
- Achieved a track record of success in analysis projects both large and small

I am writing to you now to inquire whether Bigger Brokerage of Burbank has an internship opportunity in the area of investment analyst. My education and prior experience equip me for such and both your firm and I could benefit from my services to you as an intern.

While my resume is only able to offer you an outline of my skills and abilities, I would like to meet with you to discuss how an internship could help Bigger Brokerage further achieve its financial and professional goals.

Sincerely,

Enclosure: Resume

Figure 6-2:
Sample
Exploratory
letter.

Your resume, like your cover letter, is a professional document and must look and read as such. We wish we could recommend a single, perfect style of resume for you to use, but unfortunately, this is not the case. Not only can you choose from several different styles, but if you show a resume to five different people, you'll get five different opinions about it. You just can't please all the readers all the time or even be sure which type of resume will please any given reader. That said, we help you do your best in this section.

Styles of resumes

You can choose from three basic styles of resumes, each with its own advantages and disadvantages. You decide which is best for you based on your own background and on your research about the organization you're sending it to. The three styles of resumes are as follows:

Chronological-style resume

The chronological resume, shown in Figure 6-3, is perhaps the most common format used. The focus is on your work history, and it's usually presented in reverse order: You list all of the jobs you've had, from the most recent job back to the first.

This style is a good choice if you're applying for a position in a field in which you already have some experience. The chronological-style resume is designed to show how your particular history in the field matches a company's needs. It isn't as effective at showing the skills and knowledge you have. The chronological style is, therefore, a bad choice if you're just starting your career or have no particular experience in the field to which you are applying. Unfortunately, both of these conditions are common for many student interns. After all, two of the reasons you're doing the internship are to gain experience and launch your career.

Functional-style resume

The functional resume, shown in Figure 6-4, is laid out to showcase your skills and knowledge rather than the specific jobs you've held in the past. Thus, it's a good fit for people who are early in their professional careers, people who are making a midlife or major career change, or people who have been out of the workforce for a length of time.

The functional resume may appear to be ideal for candidates with more skills than actual job experience. We must warn you, however, that most executives who review resumes for hiring say they prefer a chronological resume because it clearly and quickly shows whether a candidate has a progression of increased duties and accomplishments, has been stuck at the same level, or has gone downhill. Employers are thus skeptical of the totally functional resume because it doesn't tell which specific jobs you've held and for how long. The dilemma for many interns has been that employers are often skeptical of the functional resume, but the chronological resume hardly allows them to emphasize their knowledge and skills, making them look like a non-competitive applicant.

Sample Chronological Style Resume

Joshua Colin Donovan
readytogo@whoopee.com

2200 N. Mayflower Blvd. #24
Home Town, California 98000
(555) 543-0925

OBJECTIVE

To obtain an Investment Analyst or Consultant position with increasing responsibilities

EDUCATION

Southwestern Louisiana University, 2000
Summa Cum Laude

B.S. Finance, Accounting Collateral

WORK HISTORY

2000 – Present   Desrosiers & Sons
Broker's Analyst/Assistant. Work with Brokers to handle their analysis needs.
Conduct a wide range of financial analyses. Prepare written reports on various
investments opportunities and business organizations.

1997-1999   Crab Tree International
Facility and supplies manager. Supervise the operations of the firm's central
facility including warehouse and shipping. Maintained all records and oversaw
personnel such that operational goals were met on time and on budget.

1992-1997   U.S. Army
Specialist. Served in combat and construction units both domestically and throughout Asia.
Worked with Bradley personal transport and a variety of heavy construction equipment.
Supervised operational teams on assigned tasks and missions.

SUMMARY

- Highly responsible, mature, well organized, and self-motivated
- Dynamic leadership qualities, team player
- Excellent written and oral communication skills
- Wide ranging financial and accounting skills
- Strong computer and data management abilities

EDUCATION & AFFILIATIONS

Financial Management Association
Phi Kappa Phi Scholastic Honors Society
Com.Pets Financial Scholar

Army Commendation Medal
Army Achievement Medal
B. Bailey Initiative Medal

Figure 6-3:
Sample
Chrono-
logical Style
Resume.

Combination-style resume

The combination-style resume emphasizes your accomplishments, as does
the functional style, but it also has elements of the chronological style in that
it lists your educational and work experience in chronological order.

Sample Functional Style Resume

Joshua Colin Donovan
readytogo@whoopee.com

2200 N. Mayflower Blvd. #24
Home Town, California 98000
(555) 543-0925

OBJECTIVE

To obtain an Investment Analyst or Consultant position with increasing responsibilities

QUALIFICATIONS

- Conduct wide ranging financial data and policy research
- Supervised rapid response team in high risk situations
- Responsible for organization and dispatch of warehouse facilities and supplies
- Selected to provide instructional assistance to business and finance students
- Consistently received excellent ratings for team leadership and unit production
- Experience in living and working overseas, with emphasis in Far East

SKILLS

- Able to prepare and coordinate unit budget, properly allocating necessary funds and work hours associated with each particular task
- Can monitored budget spending on a weekly and monthly basis to ensure that expenditures do not exceed allocated funds
- Excellent written and oral communication skills
- Strong computer and data management abilities

EDUCATION

Southwestern Louisiana University, 2000
Summa Cum Laude

B.S. Finance, Accounting Collateral

WORK HISTORY

Broker's Assistant/Analyst	Desrosiers & Sons	2000 to present
Facility and supplies manager	Crab Tree International	1997-1999
Specialist	US Army	1992-1997

EDUCATION & AFFILIATIONS

Financial Management Association
Phi Kappa Phi Scholastic Honors Society
Com.Pets Financial Scholar

Army Commendation Medal
Army Achievement Medal
B. Bailey Initiative Medal

Figure 6-4: Sample Functional Style Resume.

The combination-style resume, shown in Figure 6-5, is typically broken into several short sections. It often starts with an overall summary of specific strengths and abilities and follows with specific experiences in well-defined areas for the field. In management, for example, these areas could be leadership experience, communication skills, and so on. These sections are often followed by a brief work history giving dates of employment, job titles, and names and addresses of employers; an educational history as in the functional style; and a concluding section with any special licenses, training, and so on that may be relevant.

The combination-style resume thus has the most flexibility and generally plays to the strengths of the typical intern. It is becoming more and more common and is generally well received in the professional community.

So, which style is for you? If you're applying for an internship in a field in which you already have experience and thus have a history you can point to, the chronological style is probably your best bet. The reader is looking for you to tell them not only what you can do, but what you've done to prove that you can do it. On the other hand, if you're new to a given field or to the work world in general, the functional style may be for you. This style lets you focus attention on you as a person and on what you're capable of doing, given the chance. Most organizations recognize that internships by their nature are for people who are looking to gain experience, not those who already have it by the bucketful. The combination resume has advantages in that it lets you highlight your specific and special accomplishments and the skills you can offer an employer. While one style isn't absolutely right for all situations, the combination style tends to be your safest and best bet in most situations.

A resume databank

As you craft a resume for each organization, you can mix and match not only the content but also the style so that you end up with the strongest resume possible for that particular position. To achieve this mix of content and style, start out by creating a resume databank, which should list the following items:

- ✔ Jobs I've had
- ✔ What I did in those jobs
- ✔ What results I achieved
- ✔ My top interests
- ✔ What I am best at
- ✔ Specific degrees, certificates, bodies of knowledge, skills, computer applications, languages, travel experiences, and so on that I have

In creating your resume databank, don't be shy! Give your mind free rein in brainstorming about yourself. Do this over several sessions, adding new entries and details to existing entries, and ask people who know you well to look at your databank and suggest additional points. Or ask them what they consider to be your strengths and assets. After brainstorming, check to see whether each entry can stand the light of day — that you have neither exaggerated your accomplishments nor sold yourself short.

Sample Combination Style Resume

Joshua Colin Donovan
2200 N. Mayflower Blvd. #24
Home Town, California 98000
555-543-0925
Readytogo@whoopee.com

SUMMARY

- Highly responsible, mature, well organized, and self-motivated
- Dynamic leadership qualities, team player
- Excellent written and oral communication skills
- Wide ranging financial and accounting skills
- Strong computer and data management abilities

ADMINISTRATIVE AND LEADERSHIP EXPERIENCE

- Conduct wide ranging financial data and policy research
- Supervised rapid response team in high risk situations
- Responsible for organization and dispatch of warehouse facilities and supplies
- Selected to provide instructional assistance to business and finance students
- Consistently received excellent ratings for team leadership and unit production
- Experience in living and working overseas, with emphasis in Far East

FINANCIAL SKILLS

- Prepared and coordinated unit budget with program manager, properly allocating necessary funds and work hours associated with each particular task
- Monitored budget spending on a weekly and monthly basis to ensure that expenditures did not exceed allocated funds
- Completed detailed financial analyses of corporations worldwide and their sudsidiaries

WORK HISTORY

Broker's Assistant/Analyst	Desrosiers & Sons	2000 to present
Facility and supplies manager	Crab Tree International	1997-1999
Specialist	US Army	1992-1997

EDUCATION & AFFILIATIONS

Southwestern Louisiana University, 2000   B.S. Finance, Accounting Collateral
    Summa Cum Laude

Financial Management Association   Army Commendation Medal
Phi Kappa Phi Scholastic Honors Society   Army Achievement Medal
Com.Pets Financial Scholar   B. Bailey Initiative Medal

Figure 6-5:
Sample
Combination
Style
Resume.

Your databank may well be multiple pages in length, longer than any specific resume you construct from the databank entries. To create a resume, you select the particular entries in the order and form that make the most sense for each resume you write. By keeping your databank on a computer and/or diskette (you do back up all your files regularly, don't you?), you simply insert those entries from your databank (adapted, if necessary) into a resume that you tailor to a specific internship.

So what do you say about yourself? For most people, talking (or writing, as the case may be) about themselves is as pleasant as having a tooth pulled. This can be doubly so when you're trying to make a good impression to a potential boss, spouse, or even new classmates at the start of a semester. Yet this is a critical skill to develop in order to succeed.

For most people, their biggest hang-up in selling themselves is a lack of self-confidence. Way down deep (or right there on the surface), people have a voice trying to convince themselves that they aren't good enough, they lack certain skills or experiences, and so on. Keep in mind, though, that everybody, including the person or persons who is looking at your materials and who will interview you for your position, was new at their jobs at one time. Every position is ultimately just a combination of certain skills and abilities.

So regardless of the job title or field, break the position down into manageable pieces by asking yourself the following questions and then writing out your answers:

- ✔ What specific skills and abilities are needed for this position?
- ✔ What knowledge and experiences have I had (draw from your databank) that match the skills and abilities the employer is looking for?

You then use your resume and your cover letter to paint a picture of yourself as the best possible fit for the employer's needs.

Knowledge about resume writing could fill many books — and does. Not surprisingly, *Resumes For Dummies,* 3rd Edition, by Joyce Lain Kennedy (Hungry Minds, Inc.) is very useful, as are a number of Web sites that give resume tips, including the site for the Colorado College Career Center at `www.cc.colorado.edu/CareerCenter/SummerJobsAndInternships/Intern.html`.

Making Contact

Now that you have your materials together, you can make contact with potential employers. In some cases, the first contact will be made by your internship advisor or academic advisor. Most of the time, however, making contact is up to you.

Make your first contact over the phone, for several reasons. Suppose you find a listing from a directory (see Chapter 5) with all the information you think you need. You're ready to fire off your cover letter and resume — don't! It takes months or years from the time authors submit their manuscripts to a publisher until the time a book appears on a store shelf, giving the information a year or more to change. How can you be sure what you read is still accurate? Give a quick call and say something like, "Hello, my name is Josh Jones, I am a finance major at Southeastern University. I am interested in doing an internship at your firm for next spring semester. Who is currently in charge of your internship program? May I speak with him/her please?"

Now is your chance not only to confirm whatever information you have about the company's opportunities and applications process, but also to make a small but positive impression. Keep the conversation brief but do ask about the positions and the process — and also, perhaps, a little bit more. For example, ask about their alumni and whether they keep track of them. If you can get in touch with either current or former interns, you learn as much about the organization as the organization wants to learn about you. You may even end up turning them down!

When writing your cover letter, don't forget to mention your call: "Based on Mr. Smith's instructions, I have enclosed a copy of my resume and a writing sample with this cover letter. I have had the opportunity to speak with Megan Desrosiers about her internship experience with you, and she was most positive about both the organization and the people she worked with. . . ." You're setting yourself apart from the crowd by showing that you're bright enough to first check facts and go the extra mile to learn about the firm to make sure it's a good potential fit for you both.

If you're cold calling a firm that you may like to intern for, the process is much the same. "Hello, my name is Colin Sanchez. I'm a chemistry major at Rutgers, and I understand you sometimes use student interns. Who would be the best person for me to talk to about potential opportunities? Laetitia DuFour? May I speak with her please?" If they do sometimes use interns, you'll be passed along to the right person. If they don't, you'll get a chance to make a case why they should talk to you at greater length and, perhaps, try you as an intern. After all, nothing ventured, nothing gained. The trick is to be friendly and assertive, never passive, aggressive, or pushy. This applies whether you are making contact by phone, by mail, or by e-mail, which is an increasingly common method for interns.

Surviving an Interview: It's Not the Third Degree

Start preparing long before any interviews occur by researching two areas:

✔ Knowing yourself (assessing your goals, needs, preferences, and strengths)

✔ Knowing your prospective employers (researching their goals, performance, and needs)

Speaking the part

Most people hear you on the phone before they see you in person. How does your voice sound? Do you sound positive, confident, and relaxed when speaking on the phone? Does your voice have a smile in it or a frown? If you're not sure, listen to your message on your answering machine or have a friend call you and record the conversation.

You may have heard people on the phone who sound like polished radio announcers, and heard others who sound like a scratchy CD. In both cases, you're forming a mental impression of these people just from their voices and the way they speak over the phone. People form the same attitudes about you. If your voice and speaking qualities need improvement, get help, perhaps at your school, where they teach those speech communication classes you have been avoiding. To boost your experience and confidence, look for the chance to speak in the classes you're taking, either via questions or oral reports. In addition, consider organizations like Toastmasters International, Rotary, and others that give people the chance to speak regularly in a supportive environment. Many famous speakers started this way, and these organizations are always looking for new members, especially younger ones. Read more about oral communication skills in Chapter 10.

Looking the part

You must dress like a professional person even if you're still a struggling student. This also includes a nice attaché or organizer. Book bags and backpacks are out! If you don't have a business wardrobe, put yourselves in the hands of a trustworthy salesperson at a good clothing store who can help you put together at least one suit you can wear when you need to look professional.

Playing questions and answers (but not Jeopardy!)

Prepare for the questions — and the answers — you're likely to face in an interview. We assume you're already working on speaking and looking like a confident professional; now make sure you handle questions the same way. This means thinking about the kinds of questions you're likely to be asked and having good answers ready for each question.

To help you prepare, consider the following common questions:

✔ **What are your major strengths as a person and as a worker?** Here, the trick is to sound confident, not cocky. Don't exaggerate your abilities, as that may come back to haunt you if your record doesn't match your mouth or you get the position and begin floundering. Do concentrate on the strengths that relate to the internship at hand. Talking about your best dive in the swim finals won't help much, although telling about an Outward Bound experience may show that you're a resilient team player.

✔ **What are your major weaknesses?** Woe unto the person who confidently asserts that he has no weaknesses. You may not have any, but your interviewer and the rest of the human race does have failings, and people don't want to be around the only flawless person in the world who reminds us of our own inadequacies. The tactic with this question is to honestly reflect on your shortcomings in ways that make them sound like strengths. Turn the negatives into positives. "My speaking skills are not what I would like them to be, but I know how important public speaking is in the communications field, so I have joined Toastmasters, and my speeches are getting better organized and delivered." This shows that you know and admit to your shortcoming, know how important that shortcoming is to the field you want to enter, and have taken enough initiative to improve. The added bonus to this particular answer is that it helps explain why your speaking in the interview, while not dreadful, is still less than polished. Win, win, win! This is the kind of thinking we want to encourage when talking about your weaknesses. Just be sure that what you say *is* true. Don't give a false image of yourself by only mentioning "positive" weaknesses. ("My major weaknesses are that I work too hard and am a perfectionist.") Interviewers see through such tactics if these claims are inconsistent with your overall record.

✔ **Why do you want this position?** (Often, they really mean, "Why us rather than some other organization?") This gives you a chance to show off some of the information your research uncovered about the organization's activities and strengths (and how they match yours). Also be prepared to explain why you're interested in this profession or field in general. Use knowledge you've discovered about marketing, counseling, historic restoration, law, teaching, or some other profession; what can be accomplished through this profession; and, of course, why you want to make your contribution in that profession.

✔ **Tell me a little about yourself.** This vague, poor question comes from an interviewer who may not have his or her act together. Choose those things about yourself that relate to this internship and to your strengths. "I've always been interested in art (if that is what the internship is about) and have studied various forms of painting and graphic design."

✔ **Tell about a time when you faced a major problem and tell how you handled it.** If possible, talk about an experience comparable to situations you're likely to confront in this internship or one that demonstrates skills relevant to this internship.

> ✔ **Where do you want to be in five years and how does this position fit into your plans?** Draw from your goals, needs, and preferences assessments in Chapters 2 and 3 and discuss how they link to this internship. Also, draw upon your research/scouting report (covered in Chapter 5) about the internship and the organization itself. Demonstrate your motivation and your knowledge.

Get the idea? Think about these kinds of questions beforehand and be ready with a pretty good idea of what you want to say before any interview begins.

You can find more information about the job interview in *Job Interviews For Dummies,* 2nd Edition, by Joyce Lain Kennedy (Hungry Minds, Inc.).

Closing and asking questions

The last part of the interview is the *close.* Most people are so focused on getting and surviving the interview that they tend to blow the close. Yet the interview isn't really over until you're safely out of the building.

You need to know when the interview is ending, and your clues will come through a combination of words and body language. For example, your interviewer may start looking at the clock on the wall or at her wristwatch, or she may start straightening the papers on her desk. Do your best to read the signals and act appropriately. Never overstay your welcome. Hanging around trying to get in the last word has doomed many candidates.

In many cases, the interviewer signals that you're entering the last phase of the interview by turning the tables and asking, "What questions do you have about this internship or our organization." Unacceptable responses include, 'I don't have any questions" or, "What does your organization do?" (You should have gleaned this through your research.) Some good questions we've always liked include the following:

> ✔ **Would you please tell me how you came to work here and what it is about [name of organization] that keeps you here?** This shows your concern not only for the interviewer but also about the motivation and climate in this organization. It also shows that you're serious about a potential future there after the internship.
>
> ✔ **What are some examples of recent intern projects and how they helped [name of organization]?** This shows you're serious about the work you'd be expected to do and that you want to benefit this organization, not just help yourself.
>
> ✔ **What is the track record of your interns within this profession (or industry)?** Again, this shows you want to know what value this internship typically provides and that you're serious about a career in this profession or industry.

> ✔ **What is the track record of interns who have worked here in terms of what they have learned (their professional development) and in terms of future positions?** This question is an extension and logical follow-up from the previous question. This shows you're serious about this employer and your future. It also shows you're savvy about the way the internship process often works.

If you don't already know, be sure to also ask about the next step to the selection process, whether anything more is needed from you, and when and how you will hear from them next.

Go out on a high note. You still want to look enthused and energized at the end, not like the turkey that barely survived Thanksgiving. Exit with a good smile, a firm handshake, and good eye contact. Walk confidently with your head up high. If you feel like you're going to collapse, wait until you're out of the building first and out of sight from any other employees. We hope you'll be feeling charged up and excited at this moment after a wonderful interview with an employer that seems like a perfect match.

Following up

After the interview, write out a quick summary while it's still fresh in your mind. Write down whatever you learned about the internship, the employer, the terms of employment, or the interviewer that may help you later. You want to be able to recall and learn from this interview whenever you need to.

You also want to write a brief thank you note and mail it out no later than the day after the interview. Keep the note short (it can be on a plain, professional looking notecard or on plain paper). Thank the interviewer for his or her time and for making the interview a positive experience for you. If you can, refer to something from the interview, and if you think the interviewer got the wrong impression about a point, clarify it as briefly and simply as you can. Close by saying that you're looking forward to hearing from them in the near future.

Be prepared for the organization to do some research on you. Today, many firms conduct background checks on all employees, including interns. This background check can run the gamut from calling references that you've provided to running your fingerprints through a national crime database to having a full physical and drug screen. If you know you're going to have trouble with any such checks or clearances, deal with the problem beforehand. Don't waste their time and yours if you can't or won't pass a background check.

If there is wrong information about you out there, find it and correct it by contacting the organization that is providing the information. If you have a problem in your past that could block your application, explain it in your cover letter.

Practice, practice, practice

Practice your interview. If possible, take an interviewing workshop through your school's career center or some other reputable place. Many schools offer a range of workshops relating to internships, jobs, and careers. If your school has none of these, ask faculty members or friends to conduct mock interviews for experience. You may also want to videotape yourself so that you can see how you sound, look, and come across — and also hear what you have to say. (Keep in mind that you may be unduly traumatized by a bad videotaping experience in which poor technical quality and unprofessional interviewers can make you look hopeless! Such sessions are better done at your school's organized workshops.) Practice until you come across as a relaxed yet confident individual: No slouching, nervous hand gestures, and rambling sentences full of "ums," "likes," and "uhs." For more ideas, watch TV interview shows in the fields of entertainment, politics, and business, paying close attention to the guests being interviewed. Note which people look, sound, and come across well and which ones don't. Practice until you're one of the good ones.

Before a real interview, you'll get some jitters, everyone does. Don't panic. Instead, try the following:

✔ **Breathe.** Take a deep breath or two, inhaling slowly, holding the breath, and then exhaling slowly.

✔ **Stretch.** That's right, bend over, reach out, and slowly let your body unkink from the tightness you may feel. (Both the breathing exercise and stretching are good things to try in the restroom.)

✔ **Smile.** No matter how big your butterflies are on the inside, smile and try to think happy thoughts. Keep things in perspective: This is just one interview. Over your lifetime you will do this hundreds of times for all kinds of reasons. No one has ever died from a bad interview, and the worst that can happen is someone will say "Thanks but no thanks" to you.

So You Have an Offer. Now What?

Don't think that just because you've been offered an internship the important part is over: What kind of offer is made to you and how you respond can make or break the entire process. Here is some sound advice from the University of Florida Career Resources Center, one of the Web sites we recommend in Chapter 5.

✔ **Avoid accepting an offer over the phone.** Get the offer in writing whenever possible. You will want some time to review the offer, especially if it's complicated or involves terms you haven't heard or seen before. The offer should contain key information such as the starting and ending dates, compensation (if any), other benefits (housing, transportation, or tuition), and the assignment (if it's known).

✔ **If your prospective employer can't or won't give you the offer in writing, ask for time to consider it and to call back.** Follow up with a letter from you stating your understanding of the terms (but don't exaggerate the terms).

✔ **If you receive multiple offers, consider each one carefully.** Compare your offers using the Internship Goals Checklist (see Chapter 2) and Work Preferences Checklist (in Chapter 3). The best offer isn't necessarily the one that pays the most or the one with the most prestigious employer. The internship that best meets your goals, needs, interests, and preferences will likely be the most successful one.

✔ **If the letter of offer doesn't say, find out when you need to respond.** Take some time to think through the offers, but don't wait so long that you miss the deadline. Your letter either accepting or declining the offer should be as positive and professional as all your other communications. Never burn bridges. Whether you turn a company down or they turn you down, be gracious and accentuate the positive. You may someday be back looking for a job from the same firm or being interviewed by the same person at another firm.

Part IV
The Nuts and Bolts of Working as an Intern

The 5th Wave   By Rich Tennant

©RICHTENNANT

"Tell us, Walter, in your own words, why you feel you're suited for the position of goon."

In this part . . .

We give you the information you need to be successful when you begin your internship. We provide
advice that will help you get off to a good start, make a
good impression, fit in, and perform the typical administrative, research, and other tasks you may be assigned.
This part also guides you through some potential problems for interns: sexual harassment, racism, confidentiality
violations, and other important issues. Finally, we cover
some key communication, political, and organizational
skills that can help you to be a productive intern.

Chapter 7

Making the Most of Your First Days

The first days in your new internship are crucial ones: They establish the tone and expectations for your internship — and establish your credibility. A bad start can be overcome, but a good start makes life simpler and more rewarding for you and your co-workers. This chapter includes keys to a constructive start, including making the most of the orientation, getting the lay of the land of your new company, and understanding how to fit in and begin establishing professional credibility.

Making the Most of the Orientation

Many internships, especially the large, established, structured internship programs (like the Presidential Management Internship and internships at Microsoft) have formal orientation programs. Orientation can vary, however, from a few-hour briefing on policies about attendance, office dress and behavior, and so on to multi-day orientations lasting several months that involve meetings with top officials, workshops on policy and management procedure, and skills or technical matters related to your work.

If, for some reason, your new internship supervisor fails to mention anything about an orientation, ask! Some organizations and some supervisors just don't think about having an orientation: They're from the drop-you-off-the-deep-end-of-the-pool school. For your success (and your sanity), let your supervisor know that you need some time to get the lay of the land before being expected to dive into all that vital work they have waiting for you. Perhaps your first task may be to help create a formal orientation for future interns!

Understand what's involved

Expect the following coverage at your internship orientation:

- **Introduction of top officials:** Take notes so you know who they are and what they do.

- **Introduction of interns:** Be prepared to introduce yourself or make sure the person who is introducing you has the necessary, accurate information. You don't want to be left out or get a token introduction.

- **History and mission of the organization:** Do some research in advance, and then take notes on what is said. Try to figure out how your work fits within the overall mission.

- **Organizational policies:** These policies cover absenteeism, use of organizational property, sexual harassment, safety practices, dress code, and so on. Take notes to find out what you should and shouldn't do.

- **Knowledge or skill-building sessions:** These workshops, seminars, or other sessions are aimed at building knowledge and skills relevant to your internship. These sessions vary depending on the nature of your placement, but may cover, for example, marketing techniques, teaching delivery, legislative process, graphic design principles, and counseling protocol.

Discussing and applying what you've gleaned from orientations increases the odds that you'll retain it and be able to use it later. You can do this through discussion with other interns, with your intern supervisor, or with other colleagues. If an orientation session covers specific information or skills, look for immediate opportunities to apply the information or skills while your learning is still fresh. If, for example, the orientation covers techniques for improving customer/client relations, practice these techniques when you handle customer requests or interviews with residents.

Show up

You'll have a tough time learning anything or impressing anyone if you're a no-show. The bottom line with internship orientations is to show up: Your orientation isn't an extra bonus but is the first official step for your new position. Failing to attend sends signals that you either don't care enough to make the effort, think you already know all the answers, or slipped up on your planning. None of these signals gets you off to a flying start. Arrive on time — preferably ahead of time. The company president or agency head may be standing by the coffeepot before the orientation, waiting to give the official welcome. That's a perfect opportunity to introduce yourself, glean some useful information, and begin establishing your credibility.

Be prepared (it's not just the Boy Scouts' motto)

Come prepared to learn and to make a positive impression and prepare for everything that's assigned to you. Consider the following tips:

- ✔ Do your homework, such as assigned reading about the organization's history and mission.

- ✔ Think ahead about what you would say to introduce yourself at the initial orientation session that makes you sound interesting, competent, and human. (You don't want to come off sounding too imposing.)

- ✔ Think of some intelligent questions about the organization or the specific content of the orientation before the session in order to relieve some of the pressure during the presentation itself. (Interns preoccupied with coming up with a good question to make an impression are likely to miss much of what's being said.)

If you can start building credibility by making good points or asking intelligent questions, so much the better, but be sure to avoid coming across as a know-it-all. Even if that were true (and it's highly unlikely in a new situation), you wouldn't help your cause with supervisors or other interns.

- ✔ Bring a notebook or pad and pen for taking notes on the presentations. You may be provided these at the orientation session, but not always. If appropriate (check ahead of time), bring a notebook computer, handheld device, or other equipment, if it's something you really use. Showing technical proficiency can boost your credibility, but don't bring them just for show.

Know what to do if you don't get an orientation

Many organizations in which you may intern — probably most of them, in fact — offer no orientation or give merely a token one that's along the lines of, "Here's your cubicle, the bathroom's down the hall, and you aren't allowed to make long-distance calls." If this is your situation, you have several options available.

- ✔ **Forego any orientation at all.** This is a bad choice because you miss hearing valuable information.

✔ **Work to start some kind of orientation.** This may be done by discussing the situation with other interns and diplomatically proposing to the leadership of your organization why you need an orientation, what it may contain, and how you (collectively) could go about getting it started. Getting examples of other orientations is a useful tactic because it may either embarrass your organization into following suit or provide concrete ideas for an internship program. Some options to consider include the following:

- A series of brown-bag lunches in which different employees — and different interns — explain their jobs and the issues they face.

- Guided tours of various parts of the building(s) to show where different functions are located and to get an explanation of those functions. If your organization has multiple units in different locations, this may mean traveling to some of these locations.

- Tours of the organization's market area or service area. This helps you learn about the people your company serves.

- Organized discussions of significant books or reports that are relevant to your work.

Proposing new training may lead to several benefits: It can improve intern unity and help establish your leadership role among interns. It can also show your intern supervisor and top management that you can take initiative and show leadership. It will also likely lead to more learning than if you hadn't made this effort. If you launch such a campaign for an internship, be sure you're willing to follow through to do your share of the necessary work: finding out what other organizations do for an orientation, contacting potential speakers or trainers, making logistical arrangements, and so on.

You or someone else may have made an honest effort to get an internship program started and it doesn't fly. Or you may be the only intern in that organization so that a big production wouldn't make much sense. In such cases, you need to create your own internship orientation by doing the following:

✔ **Read all you can find about your organization and its mission and history.** Your reading should include recent annual reports, the budget, other major new publications, news clippings about your organization, recent consulting reports or evaluations, and so on. The company or agency library and public relations unit are good sources for this information.

✔ **Deliberately arrange to meet key people in the organization who would likely have been at an orientation.** This can be over lunch, in the hallway, in their offices, or at other places at their convenience. Meeting key people provides an opportunity to determine whether you have common interests and goals. Also, be sure to ask these people what they do and whether they have any advice for you as an intern. In addition to benefiting from the enhanced knowledge, you demonstrate your initiative and commitment. Don't forget to talk with secretaries, office managers, and others who possess detailed knowledge about procedures and whose cooperation you need to succeed as an intern.

✔ **Take advantage of any workshops, seminars, conferences, or meetings that may speed your learning curve.** Even if these are primarily for permanent staff rather than interns, ask your supervisor if you're allowed to attend. This shows initiative and ties you with the permanent staff. After all, isn't that what you want — to be identified with the permanent staff and perhaps to be hired to work with that staff?

Even if your intern organization has an orientation program, supplement that with these efforts of your own.

Getting the Lay of the Land

When entering any organization, whether as an intern or a CEO, you need to get the lay of the land, finding out what makes this organization tick. A solid orientation, whether formal or self-created helps with this. You also acclimate yourself through meetings, conversations with your supervisor and other people inside and outside the organization, reading, searching Web sites, and so on. Crucial information to learn about your organization is covered in the following checklist. Many of these are items you may have scouted out in your investigation of the organization before taking the internship.

✔ **What are the key missions of your organization?** To make products and money? To educate? To protect the environment? To represent people? Have these missions changed recently? Does agreement exist over what the mission really is?

✔ **What has been the organization's history?** Has it been through crises or traumas that influence the organization's current behavior? When did these occur and what was the nature of these crises?

✔ **How would you describe your organization's culture?** Competitive? Nurturing? Controlling? Future-oriented or past-oriented?

✔ **What are the organization's principal sources of revenue?** Sale of products or services? Taxes? Grants or contracts? Donations? In addition, what are its principal expenditures: salaries, contracts to provide products or services, or equipment?

✔ **What are key professions represented in your organization?** Is your organization dominated by educators, engineers, managers, counselors, lawyers, doctors, or some other professional group? Knowing this should tell you something about your future in this organization. If you're in the dominant profession or are preparing for that profession, you'll likely have an easier time fitting in, and you're more likely to be hired permanently.

If, on the other hand, you're interning in a social services agency and discover that all top officials are social workers by profession (and you don't plan to be one), don't count on making this organization your career-long home. In any case, you need to educate yourself to some of the language of the dominant profession and work at relating to those professionals.

✔ **What is the preferred medium of communication?** E-mail? Paper memos or reports? Formal meetings? Informal conversations? Are you comfortable and skilled in using the preferred methods of communication?

✔ **What are the preferences and pet peeves of top officials and of your supervisor(s)?** Examples include detesting lateness, abhorring casual dress, appreciating hearing all sides, and being uncomfortable with small talk.

✔ **What types of behavior are rewarded or punished?** Risk-taking or risk-avoidance? Being proactive or reactive? Thinking on your feet or reflecting and responding later?

Discovering these and other relevant pieces of information helps you know how to fit in with your new organization (see the following section).

Fitting In and Establishing Credibility Early On

Fitting in involves being accepted socially and professionally — both for the person you are and for what you bring to your internship and the organization. Your professional credibility also hinges on your behavior in the first days of an internship. The following do's and don'ts also are worth heeding.

To fit in and establish credibility, do the following:

✔ Listen more than you talk. You don't pick up much information when you're doing the talking.

✔ Show respect for other people, including secretaries, mail clerks, and others who often don't get respect but whose cooperation is necessary for you to succeed.

✔ Show interest and commitment by attending organized sessions for interns and requesting permissions to attend other sessions, as well.

✔ Come prepared for work and for the learning sessions that are offered to you.

✔ Come groomed and dressed appropriately. We think the dress-for-success mantra is overdone, but you do need to be clean, neat, and professional-looking.

✔ Show your support for the organization and your colleagues by attending celebrations or social occasions such as promotion or retirement receptions and contract-winning parties.

✔ Treat your colleagues as you would want to be treated. Show interest and provide emotional support.

✔ Willingly help out when asked rather than refuse to help or complain while helping.

Steer clear, however, of the following:

✔ Criticizing people, policies, or procedures until you really understand the situation.

✔ Working on your school homework or other tasks — especially in front of others — when on your internship job.

✔ Spending so much time cozying up to key people that you don't do your job well. When starting your professional network via lunches or meetings, be sure you've covered home base by doing your assigned work. We have a friend who was so busy networking with the top brass of the General Accounting Office that he let his job performance slip. Needless to say, he lost credibility with his immediate boss, and he eventually left that office.

✔ Acting like a know-it-all, but failing to demonstrate competence in the tasks assigned.

The best way to fit in and establish your professional credibility is to perform your job competently. Chapter 9 provides specifics on performing common but important internship tasks.

Chapter 8

Problems and Issues You Need to Be Prepared For

● ●

In This Chapter

▶ Working with a difficult boss

▶ Understanding confidentiality

▶ Avoiding improper behaviors

● ●

This chapter helps you prepare for some of the problems that occasionally arise during an internship. Like any other position, an internship can bring troubles and troubling decisions to the worker (that's you), and the worker (yep, still you) can, on occasion, bring troubles and troubling decisions to the organization. We want to help you prepare for the former and avoid the latter. We address these sensitive issues and potential problems before covering all the intern skills because these problems can arise at any time, even the first day. Being aware of these potential situations ahead of time and preparing for them is your best course of action.

Dealing with Problem Bosses

Sometimes you may be working away, minding your own business, when wham, a boss or co-worker starts to make your life miserable. While you can't avoid this, you can be prepared. But how? Beyond reading *Dilbert,* we have some wisdom to share with you.

Stepping into your boss's shoes

Consider the role of a boss or supervisor. Some people start their internships with false conceptions about supervisors that get in the way of forming a good and positive relationship and usually lead to problems with the boss. For example, here are some common misperceptions about supervisors:

- Supervisors never make mistakes or bad decisions.
- Supervisors never have bad days, never feel ill, and never have their own problems at work or at home.
- Supervisors have all the time and resources in the world to fix every problem, especially yours.
- Supervisors can fix any problem they face.
- Supervisors have limitless time and energy to pay attention to you and your problems.
- Supervisors can read minds, especially yours.

Most supervisors and co-workers are people just like you who have good days and bad days. They have their own problems and pressures and are trying to do the best they can with the resources they have. They also have feelings, just like you do. The best advice is to follow the golden rule: Treat others, including your boss and your co-workers, as you would like to be treated.

Don't think your boss is neglecting you if he or she isn't spending as much time with you as you would like. While no one wants to be neglected, the more people managers have to oversee, the less time per person they have to spend. For a typical 40-hour work week, a supervisor with just ten people to oversee has only about one-and-a half hours per person per week, after taking into account all of the other duties and responsibilities that must be handled (everything from mail, phone calls, e-mails, meetings, and so on).

Your supervisor is also somebody else's worker. He or she also has supervisors to worry about and has limits and responsibilities. Sometimes, your supervisor may see your problem, but has to do what he or she thinks is best for the entire workplace. Seeing your supervisor as a fellow worker in the organization can help to defuse some of the tensions that may develop.

Getting along with your boss

An old proverb says the first step in a battle is to know and understand your enemy. While we would not call your supervisor and fellow workers the enemy, we would agree that one of the best ways to get along with others is to understand their likes, dislikes, and personality traits. If you understand these details, you're much more likely to succeed.

The following sections share some basic questions for you to answer to help you get along (and get ahead).

Communications

Supervisors and managers, like other people, have their own preferences for how they want interns — and others — to communicate with them.

Understanding and following their preferences, while avoiding their dislikes, will help you communicate better with them. Answering the following questions will help you find out about the communication preferences of your bosses. See Chapter 10 for other advice about communicating.

✔ **How does your manager prefer to communicate with others?**

- In-person, face-to face
- Over the phone
- By e-mail
- Written memos and notes
- Smoke signals or other means

✔ **How does your manager prefer your communications?**

- In great and specific details
- In summary format
- Just the facts, save the conclusions
- In Morse code

✔ **When does your manager prefer to meet with you?**

- First thing in the day
- In the morning
- During lunch
- In the afternoon
- At the end of the day
- Around midnight, just as you are getting to sleep
- The Twelfth of Never

✔ **How often does your manager want to see you?**

- Once a day without fail
- Whenever you need guidance on a project
- Only when you have exhausted all of your own ideas and are stymied
- As little as possible — and it better be important!
- When hell freezes over

Punctiliousness

Some people are pretty easy going when it comes to issues like how you are dressed, whether you are exactly on time, or other matters of what might loosely be called etiquette. If your boss is easy going, you can be too. On the other hand, if your boss is a stickler for the right way, you'd better be also.

✔ **Dress code:**

- My boss is relaxed about my attire as long as it is appropriate.
- My boss accepts casual day only with the greatest reluctance.
- My boss probably wears a suit and tie in the shower .

✔ **Timeliness:**

- Being late is not okay, but getting work accomplished is what's important.
- Nothing wrong with a little flextime.
- A minute late from lunch is the same as an hour late.
- You could set your atomic watch by when she arrives in the morning.

✔ **Circadian rhythms:**

- My supervisor is definitely a morning person.
- Long lunches are occasionally fine.
- What's lunch?
- We *all* like to work late, don't we?
- What's more fun than spending the weekend at work?

You probably get the idea. Try to understand what your supervisor does and doesn't like, what sets her off, and what makes her happy, and you'll have far fewer problems. Some managers/supervisors get irritated if interns come to them for every little problem. Others want constant interaction with interns.

Solving common office problems

And if your boss really is a problem? The following sections give you some common problems and solutions to try.

Problem: My boss is too bossy

Is micromanaging everyone and everything a prerequisite to promotion these days? Some bosses really are anal retentive from birth, while others have learned to be this way. In some cases, they fear that if they don't oversee every detail of every worker, tasks will be done wrong. In other cases, they feel most workers are out to get them and will mess up given half a chance (and this becomes a self-fulfilling prophecy). Sometimes bosses have been burned by workers who failed to deliver, so they protect themselves by hovering over every worker. Finally, many mangers are promoted not because they're good at managing but because they were really good at doing what their workers do. This results in some bosses believing they truly can do your job better than you, so they either second guess you every step of the way or do it all themselves.

TIP

When your co-worker is a nightmare

You may think you have co-workers who are sprouting horns underneath their hair. One or more co-workers may appear to have it in for you and may be doing everything possible to make your life miserable. On the other hand, the situation could be a misunderstanding. In either case, the ball is in your court. You must take the first step: Communicate. That's right, you must sit down and talk with your co-worker about how his or her behavior bothers you. (Your tendency may be to go to your boss — don't. At least not until you've first spoken with your co-worker. Your boss's first question is likely to be: "Have you spoken with him/her about this first?" If you answer no, your goose is cooked. You come across as unprofessional at best and a whiner and/or loser at worst.)

When you're ready, seek out this person and make a time to meet that's quiet and calm for you both. Vent your anger before you meet. Don't see this as a hollering session. Instead, consider beforehand which of your co-workers actions (or inactions), words, or behaviors are bothering you. What would you have him or her change to make things better? When you do speak with this co-worker, focus on specific things, with reference to your feelings. Accept that you're at least a little part of the problem. In addition, focus on specific changes you each can make to improve the situation.

Give it a try. If the other person is reasonable, the meeting may work. If you both try and fail or the other person won't try at all, go to your supervisor. You can talk about not just the problem but all you have done to try and deal with it as a professional. You'll strengthen your reputation, whatever the outcome.

Do any of these sound like your boss? Try the following: Think of your boss as your parent and you as a teenager. Break a new assignment down into discrete baby steps. Ask for responsibility for some of the steps you know you can accomplish with your eyes blindfolded. The first time around, run everything you plan to do by your boss first, then do it as well as possible. Keep this up, each time expanding slightly the number and scope of steps you're responsible for. Eventually, you will be trusted to do more and more on your own without being micromanaged. Trust is earned from these bosses the hard way, so be careful not to fail — missing one curfew can get you grounded for a month or more.

Problem: My boss is never around

We recall at time at a major university where seeing the president on campus was such a rare event that the school newspaper offered a special T-shirt to anyone who called in a confirmed sighting of the president anywhere on the campus grounds. Compared to the too bossy boss, coping with the hard-to-find boss is probably less stressful but still affects work performance and learning.

You're not going to change your supervisor's habits or work schedule. What you have to do, instead, is to efficiently use the rare time that you do have. Either by checking with his or her secretary or through a coordinated team effort, scope out the boss's in-office schedule. Most bosses are fairly predictable after you get their schedules down. After you know the schedule, you can arrange either formal or drop-by meetings when you know the boss is in. Just be sure that you're thoroughly prepared for such encounters so you don't waste one of these rare and special close encounters.

Another tactic involves walking or traveling with the boss to give you contact time. Catching his or her ear on the way to a meeting is better than no contact at all. If all your tactics to increase access to your supervisor fail, you may want to ask him or her to assign you to another supervisor (preferably one with whom you've already established rapport) or to suggest other staff members you can turn to for guidance and learning.

Problem: My boss just grunts when I ask how I'm doing

Men are from Mars, women are from Venus, and many supervisors are from Pluto. Or, at least, many supervisors are uncommunicative, at least when letting you know how you're doing. Some bosses are like this because it just doesn't occur to them to give you feedback. Other bosses are actually a bit on the shy side, especially when giving feedback. They may have to say something negative or are afraid you may get confrontational, so they avoid giving any feedback at all. Other bosses don't tell you how you're doing because they haven't got a clue; they are hardly around or they show no interest.

This can be a double-edged sword because many people like to pretend that no news is good news. On the other hand, you're completing this internship to learn and to be seen as a successful future employee (at that company or somewhere else). Neither of these is going to occur if you're as visible as Casper the friendly ghost. So make an appointment. Go in and talk about your need to know how you are doing, not just right then but on an ongoing basis. Try to arrange a schedule for future feedback sessions. This will help you to improve your work and get you known as a person, not just a temp.

Because interns are usually fairly new to their workplace, it may be that their supervisors don't feel they have enough information to give good feedback yet. On the other hand, because some supervisors may view interns as temporary, they may not feel they have to bother monitoring interns or giving interns feedback. The best remedy for this problem is to show with your enthusiasm and your performance that you're a bona fide member of the work team and worthy of getting feedback. (See Chapters 13 and 15 for more on evaluation and feedback.)

Problem: My boss is unreasonable

Being unreasonable comes in two main flavors, and you need to deal with each differently. The first type is the too-much-work-in-too-little-time variety. Some bosses just don't seem to have any idea of what you're working on or how long it should take you. We once experienced a college professor like that, assigning four textbooks to read and master over four weeks. To him, that was most fair. When we complained about the overwhelming amount of material we were being asked to cover, he replied that these were the same four texts he had had to learn in the same four weeks when he was a student. Upon further investigation, we found out he was right. But by checking the shelves in his office, we noticed that the early editions he had used some 35 years earlier were a good deal briefer: The total width was five inches. The same four titles in our editions were close to three inches thick each! That's nearly three times as much total material. Confronted with this information, we won a reprieve and more time. This is your best strategy, too. Document over a couple of weeks all that you're expected to do and how much time is required. Then meet to negotiate a more appropriate workload.

The second type of unreasonableness is less about the amount of work than the variety of work expected. Some bosses see all workers as a cross between a gofer and a personal servant. They think nothing of having you run their personal errands before, during, and after work hours. Partly, bosses assign such tasks because some work places encourage or at least allow such behaviors. If you find you're not being used to do the types of work you were brought in for, you have a couple of choices:

- **Go along with these requests for the sake of being an intern at that company.** If this is truly the norm, all former interns and workers will know it, and you will have a certain cache for having survived the same ordeals.

- **Meet with your advisor.** Document what you're being asked to do, when, and so on, and the two of you can then decide whether to take action. You can try to get your workload changed or look for another situation.

Maintaining Confidentiality

In your internship, you may have information that other people shouldn't have — secrets, if you will. This is perhaps most obvious for interns in government or politics, business, law, and health care, but it also holds true for internships in social work, education, journalism, and other fields. Even though access to information may be limited for interns, you may still learn things that involve future policy decisions, business plans, patient treatment, student profiles, or other confidential information. Some of this information must be withheld from other interns and co-workers, some from other managers, some from your friends or your family.

Organizations take confidentiality very seriously, and so should you. In fact, some companies have strict rules about confidentiality in their employee manuals/guidelines. You may also be required to sign a specific confidentiality agreement as part of your employment. Take these seriously!

Information that's considered the property of and valuable to the organization is called *proprietary information.* For example, say you're part of a group that's working on a new product or service. This is pretty heady stuff you're working on. The information is of great value to your company, and other firms would love to know about it. It's your responsibility to keep this proprietary information to yourself, to keep it confidential. Even the fact that you're working on it at all may itself be confidential. Within the organization, many documents, reports, and so on will also be confidential, and access to them (or knowledge of what's in them) will be severely limited. It is up to you not to allow others access to these documents or to share what's in them.

The confidential information you have and use is up to you to protect, both in your home and work space:

- ✔ Don't leave sensitive documents lying around.
- ✔ Lock up your desk and files when you leave (even for just a moment).
- ✔ Make sure your computer and screen aren't open to casual perusal by others.
- ✔ Don't take confidential information with you (say to home or to a meeting) unless you've first asked if it is okay.
- ✔ If you're sending confidential information, make sure it is clearly sealed and labeled "confidential" and follow any specific security guidelines your organization has.
- ✔ Be careful of what you throw away. If you have the slightest doubt, shred it.

In addition to official secrets, you may run into another type of confidential information, information about people in personnel files or student files. You wouldn't want just anyone at work being able to see your files, would you?

Sometimes, you'll become privy to knowledge you shouldn't have because others will tell you things they shouldn't, or you may overhear or see things you shouldn't. How you handle these situations comes from your own sense of ethics. If a good friend at work asks you about something confidential, how do you handle it? One way to handle such a situation would be, of course, to tell her. After all, she's a friend and works there, too! On the other hand, it's not your secret to share, even with a friend. A better response would be to simply reply that you can't respond because the information is confidential. If she continues to ask, tell her she is out of line. And keep in mind that a friend who tries to get information out of you is no friend.

Ask your supervisor about confidentiality early on. Ask him or her just what sort of information you'll be coming across during your work and what's considered confidential.

Defining Improper Behaviors

In today's environment, you've probably heard of an endless supply of improper behaviors. They almost all involve prejudicial beliefs and actions of one type or another. Of these, be conscious of three behaviors in particular: sexism, racism, and sexual harassment.

Sexism

Sexism (also called gender bias) involves stereotyping and possibly discriminating against people because of their gender. It is also defined as the belief that rights and roles in society and work should be governed by one's sex. You may have heard it referred to as *chauvinism*. Historically, sexism has been male-driven and accompanied by a belief in the inferiority of women, hence the term *male chauvinism*.

What this means for the typical worker is that in some unenlightened work environments, half the workforce (nearly always the female half) is treated either covertly or openly as second-rate. One example of this is the *glass ceiling,* a term that refers to the inability of women to be hired and promoted to top positions within a firm. After being promoted at lower levels, these women reach a glass (invisible but quite firm) ceiling or barrier that keeps them out of top positions.

What does this mean to you as an intern? Two things. On one hand, you may be the victim of sexism. Yep, that's right! Just because you're female (or male), you may be treated differently. You may be kept away from the most important and best opportunities. You may be stuck doing the least important and least glamorous tasks. People may make you (and/or your gender) the brunt of jokes, remarks, or certain looks, all of which are hurtful personally and professionally. Sexism is, in fact, one form of sexual harassment which we discuss in the "Sexual harassment" section of this chapter.

Unfortunately, you may be the source of the problem as easily as you may be the victim. High schools and colleges today are still a fermenting site of sexist beliefs and attitudes, adding to this brewing problem rather than reducing it. We use the term fermenting carefully. While chauvinistic attitudes are formed long before one gets to high school or college, even at the high school or college level, some school experiences still contribute to sexism instead of eliminating it.

One of the biggest mistakes you can make is to be a prejudicial chauvinist of any kind, *active* or *passive*. Here's an example: Suppose you're with a group of co-workers and one starts to tell a joke about dumb blondes (referring to females — you don't hear jokes or assumptions about males who are blond being stupid). What do you do?

- Laugh loud and hard to fit in, and then tell your favorite dumb blond joke?
- Laugh, but keep your joke to yourself.
- Don't laugh, trying to look at least as uncomfortable as you should be feeling.

The first response is an example of active prejudice. You actively go around making these kinds of remarks, telling these kinds of stories, and so forth. The second response is an example of passive prejudice. If you go along with such a joke or remark, even if you never initiate them, you say such ideas are acceptable. Only by expressing through your disapproval that such jokes and remarks are wrong are you fighting prejudice rather than contributing to it.

(If you have difficulty imagining why anyone would be uncomfortable with a dumb blond joke, imagine an important female in your life (say, your sister) and imagine that the joke is about her and everyone is laughing at how stupid she is. This generally takes a lot of the fun out of it for you.)

We hope you see that the best answer in this situation is the final one. As an intern, you are hardly in a position of authority to remake the organization, but at the same time, you go a long way in positioning yourself by how you act toward others and how you react to the bad behavior of others.

You also have one other potential response: You can also tell the group that you know some highly intelligent blonde women and that you can't see the humor in dumb blonde jokes. This response may not earn you the office humor award, but it does let others know that you draw the line at laughing at the expense of others. This becomes equally important when confronted with racial put-downs, which are discussed in the following section.

Racism

Racism, in the same vein as sexism, arises from a warped belief that one group of people (and all the individuals therein) are somehow better than or inferior to others just because of their skin color or ethnicity. Racial prejudice comes in as many colors and flavors as there are people, but sometime in your working life, you'll probably run into someone who tries to make himself feel better not by raising his own achievements but by putting down others.

Racial discrimination comes into play if one or more groups are mistreated because of skin color or ethnicity. This applies to discrimination in hiring, job assignments, access to training, working conditions, disciplinary actions, and other aspects of employment. Because interns are typically at the lower end of the pecking order, they are more likely to be discriminated against than to do the discriminating, but being the one who discriminates is possible, too. Ask yourself the following question:

✔ Do I primarily interact with other interns and employees who are of the same skin color or ethnicity I am?

✔ Do I find myself selectively including people of the same skin color or ethnicity in my communication loop and/or excluding others of a different skin color or ethnicity?

✔ Do I only look for mentors who are of the same skin color or ethnicity I am?

✔ When forming work teams, do I automatically avoid groups with interns or employees who have different skin color or ethnicity than I have?

If you answer yes to one or more of these questions, you may be guilty of some form of racism. Not only could this deprive you of benefiting from the experience and knowledge people of other skin colors and ethnicities have to offer, but this makes you part of the problem rather than the solution. Racism has no more place at work than does sexism or *ageism* (discriminating on the basis of age, usually older age).

If you're systematically disadvantaged by other people's discriminatory practices in terms of assignments, promotions, access to training, and so on because of your skin color or ethnicity, you're the victim of racism. If you're the victim of racism (or any other form of discrimination) at work, go directly to your supervisor to discuss the matter. If he or she fails to act, go to the human resources office directly. That department exists, in part, to stop such activities. Be sure to tell your academic advisor, as well.

Making a charge of racism (or any other form of discrimination) is a serious response to a serious action. Such charges must not be taken lightly or made hastily. After a formal charge is made, or even when a supervisor is told about a problem, the situation can escalate and may become more difficult to resolve. For that reason, we recommend attempting to resolve the problem at the lowest possible level. If the problem is racially offensive humor from another intern or employee, talk it out with that person. Tell that person why you're offended. If the offensive humor persists, tell your supervisor. If the offensive practice involves your supervisor (for example, regularly excluding you from choice assignments), make your feelings known to your supervisor directly.

Get the supervisor's side of the picture, as he or she may have reasons you aren't sent to represent your not-for-profit agency at legislative budget hearings. Maybe you're not getting this assignment because of your lack of experience, not because of your skin color or ethnicity. To play the race card in such a situation would be inappropriate and probably counterproductive, leading to strained relations with your supervisor and less chance of getting what you want: more challenging assignments. You need to be sensitive, of course, to *rationalizing* (being told it's a matter of experience when the underlying reason is racial discrimination). If you aren't sure, consult with your academic advisor on how to proceed within your organization.

Sexual harassment

Flirting (and sexual attraction) has been around as long as two people have been in existence. Some people find flirting fun and enjoyable; others find it annoying. Office romances can be both exciting and dangerous (and sometimes forbidden by company policy), but sexual harassment is always — always! — both wrong and illegal.

So just what is sexual harassment? Harassment based on sex occurs specifically when the following happens:

- ✔ Someone insinuates (hints or suggests) that a job or a promotion will be made in exchange for sexual favors or insinuates the opposite — a job will be lost or a demotion will occur if sexual favors are not provided.

- ✔ A hostile work environment is created through the presence of offensive (sexual or otherwise) images, language, or behaviors.

- ✔ Someone makes clear (as opposed to hinting) that to get or keep your job, raise, promotion, and so on, you must provide sexual favors.

The first type of sexual harassment is known as *quid pro quo* (that is, you do something for me, and I'll do something for you). In this case, a person in a position of authority tells an employee in a lower position that he or she will reward (or punish) the employee for sexual favors. Because it is usually just hinted at, suggested, and so on, this type of sexual harassment can be difficult to pin down. Potentially, someone could be sending or misperceiving messages where none exists.

One successful technique is the "Huh?" routine. When someone makes a sexually suggestive offer, don't ignore it or respond in anger. Instead, with a you-can't-believe-he(or she)-really-said-that expression, respond by saying, "Huh? What exactly are you asking me to do?" and just look at him or her with that highly puzzled look. By forcing the other party to repeat the innuendo in open and clear terms, you expose it as either the stupid remark that it was or for the explicit type three harassment it is about to become. If the requirements are brought clearly out in to the open (this is the third type of harassment), run — don't walk — to your HR department and your advisor.

The second type of harassment is more most difficult to deal with. Just what is a hostile work environment? Many courts have been arguing over this topic for years and without a clear definition, you can't be sure whether you're being subjected to (or creating) a hostile environment. Generally, a hostile environment is a set of conditions (debasing pictures, repeated off-color jokes, and so forth) that are offensive to some workers and interfere with work.

The trend seems to be for sexual harassment to be treated as one form of harassment or discrimination just as discrimination on the basis of age ethnicity, sexual preference, and other forms of diversity are treated. If a "pattern or practice" of harassment or discrimination has occurred, then you can protect yourself against your supervisor, other employee, or other intern. Since the law on this point is changing and differs by state, you are well advised to take a workshop on coping with harassment and request your employer's policies on harassment and discrimination.

If something like discrimination or sexual harassment is bothering you about your workplace, be clear about exactly what the problem is and have a plan to follow. Start small by discussing it first with your advisor, then with your supervisor. Most problems are handled best by quiet, discrete actions on all fronts. You can always escalate the situation by moving up the chain of command or filing a formal complaint or grievance, but you can't take back or undo any actions you take or charges you make.

There is a fine and tricky line between office romance and sexual harassment. You may think that all the warnings and stories you have heard about office romances don't apply to you because you're "just an intern." Cautions about love and romance, like truth and consequences, apply to interns too. Before making any type of personal connection in a workplace setting, act only after careful consideration.

Chapter 9

Typical Internship Tasks and Requirements

*P*eople take internships for all kinds of reasons, some valid and some defective. Some illogical reasons include getting away from a bad relationship, having opportunities to show off new outfits, and imitating what your friends are doing. Some valid reasons for taking an internship include expanding your horizons, getting a change of pace from school, and meeting different people. The main reason to take an internship, however, is to get firsthand work experience in a career that you plan to pursue and to discover whether that work is right for you. That work experience typically includes three basic types of tasks: specialized or technical, managerial, and research. Not every internship requires all three types of tasks in equal amounts. For example, internships with Microsoft tend to emphasize the technical and managerial side of things, although research work may also be included. Peace Corps placements have been traditionally heavy on technical or specialized work, such as building safe water supplies and preventing infectious disease, but many assignments have become more managerial-focused. This chapter addresses all three kinds of tasks that interns perform and also describes basic requirements for working successfully as an intern.

Specialized or Technical Tasks: The Devil Is in the Details

Internships span an incredible range of specialized and technical tasks. Some interns fill out tax forms; others build latrines. Some take hotel reservations;

others teach on reservations. Some create CDs; others combat VD. Because the range of specialized or technical tasks that interns may be called upon to perform is so great, we can't possibly explain how to do all these different tasks. We trust that you've studied most of these tasks in school and that you've taken on an internship to learn how to do these specialized duties in a real-world environment. However, we can offer several pieces of advice about the technical/specialized part of your internship.

Asking for help

Interns aren't expected to know all the intricacies of the job. That's why you're interning. Your intern status is your golden opportunity to ask your colleagues and others for help. If you've majored in accounting but haven't had to do a corporate tax return, ask for guidance. The same goes for other specialized kinds of work you may be called upon to do. Asking for help isn't a sign of weakness but rather a sign that you have enough confidence in your abilities and reputation to risk admitting that you need help. Asking for guidance on specialized projects helps you learn faster, and it's a good way to find out who's willing to take the time for and interest in you. Those who do may make a good mentor. (See Chapter 14 for advice about choosing and working with a mentor.)

Try to avoid asking for help on such basic and simple tasks that people *would* start to wonder whether you deserve to be there. We're talking very basic here, such as constructing a table of data. If you somehow get into a situation where you don't know even the most basic tasks, you have several options. You can ask for help from a friendly source such as a fellow intern or close coworker — someone who will help you but not blow your credibility. Or you can do extra homework on those tasks by doing extra reading or completing a tutorial. If the knowledge gap is serious, consult your academic advisor. Maybe you got placed in the wrong internship. Perhaps your advisor can work out some extra training for you with your supervisor.

Trying a range of tasks

You're there to learn and build your tool kit of skills. If your internship has a built-in rotation among several different kinds of work, you're ahead of the game. If no such rotation exists, tactfully request the opportunity to try several different technical assignments. Trying different specialized tasks also helps you achieve your goal of discovering whether this kind of work is really what you want to do with your life.

Carving out a specialty niche

Just as getting a range of experiences increases your learning and your versatility, finding and staking claim to a specialized niche advances your career and makes you more valuable to your organization. Being the only one — or one of the few — who can perform a particular specialized task makes you more indispensable and more valuable. Being more valuable in turn increases your influence within your organization. You have knowledge, and knowledge is power, as the adage goes. Because students and younger workers tend to have more computer skills, many interns make their special niche by creating databases or Web pages. Your niche, however, can be anything that the organization needs and no one else, or few others, can do. Chapter 11 covers more fully the ways to get and use power in an organization.

Managerial Tasks: Even Interns Have to Manage

Many internships, especially those in business, government, and the nonprofit sector, center on management tasks. The titles administrative intern or management intern are probably the most common intern titles in this category. Typical assignments might be working in project management for Coors Brewing Company or serving as a Presidential Management Intern in the U.S. Environmental Protection Agency.

But many interns in other kinds of assignments also may find themselves performing certain managerial tasks, such as staffing committees, writing memos, and representing their unit at meetings or hearings. It pays to know something about the kinds of managerial tasks you may be asked to perform.

Committee tasks: Be committed to being committeed

Interns, even those in technical or research placements, may be asked to serve as staff to a company or agency committee or board. Some interns handle the gofer duties, which may include photocopying agendas and other documents for meetings, fetching audiovisual equipment, and performing other similar routine tasks . But if the organization is smaller — and/or your supervisor has lots of confidence in you — staffing a committee can be more challenging. You may get to help prepare an agenda, for example, or take minutes at a committee meeting. Being an effective secretary is a valued skill worth cultivating. Don't dismiss taking minutes as boring. The job of following a discussion, recording the main points, and recording any decisions is a challenge. In some cases you may even be asked to serve as a member of the committee to interject your knowledge or represent your unit.

Know the role of the board or committee to which you're assigned

Not all boards serve the same purposes. A governing board or board of directors typically has the final say on decisions. Be aware that sometimes a board of directors really sees its role to rubber-stamp management's decisions. In such cases, it acts more like an advisory board or really an "approval" board. An advisory board's role may be simply that, offering advice that can be accepted or ignored. However, some advisory boards have so much knowledge and clout that they're hard to ignore.

Committees likewise have different roles. Planning committees are formed, as you might suspect, to plan an event (for example, a conference or annual meeting) or a change (such as a move to new offices). Budget and finance committees deal with money issues (costs and revenues). Program development committees work on creating new programs or policies for the organization. Executive committees typically have more clout than other committees and may make key decisions when the board of directors isn't meeting — and sometimes even when it is. Always try to find out what a committee's central role is within the grand scheme of things.

Know your role for each committee

Are you a gofer, a serious staffer, or a member of the committee itself? Understanding your overall role helps you know what to say and do while on the job. If you're an actual member of the committee, you should be able to interact with other members on a fairly equal basis — unless you're seen as the token intern who needs something to keep busy. You can tell that you're considered a token intern if that committee is your only assignment and you still don't have much to do for the committee. As a committee member, you're probably allowed to make motions during meetings, respond to other people's points, and vote on any motions. Staff members usually don't speak unless called upon, and they don't vote. Gofers are unlikely to be called upon unless they're needed to distribute papers or deliver equipment or food or run some other errand.

If you're operating in AIM (Active Intern Mode) as we advocate throughout his book, you're more likely to be alert to opportunities to expand your role — tactfully and deliberately. If cast as a committee gofer, look for ways to show your competence and initiative, earning you more responsibility. Anticipating needs for extra information is one way to do this. For example, in a meeting to prepare an organization's new promotion brochure, you could have copies of past years' brochures available to members. You may be the only one who thought to dig up recent brochures and bring them to the meeting. When someone asks what the committee did last year, you can produce your stack of back copies. Even if others at the meeting thought to bring last year's copy, you'll still earn respect for thinking of these details as an intern — and for bringing brochures for several years so a trend can be spotted. You can also build credibility by making sure that the necessary equipment is present and working and by being the guru whom others turn to when having trouble with their audiovisual slides or equipment.

If you're a staffer, you can expand your role by having answers to committee members' questions when they arise. Anticipate the kinds of questions that may come up and do your homework ahead of time. Many kinds of questions are fairly predictable. What are we doing now? If we do this, how much will it cost? Who else is doing this? Is it working for them? What do the experts think about this now? You can find out what experts think by recalling what you learned in your classroom study, reading up on your own, and asking knowledgeable people ahead of time (especially if they won't be at the meeting). If you have knowledge to offer, you can even start volunteering it without being asked. Offering information works best after you've established some credibility by being able to answer questions that arise. And your contributions will always be received better when done tactfully. "I did some research on that. Do you mind if I tell what I found out?" is better received than "This is what you should all know on the issue."

Know all the players

If you're assigned to a committee, find out who is on that committee. Learn their names, job titles, official roles on the committee (chairperson, recorder, treasurer, and so on), and unofficial roles (devil's advocate, committee conscience, grandstander, and so on). Knowing the member's basic positions on key issues is also helpful. Some of this information is easy to get. Names, titles, and official roles usually come on a committee roster. If no roster exists, you can assist the committee by crafting one that includes this information and contact information: phone, fax, e-mail, and address. Brief biographical descriptions, often referred to as bios, of the members may also be available in manuals or other printed form. If these bios don't exist, you can contribute by compiling them, which would help you and other people. Other information about committee members may have to come from talking with them, observing them, or talking with other people.

Learn the rules of procedure

Every board or committee has rules of procedure that explain how meetings are conducted, whether minutes are taken and distributed, who has voting rights, and other matters. Learning these rules of procedures helps you function better as a staff member or committee member. The rules of procedure often are contained in the committee's or organizations bylaws or charter. In many cases, board or committees adopt standard rules of procedure, such as *Robert's Rules of Order*. Learning these rules early will stand you in good stead later.

Prepare for any meetings

Read the agenda and anything else distributed beforehand and bring these materials with you to the meeting so that you can refer to them. In fact, interns can play a useful role by bringing an extra set of key materials in case someone needs them. Interns also can help by anticipating questions or issues that may arise and doing some homework on them.

Writing tasks

Almost every intern has to write on the job. Interns have to do a variety of writing, including the following:

- Reports (short or long) on research or analyses
- Memos about their work or on issues within their organization
- Letters to customers, clients, citizens, or others outside their organization
- Briefs, which are written discussions of a legal case or situation or policy issue
- E-mail messages (typically short) on work-related issues (reports, memos, letters, and other types of documents can also be conveyed by e-mail)
- Diaries or logs, which interns are frequently required to keep as a record of their activities

A growing number of internship programs now require interns to compile an internship profile that typically includes a resume, goals, an internship report or diary, and samples of written or creative work. Work samples include reports, briefs, memos, or other documents that interns write during their internship.

Liaison tasks: Dangerous or innocent

Interns frequently act as a *liaison*, or link, with other organizations or units within their organization. This type of liaison isn't the kind you see in the movies, at least not usually, and the kinds of social or sexual liaisons discussed in Chapter 8 can be dangerous to your career. Intern liaison tasks usually are tamer but still important. Liaison/linking can be done internally or externally.

Internal liaison tasks

The part of the organization where you work frequently needs to be represented with other units in the same organization. For example, maybe several departments, such as sales, marketing, production, and research, are involved in a joint project. If you're the research unit's representative on this project team, you're playing the role of liaison *within* your organization.

Beginning interns usually represent their particular unit at meetings that nobody else wants to attend or has the time to attend. Make this task work for you by turning it into an opportunity to develop your liaison and other communication skills and to develop your contacts. This role can be a chance for you to show what you can do so that you get more challenging assignments next time. Something really important occasionally happens at these meetings, and you're the one representing your unit. Beware of being put on the spot and asked to represent or commit your unit in such situations. Don't make foolish mistakes. If you're unsure what your supervisor thinks or would do in a certain situation, explain that you can't respond at this time but that you'll get the answer as quickly as possible. Then do so. You're more likely to gain experience in the internal liaison role first because that generally is less difficult and less risky than the external liaison role.

External liaison tasks

Interns may be called on to serve as liaisons outside the organization. For example, business interns may be assigned to make calls to prospective customers, government interns may represent their department (or employer) at a citizens group meeting, and an intern for a nonprofit housing agency may serve as the agency's delegate at a meeting of other nonprofits.

Research Tasks

Some internships are primarily research internships. The kinds of research involved could vary from tracking stock earnings to identifying the kinds of recreation available in a community to studying the plant life in a forest to searching for innovations in government communication. You get the picture. Interns get to do all kinds of research in every field you can imagine. Interns often do research because regular employees are too busy with other duties. For example, that search for innovations in the ways governments communicate may be something a state agency wants done but can't free up any staff to do. Voilà! Interns to the rescue! Interns provide the extra help and typically are more acclimated in research methods, having recently done mountains of research in college or graduate school.

Other internships aren't primarily for research but involve some research along with other tasks. A legislative intern who has to research the contents and consequences of different bills (along with handling citizen questions, answering letters, and performing other duties) fits this type. Whether your internship deals mainly with research or just includes it with other tasks, you need to know something about both formal research and informal research.

Formal research

Formal research is research done in a systematic, rigorous way. It can be laboratory research that relies on the scientific method or telephone survey research of consumer preferences using random sampling. Formal research usually involves designing the research, gathering data, analyzing those data, and reporting the results.

The kinds of research and methods used vary considerably from field to field. We can't presume to cover the knowledge and skills important for research in law, business, psychology and counseling, the natural sciences, and social sciences. That's why you take courses and do lab or fieldwork. But we can give general advice in the form of Table 9-1. If you're hired as a research intern, you presumably have some training and skills in research. What you need is the chance to apply your knowledge and skills via your internship. Even though it would be foolhardy — not to mention darn long — for us to try to cover all research basics, Table 9-1 offers a few tips we've picked up from experience that apply to any research you do.

Table 9-1	Some Research Do's and Don'ts for Interns
Don't	*Do*
Start your research without getting necessary guidance.	Take the time before you start your research to learn about prior, similar studies attempted; special precautions that apply now; deadlines; who can help you; and other relevant points.
Act as if it is the first time research has ever been done on this topic.	Take advantage of previous research on your topic or similar topics to see how it was set up, what methods were used, what findings were obtained, and what the conclusions were. You need to know this to find out how your research should be similar or different.
Base your conclusions on a single interview, several survey responses, or a few field specimens. These results may be limited and biased and lead you astray.	Try to gather an appropriate amount and diversity of data. Drawing from ten interviews of people in different positions will likely be more accurate, for example, than one or two interviews of people who hold similar positions. Supplementing these ten interviews with information from other kinds of sources (official records, observations, surveys) is even better.

Don't	Do
Prejudge your conclusions before you've completed your analysis.	Make a list of tentative conclusions that come to you as you conduct your research. You may not be able to remember these later on. Be sure these tentative conclusions are actually supported by your final results, however.
Assume that your "facts" and conclusions will speak for themselves.	Document your research carefully and support your conclusions with evidence that the users of your research will accept.

Informal "quick and dirty" research

Another type of research is typically less rigorous, systematic, and painstaking than the kind of research we've just described. Informal research is sometimes called "quick and dirty" research because speed and relevance typically are more important than painstaking method and accuracy. This doesn't mean that informal research is less important, however. In fact, more critical decisions in business, government, and nonprofit sectors tend to be made on the basis of informal research than on the more formal, systematic research. Examples of informal research include determining whether enough senators will vote for your senator's bill, finding out what other companies are doing that could mean more (or less) competition for your company, or looking into how other nonprofits do their fundraising. You could research those issues by using formal methods, but typically that's not the case. Formal, systematic studies tend to take too long and may not be substantially more accurate than informal research — if the informal variety is done right.

Work Requirements for Interns

Just completing your tasks competently isn't enough. No matter what your tasks, all interns need to meet certain general work requirements. For those of you who are well into your career and are reading this book to help you launch a different career, we apologize. You are undoubtedly already familiar with most of these basics. They are important nonetheless. Sometimes even the most seasoned employees start thinking that these basic rules don't apply to them. They do!

- ✔ Report when scheduled. You'll build credibility and increase your learning.
- ✔ Notify your supervisor if you can't be at work. Failure to do this causes problems for many interns.

✔ Keep your supervisor informed of what you are working on and where you are working (if not on the actual work site).

✔ Take appropriate safety precautions for yourself and for other people and for equipment.

Chapter 10

Communication Skills for Interns

• •

• •

*I*nterns — and managers, attorneys, architects, accountants, designers, curators, engineers, counselors, and almost everyone else in the workforce — spend much of their time and effort communicating. Think about it. A sizeable chunk of most employees' time is spent talking, listening, reading, writing, participating in meetings, and communicating in other ways. Communication skills are probably the key skills that enable you to apply your other knowledge and skills effectively. Effective communication doesn't guarantee success, but it certainly increases the odds.

Here are a few examples of how the failure to communicate can prevent what would otherwise be a successful outcome:

✔ Intern Bryant wastes a brilliant budget analysis because she couldn't explain it clearly to her supervisor.

✔ Intern Rosen's proposal to his nonprofit board of directors recommending new fundraising strategies is compelling but comes unglued when questions start flying.

✔ Intern Garcia does a superb job of researching local plant life but can't translate that research into an organized, readable report that others could use.

This chapter covers behavioral and communication skills. Although communication could be — and is — the subject of entire books, we concentrate here on those skills most crucial to interns: listening and talking skills, skills for working effectively in teams, skills for making presentations, and writing skills.

Listening and Talking Skills: Did You Say What I Think You Said?

Listening and talking are the building blocks of oral communication just as reading and writing are the fundamental skills of written communication. We use the word "talking" here because to many people the term "speaking" means formal speaking, such as giving speeches, briefings, and presentations. We address that set of skills later in this chapter. In this section, we discuss those basic skills used in carrying on an intelligent exchange (a conversation) between two or more people.

Listening well

Most workers, and certainly most interns, have to listen much more than talk. And if you're typical, you've probably had more instruction on talking than on listening. That's why we start with listening. The following sections present some basic pointers for listening effectively.

Avoid unnecessary noise and distractions

Listening is more difficult if a radio or TV is blaring in the background, if several conversations are happening nearby, and if you're sitting in front of your computer with your Web design work beckoning. To give yourself a fighting chance at listening carefully, find a place without noises or other distractions, or create that place by turning off the radio, asking others to take their conversation elsewhere, and turning off your computer.

Get physically ready to listen

You won't be able to put much energy into listening if you're slouched over or have your legs up. To listen effectively, face the person who's talking and sit or stand basically erect while leaning slightly toward the speaker. This posture not only makes you more physically ready to listen but also gives others the signal that you're listening attentively, encouraging them to talk.

Be careful, though, about falling into the trap of looking like you're listening carefully when you really aren't. If you learned the habit of faking attention in school or at home, it's time to break the habit. People expect you to hear and understand what they're saying, and if you don't, that can lead to some unfortunate blunders. If you carry this bad habit to the extreme, you could get the reputation of not really caring about what other people say, thereby damaging your credibility.

Don't let delivery throw you off

Many listeners tune out the second they hear someone talking in a flat, monotone voice or with a slow, unexciting delivery. Not everyone sounds like Tom Hanks. (And Tom Hanks didn't always sound like Tom Hanks, either.) By letting someone's delivery throw you off, you may be missing some good ideas and information that could help you in your job or career. Concentrating on content rather than style takes some practice, but work on it.

Listen for ideas, not just words

Listen for the overall meaning of what people say rather than for the specific words they use. Words can throw you off, just as delivery can. Many people have red flag words — words that send them up the emotional wall when they hear them. Sometimes these red flag words can be jargon, such as computerese or bureaucratese. Other people may be bothered by words that are misused, such as saying "verbal" when "oral" is really correct. Whatever the type, these red flag words have the effect of turning listeners off and tuning them out, at least temporarily. By the time someone mentally notes that they really meant "oral" and not "verbal," he may be two sentences behind and miss some key ideas.

Find something that hooks your interest

If you can find something interesting about what the speaker is saying, you're ahead of the game. This listening technique turns up your mental and physical energies. You hope the key message, whether in a conversation or a presentation, is interesting enough to hook your attention. If it isn't, listen for other possible ideas that interest you. These may be side points, examples, or stories, but listen for them. If you can't find anything else to catch and hold your attention, look and listen for what the speaker is doing wrong and how you might do it differently. Remember that this last suggestion is only a last resort because focusing on the negatives will probably cause you to miss a lot of what's being said while you mentally criticize and revise the message. The alternative, though, may be tuning out completely, meaning that you would miss everything.

Don't talk while listening

Some people are so thrilled with their own voice that they do far more talking than listening. It's hard to learn anything new while you're talking. If you fall into this group, work on holding your tongue until the other person is finished. While you're listening, don't be thinking of what to say next or jumping in with your counterargument or other brilliant point. You'll miss many of the other person's points. In addition, the person talking will either be distracted into reacting to your point or be turned off and stop talking. Listening while listening is probably the most critical listening skill of all.

Don't be thinking about what you're going to say

Another bad habit to avoid is when you stop listening and start thinking about what you are going to say when it's your turn to talk. What can happen is that you start to listen, sort of get the gist of the other person's thoughts, and then tune out to think of what you'll say in reply. Some people think that they're listening as long as they aren't themselves speaking. But being tuned out to others while you concoct your own brilliant, pithy reply is just as bad.

Talking (but not presenting)

Sometimes you need to talk. As important as listening is, you need to advance your ideas or react to the other person's ideas (after listening attentively of course).

Use specific words rather than general ones

One of the surest ways to get your listeners confused is to talk in generalities. Consider these examples of both general and specific language:

> General: "The facility needs restoration to be more functional."
>
> Translation: "The toilet needs cleaning before anyone can use it."
>
> General: "If organizations like ours are to improve their performance capabilities, we need to improve our communication equipment."
>
> Translation: "We need a modern telephone system to keep up with requests for our products and services."

Too often along the way, we learn (usually incorrectly) that more general, lofty language is better than simpler, more direct language. If your teachers made you think that, we apologize on behalf of educators everywhere. The trends are toward simpler, more direct speech and writing in order to improve communication. Keep that in mind the next time you're tempted to let fly with grandiose but meaningless prose.

Don't use a four-dollar word when a fifty-cent one will do

Avoid stuffy, overblown words. Be careful of using jargon, and don't use big words when small ones work better. Ignore this rule, and you risk confusing your listener and looking like a showoff.

Identify your opinions

Your opinions are valid and important. You should share them — selectively. But avoid passing them off as statements of fact. If you say, "People waste most of their time surfing the Internet," you give an opinion. This statement is not something that can be proved or disproved accurately. Do yourself and your listeners a favor and signal when giving an opinion: "I think surfing the

Internet is more a waste of time than a help, based on my experience at our training session last month." This signals your opinion and gives the date and context for your opinion. Doing this allows other people to understand you more clearly. The hidden bonus is that you will understand yourself better and be aware of whether you're stating facts or opinion.

Don't be afraid to express feelings

Drummed into most of us from a wee age is a fear of expressing our feelings, especially in the workplace. The message often sent is "Don't show emotion. Doing so reveals your weakness." Today, however, many people believe that feelings are as valid as facts and also need to be communicated. For example, if you're willing to say, "I feel uncomfortable doing these neighborhood interviews on my own," you could prevent some real problems for you, your employer, and the people you interview. If you're unsure about your internship performance, saying something like "I feel uncertain about how I'm doing" should prompt an assessment from your supervisor or other colleague.

Clarify what you don't mean

Often it helps to say what you *don't* mean as well as what you do mean. Doing so helps listeners rule out possible interpretations as not the ones you intend. Consider this example. "I recommend that a new handbook for interns be written, but I don't mean that interns should just have the handbook dumped on them without any training." This statement says what is intended (a new intern handbook is needed) and what is not meant (the handbook shouldn't be the only form of preparation). By clarifying what you don't mean, you further clarify what you do mean: A new handbook and training are needed.

Communicating in Teams

Today, work often gets done in teams, whether the field is business, government, or nonprofit organizations. Teams are particularly vital in technical and intellectual kinds of work. As a result of this trend in the workplace, interns need to be able to function effectively in teams, both teams of interns and teams with other workers, including workers of different ranks and professions. To function successfully in teams, you need to understand and practice the following guidelines.

Constructive communication behaviors

When performing task functions, that is, behaviors that help accomplish a goal or task, work on the following behaviors. This list is adapted from a list circulated by the United States Office of Personnel Management as is the list of destructive communication behaviors.

✔ **Initiating:** Propose tasks or goals for the team to consider. Define a team problem. Suggest a procedure or ideas for solving a problem.

✔ **Information or opinion seeking:** Request facts the team needs. Seek relevant information about a concern of the team. Ask for suggestions or ideas from other team members.

✔ **Information or opinion giving:** State a belief. Provide relevant information about a team concern. Give suggestions or ideas.

✔ **Clarifying:** Elaborate, interpret, or reflect ideas and suggestions. Clear up confusions. Indicate alternatives and issues before the team. Give examples to illustrate points.

✔ **Summarizing:** Pull together related ideas. Restate suggestions after the team has discussed them. Offer a decision or conclusion for the team to accept or reject.

✔ **Consensus testing:** Send up "trial balloons" to see whether the team is nearing a conclusion. Check with the team to see how much agreement has been reached.

Be sure to recognize that these "task" roles are as important for group members as for the leader. The leader needs help from every member to make the team function. When performing team relations functions — trying to improve relations within your group or work team — these skills can come in handy:

✔ **Encouraging:** Be friendly, warm, and responsive to others. Accept others and their contributions. Give others an opportunity for recognition.

✔ **Expressing team feelings:** Sense feeling, mood, and relationships within the team. Share one's feelings with other members.

✔ **Harmonizing:** Attempt to reconcile disagreements within the team. Reduce tension. Get people to explore their differences.

✔ **Modifying:** Be willing to modify your position even when your status is challenged. Admit error rather than clinging to your position. Discipline yourself to maintain team cohesion even when you're tempted to criticize the team. (There may well be times when criticizing the team is necessary. But try to do it in a way that educates rather than divides the team.)

✔ **Gatekeeping:** Attempt to keep communication channels open. Facilitate the participation of others. Suggest procedures for sharing opportunities to discuss team problems.

✔ **Evaluating:** Evaluate team functioning and performance. Express standards for the team to achieve. Measure results.

Destructive communication roles

Some communication roles aren't healthy for a group, team, or meeting. Here are some of these destructive behaviors:

- **Sidetracking:** Dragging the team off the track. Preventing or postponing dealing with the agenda. Referring back to issues that have already been discussed or leaping ahead of other participants.

- **Dividing:** Looking for ways to set one side against another. Disrupting any unifying forces that may occur.

- **Nitpicking:** Finding fault with most proposals, procedures, and people's efforts. Shooting down ideas before they have a chance to be developed.

- **Foot-dragging:** Coming up with reasons why an idea can't work or why a proposal can't succeed.

- **Dominating:** Taking charge of a team or meeting or running the whole show. Not allowing others to participate, a practice known as negative gate-keeping (keeping the gate closed). Hoarding information so that others can't participate effectively.

Regularly monitor how you communicate. If you find that you're playing any of these negative roles, you need to stamp them out like they were a creeping menace (which they are). Once these behaviors become ingrained habits, they're much harder to change. You can monitor your behavior on these roles by doing the following:

- Deliberately noting what you say and do in groups and noting the reactions of others. You might even want to keep a log of your contributions in groups and the reactions to what you say or do.

- Asking other supervisors, other interns, or other employees to give you feedback on what you're doing wrong — and right. If you don't ever hear what you're doing well, you may stop doing it. Besides, everyone needs some positive stroking from time to time. This feedback probably works better after your team meeting or group discussion is over. If your colleague is flashing you secret hand signals alerting you to some mistake during a meeting, you may get rattled and compound your mistake. So ask your coworkers to hold their feedback until after the meeting when you can better absorb their feedback and react to it.

- Observing the effective and ineffective communication behaviors of other people. Take notes of what you particularly like and don't like about this behavior. Try out any practices that seem like they might work for you. But don't try out too much too fast, or you won't have your act together, and other people won't know what to make of this different you.

By Your Writing You Are Known

We want to add to your knowledge of sound writing practice by covering two basics of good writing: organization and tone. These two factors usually don't get as much attention as style, but organization and tone are probably even more likely to boost (or damage) your credibility as an intern than any other aspect of writing. If you've had any instruction on writing at all, it probably involved your writing style and usage. If you use those effective listening skills, you can probably still hear your writing teacher counseling you: "Don't make your sentences too long. Don't use a singular verb with a plural noun. Don't end a sentence with a preposition."

These rules are important, but they rarely are the aspects of writing that get interns into trouble with their supervisor or earn them praise for a job well done. And some of these rules no longer have the force they used to. Notice that the preceding sentence ends with a preposition. It's no longer the cardinal sin that it used to be. Other rules on writing have changed as well. Find out what the style and usage guidelines are at your workplace. Also ask whether your organization uses a certain published set of style guidelines, such as *The Chicago Manual of Style* or *The Associated Press Stylebook and Libel Manual*, or whether it has its own workplace-specific guidelines.

For these reasons, we concentrate here on organization and tone. We assume that you are already familiar with the basic building blocks of style and usage.

Organizing your writing

The biggest problem for beginning writers involves organization: presenting your ideas and information so that readers can follow your train of thought. You should have learned how to write a coherent sentence by the time you do an internship. What you may not know how to do is organize your ideas to the best advantage.

Good organization of your writing involves three basic ingredients: a sound introduction, appropriate sequencing, and effective use of organizing devices. Because the purpose of sound organization is to guide readers, the process is similar to planning a trip.

The introduction: Mapping your route

Like a good trip plan, a sound introduction tells where you're starting from and where you intend to go. Whether you call it an introduction, something else, or give it no heading, the intro gets you off to a good start. Essential parts of a sound introduction include the following:

✔ **Opening:** Use this part to motivate the reader to read further. Do this by demonstrating the seriousness of the topic, showing how the message affects the reader, or linking to the reader's interests. Here's an example: "The United States, the wealthiest nation in the world, has a higher rate of child poverty than do the Slovak Republic, Hungary, Poland, Spain, and Ireland." This sentence grabs attention because it conflicts with readers' expectations.

✔ **Context:** Explain why the reader is getting this message. Readers may be getting this message for different reasons. Maybe you're preparing a report that's required by law or administrative procedure: "This annual report is sent to you to comply with the bylaws of the Center on Child Poverty." Perhaps you're writing a message in response to a direct request: "This report, 'Child Poverty: An International Comparison,' responds to your request for a detailed analysis of this issue." The message may come at your initiative: "Ms. Renaldo, I did some research on my own about child poverty and thought you might be interested in these findings."

✔ **Statement of purpose:** Describe your objectives for this letter, memo, report, or message. Here's an example: "The purposes of this report are to raise awareness about the high rate of childhood poverty in the United States and to motivate actions that would decrease the rate of children living in poverty."

✔ **Statement of subject:** Let readers know the primary subject of your message. For example, "This report analyzes the levels and causes of child poverty in the United States." You can often combine the statement of subject with the statement of purpose.

✔ **Preview:** Let readers know what follows. Think of this as a preview of coming attractions. Be sure that your preview lists the topics you will cover and in the order in which they appear. If you number topics in your preview (a helpful idea), use the same numbering scheme and sequence in the body of your message. "This report 1. Compares the rate of child poverty in the United States with that of other nations; 2. Examines causes for child poverty; and 3. Recommends actions for reducing child poverty."

Sequencing: Crafting your itinerary

You can't really map out your trip until you've decided what destinations will be in your itinerary and in what order you will encounter them. In writing, a sound introduction gets you off to the right start. But before you know what to put in your preview, you need to know what your basic sequence should be. The following sections describe some of the most common patterns of sequencing.

Order of importance

With this pattern, you present your points in the order of importance (as you perceive them or as you think the readers will perceive them). In most cases you want to lead with your strongest point so the order goes from most important point to least important. This is probably the most useful of all organizing sequences. Importance can be measured in many ways. Some of them include the following:

- Most serious issue to the least serious
- Largest to the smallest
- Discovery with the biggest implications to the one with the smallest

Receptivity

In receptivity sequencing, you order your points not by importance but on the basis of how receptive you think readers will be to them. By leading with the idea, proposal, or example that you think your readers will likely prefer, you can often get them in a better mood for accepting the ideas, proposals, or examples to follow. This pattern isn't used nearly as much as it should be. Use it carefully, however, or readers may seize on that first point (their pet idea) and totally miss the most important point that follows.

Logical order

"Logical" as we use it here doesn't automatically mean that the order is literally "logical" (meaning that it makes sense) for every situation. Situations exist, though, where one topic logically comes before another. When readers need to know topic A before being able to understand topic B, then logical order is called for. Here are some examples:

- Discuss your research methods and findings before giving your recommendations. Logically, your methods lead to your findings, which lead to recommendations. Note, however, that some bosses prefer to see the findings first and look at your methods if they have questions. Other readers may want to cut right to the chase and see your recommendations first. In these cases, use the pattern based on receptivity.
- Explain the basic features of a program or product before describing more advanced features.

Chronological order

If you need to organize your information in a time sequence, either in chronological order or reverse order (most recent to farthest back) use the chronological order of sequencing. This pattern gets overused because people often think they need to report events in the order they occurred. Chronological order is most appropriate when you must relate events in the order in which they happen. Here are some examples of when to use chronological order:

- Reporting on a crime from beginning to end
- Describing the historical background on an issue or problem

✔ Complaining about a product or service and steps taken to rectify those problems

✔ Preparing a resume

Don't use chronological order when importance, logical order, or receptivity would be more helpful to the reader.

Sign posting: Marking the way

The third major way to organize your writing is to do some sign posting, or placing markers that guide your readers and you.

Headings

Headings are the most important kinds of signposts. Notice how many headings and subheadings this book has. Imagine trying to wade through this book or any other writing if there were no headings or subheadings to guide the way. Topic or subject headings mark key topics; for example, *Managing Art Museums*. Caption headings are more like newspaper headlines: *Managing art museums becomes more businesslike.*

Using boldface or italics makes headings stand out clearer, as does a larger font. Headings also come in different levels. This book uses four levels of headings. Be sure to put related points under the appropriate heading. There are different ways to show which headings are more important than others. For example, larger headings usually indicate more important information.

Your employer probably will have style guides for you to follow concerning headings. Don't be afraid to use headings and subheadings frequently.

Other signposts

Numbering, bullets, and other devices also help to highlight key points for your readers. For example, we use bulleted lists in this book to concisely present points we want to make.

Setting the right tone

Tone is another key ingredient in writing. Tone is the way your writing or speaking sounds. Tone can sound polite or rude, businesslike or casual, timid or aggressive, negative or positive. In fact, tone can have many different sounds. A key to writing effectively is to use the tone appropriate to your purpose. If you're writing to get others to apply as interns, a positive, encouraging tone is called for. If you're writing to let someone know that a request has been denied, a polite yet businesslike tone is more appropriate.

How do you create the right tone? Tone is created by the following:

- The content of the message: If readers get a rejection message, they're likely to see the tone as negative even if it is tactfully worded.

- Your choice of words: For example, the words *fault, damage,* and *loss* create a negative tone while *hope, pride,* and *gain* convey a positive tone.

Because you're an intern probably near the bottom of the totem pole, it's especially important for you to use an appropriate tone when writing to or talking to your bosses or organizational superiors. You don't want to come on too strong with your superiors, but you don't want to sound too timid or mousy either. The following examples give you an idea of how to set the right tone or avoid inappropriate tone.

- **Overly aggressive tone:** "You have to follow my recommendation if you know what's good for our organization." This tone oversteps the intern's authority. The boss doesn't "have to" do anything the intern says — unless she's convinced that it makes sense.

- **Appropriate tone for Superiors:** "I have prepared these recommendations for your careful consideration. They are based on three weeks of research that I have summarized here as well." This statement hits the right balance between standing up for your ideas and respecting the authority and rights of your superior.

- **Overly humble tone:** "I know this isn't going to be very good, but you might be able to see some possible merit in what I suggest. But if you don't like my ideas, I will understand." This overly humble, timid statement reflects an intern who's groveling. Most employers want interns who say what they think — but tactfully. If you have a supervisor who likes you to grovel, find another supervisor or another internship.

E-Mail Writing: Don't Forget the Good Stuff

Much writing now occurs in e-mail. E-mail makes it easier and quicker to send and receive messages. Writing by e-mail has its pitfalls, though. Because people tend to write and send e-mails so quickly and so often, they often underestimate the importance of good writing in e-mail. Many e-mails are poorly organized, have the wrong tone or mixed tone, and contain grammatical and spelling errors. You may not realize it, but your e-mail messages give others an impression of your capability just as your hard-copy writing does. Observing some simple guidelines can help make your e-mail writing a credit to you.

Here are some e-mail don'ts:

- Don't fall into the trap of thinking that because the message came to you quickly that you have to whip off a reply immediately.

- Don't think that because e-mail appears to be a more informal format that you can write whatever pops into your head at the time.

- Don't assume that headings, numbering, and other types of organizing devices aren't needed in e-mail.

Now for some do's of e-mail writing:

- Do think through your reply before writing and sending it. Hasty messages are often regretted later.

- Do put as much careful planning and thought into an e-mail message as into your hard-copy letters, memos, and reports. You're still being judged by how well you write.

- Do use headings, numbering, boldface, italics, color, and so on where appropriate to guide readers and to emphasize points. As with your other writing, don't overdo it with special effects, making it more confusing instead of clearer.

- Proof your message before sending and use the spell checker, grammar checker, and other safeguards. If your browser has a composer feature, you may want to write and polish your message on a composer first before sending. This feature decreases the urge to whip something off without thinking. Likewise, writing your message with a word processor and attaching it to your message or pasting it in makes your writing look better and probably means you've put more care into it.

Writing on Behalf of Someone Else

Many managers, scientists, attorneys, and other professionals increasingly write their own work today because almost everyone has computers with word processing software. As an intern starting into your career or entering a new career, you will need to do most of your own writing now and later. Sometimes, however, you may be asked to write a memo *for* your boss — not *to* your boss — or answer some of your boss's correspondence. If so, follow the pointers in the following sections.

Clarify the sender

Most of the time, you write the memo, letter, report, or message with your boss's name as the sender. Sometimes, however, especially with routine correspondence, you may need to write something like, "Senator Walsh has asked me to respond to your October 4th letter about campaign finance reform." Find out before starting the project whether you or your boss will be the sender.

Find out the sender's writing preferences

Does your boss — or anyone else for whom you're asked to write — prefer short, breezy messages or long, eloquent ones? Does the person like or detest technical jargon? You can't write convincingly for someone else unless you know how that person would write it. Ask for copies of letters, memos, briefs, and reports that the boss has actually written. Pattern your work after those examples. If you find serious fault with some of the boss's writing practices, insert your improvements gradually and tactfully. Your boss may be thankful that you make these improvements. But also be prepared for criticisms that you have changed the sacred style.

Learn as much as you can about the recipients of the message

You can't possibly know everything about all your audiences, and in many cases you don't need to. Mass mailings and replies to routine correspondence don't generally require knowing about each individual recipient. But when sending important messages, find out something about the background, positions, and basic preferences of your audiences. And sometimes you need to ask what the relationship is between the recipient and the sender. One of the authors, Jim, once worked for the governor of New York and was asked to write a reply to a farmer who wanted the governor to help farmers. Jim wrote a polite, respectful but businesslike reply, only to be told later (before the letter was sent, fortunately) that the farmer was the governor's cousin.

Get feedback on your writing

Follow up to find out whether your writing hits or misses the mark. Feedback is especially important when you're writing on behalf of someone else. If you want feedback, ask your supervisor (or whomever you're writing for) to make revisions and comment on your writing. When you get your draft back marked up, you can find out more about your supervisor's writing style. After you see the comments and make these changes a few times, you'll have a better idea of how your supervisor wants you to write. Ask your supervisor and anyone else for whom you are writing to share with you any feedback they get from other people about your writing. Such feedback can help your writing and boost your morale.

Making Presentations That Don't Scare Others — or You

If public speaking scares you, you're not alone. For example, one national survey found that while 18 percent of the American population feared death, more than twice as many (41 percent) feared public speaking. Obviously, interns aren't the only ones who need to speak in public yet find it terrifying. Even experienced professionals get nervous when they have to speak in public. We read that Johnny Carson, Jay Leno's predecessor as host of The Tonight Show, used to get butterflies so badly before going on the air that he would regularly "lose his lunch." And this happened even after years of hosting. Our point is *not* that you will have years of nervousness to combat. Most people don't face a live studio and an international TV audience. And people vary considerably in how much public speaking affects them. Some people go into catatonic shock; others thrive on public speaking and get an adrenaline rush in front of a crowd. If you're like most people, you fall somewhere in between. That means you can learn to become more comfortable with public speaking and can profit from some pointers on how to make oral presentations.

As with other kinds of skills, preparation and practice are the keys to succeeding with your presentation and to gaining confidence in your speaking skills.

Preparation and practice

The following steps discuss how to prepare for your presentation.

Step 1: Clarify the goals for your presentation. What do you intend to accomplish with your presentation?

Suppose that you want to show the staff how to create a Web page. Or maybe you want to boost your reputation as an able intern. Perhaps you want to raise a concern that you think needs attention. Almost all presentations — and all communication in general for that matter — have one or more of the following goals:

- ✔ To inform and educate
- ✔ To change opinions
- ✔ To change behaviors

If making a presentation about constructing and using Web pages, you probably want to increase the staff's knowledge level about the Web, Web page design, and use. But you also probably hope to change some opinions, such as about how useful the Web can be, how much easier pages are to design than many people think, and so on. And if your supervisor has asked you to make this presentation, she probably wants some behavior change as well in terms of how staff members use the organization's Web page and how many can help design and maintain it. In addition, you probably want to improve staff members' opinions of you and your abilities. When clarifying these goals, talk with your supervisor or whoever has asked you to make this presentation, and find out about the projected audience and its needs.

Step 2: Scope out your audience

Knowing some key information about your audience can be helpful. Suppose the staff is your audience for a presentation you're giving on Web page construction. You need to find out who is likely to be present in the audience when you make your presentation and determine the audience's level of interest in your topic. If the audience is uninterested or has only casual interest, you'll have to work harder to get its attention and maintain interest.

You also must figure out what your audience already knows about the topic. If most people already surf the Web but don't know about designing and maintaining Web pages, you can concentrate on this aspect. How will the audience be affected by your presentation? Does your presentation bring good news? Bad news? Mean more work? If staff members will now be expected to work on Web pages and your presentation is supposed to get this started, you may need to put more time into preparation and put together some instructions that members of the audience can take with them. You can find out an audience's knowledge on the topic by asking the person who gave you the assignment and by talking informally in advance with people who will likely be in the audience.

Step 3: Identify and develop your main points

Based on your goals for the presentation and the needs of your audience, you can now work on your main points. Most experts on public speaking counsel against having more than three main points you want to get across. That's the good news! But the bad news is that you have to work harder to identify and refine the most crucial points.

Step 4: Organize your presentation

Once you've come up with your two or three main points, you can start organizing the presentation. Presentations — whether they're called speeches, briefings, lectures, or just talks — have three principal parts: introduction, body, and conclusion or closing.

✔ **Introduction:** Introductions for oral presentations have the same parts and functions as introductions in writing.

You need an opening that attracts interest and sets the tone for your talk. Good opening tools include vivid illustrations of your topic, compelling statistics, reasons why the topic deserves the audience's attention, good stories, or even jokes. Use a story or joke that relates to your topic because doing so avoids the awkward transition of "Now to get down to the topic at hand."

The purpose, context, and subject of your presentation should also come within the first few minutes of your talk, followed by your preview. The preview of your presentation should highlight coming topics in the order you will cover them.

✔ **Body:** This is the "meat" of your presentation, where you make your two or three main points. Support these main points with sub-points, examples, data, and information from other sources. Keep in mind that the body should be the longest part of your presentation, typically at least 80 percent. Avoid the mistake that many beginning speakers make of spending so much time on their introductions that they don't have time left to cover the "meat" thoroughly and have to skip or rush through their closing. Or they take so long getting to their key points that the audience has lost interest by the time those points come.

✔ **Conclusion:** This is where you wrap everything up in grand style. Most closings include a summary of the key points. You can follow the time-tested advice to speakers: "Tell them what you're going to tell them" (your preview), "Tell them" (body), and "Tell them what you've told them" (summary). Don't make the mistake of rehashing virtually everything you've just covered in the body. Doing so will bore the audience and certainly detract from the impact of your closing. Signal that your closing is coming by saying something like, "In conclusion" or "In closing." These words often help refocus people's attention if it has wandered. You want everyone to be fixated on your closing pearls of wisdom.

Your closing is also an ideal place to say what you think should happen next — if doing so is appropriate. For example, you may want to say something like, "Now that we have covered the basics of Web page design and construction today, I stand ready to help you with your own pages over the next several weeks. Don't worry. It took me some time to get the hang of it. Before you know it, you won't just be surfing the Web. You will also be creating your own destinations for others to discover and use."

Step 5: Develop audiovisual materials to use during your presentation

Here are some pointers for lining up the audiovisual aids for your talk:

✔ Keep your audiovisual aids appropriate to your audience and place of your talk. If your audience isn't comfortable with high tech and the site of your presentation doesn't have reliable equipment or electricity, think twice about using computer presentation graphics.

✔ Limit the content on each visual to what can be easily grasped. Many presenters clutter each slide or transparency with information overload. Doing so frustrates and confuses the audience.

✔ Be sure that your visuals can be seen and any audio aids can be heard. Test each one ahead of time by viewing and listening from the far corners of the room where you'll be presenting.

✔ Limit the number of aids so that the ones you do use will have maximum impact.

✔ Don't simply read your presentation. Many beginning speakers find it more comfortable to read their presentation, but we don't recommend this approach, and certainly not for the long run. The sooner you can move beyond reading your talk, the sooner you can put more spontaneity into it and the sooner audiences will stop yawning. Showing a series of slides containing an outline of your talk and then reading from each slide is not the way to get maximum impact. Presentations that are read word-for-word from a screen are just as boring as if they're read from notes. Throw away that crutch as soon as you can.

Step 6: Practice delivery

Practice your presentation under actual conditions to the extent possible. Keep to the same time limits, practice in the same room and with the same equipment (if possible), and field questions from a practice audience if that's part of your actual presentation. The closer your practice audience resembles your actual audience, the better. In fact, try to get some members of your actual audience to hear you in advance and give you feedback. This type of practice helps more than going through your talk in front of a mirror in your room. Will you need to go to such lengths to practice for every presentation? Probably not, but we recommend it for your first few presentations until you get experience and confidence and for the really crucial presentations after that.

Step 7: Get feedback on practice

You can get feedback on your trial presentation in several ways. While speaking, you can observe the reactions of your trial audience to your introduction, main points, and closing. Expressions showing interest mean that you're on the right track. Boredom or scowls indicate that you have some revising to do. Another way to get feedback is to ask for reactions from your test audience after you're finished. What did they find effective? What needs to be improved or scrapped?

Making the presentation: Putting it all together

If you've carefully followed these steps to prepare and practice your presentation, you should be feeling fairly confident about how well your actual talk will go. At least you'll know that you're as ready as you'll ever be. You can't be faulted for lack of preparation.

When actually delivering your presentation, follow these guidelines:

- ✔ **Establish eye contact with a few key people in your audience and talk especially to them.** This technique helps you establish more personal contact with your audience and certainly helps with those key members you need to reach. Make sure these "targets" are in different locations in the audience.

- ✔ **Speak deliberately and distinctly.** You can't typically talk as fast in public speaking as you do while chatting with a few friends. Many beginning speakers talk too fast and indistinctly, causing the audience to miss many of the ideas presented. Your practice sessions should help you find out whether you're talking too fast or too slowly and whether you can be clearly understood.

- ✔ **Have your opening under control that you get off to a good start.** Doing so will also boost your confidence before you speak and while you're speaking.

- ✔ **Be sure your visuals are shown only while you're talking about them.** Audiences will likely be distracted if they see a visual long after or before you explain it or talk about it. The same rule applies to tape recordings or other audio effects.

- ✔ **Establish some tactics for handling questions.** Many presenters do fine on their prepared remarks but fall apart during questioning. Unless the ground rules say otherwise, near the beginning of your talk, ask the audience to hold questions until you have finished. This technique helps prevent the chances of getting dragged off the subject during early questioning and never getting back on the subject, never finishing, or getting "destroyed" before you've even had a chance to say your piece. While fielding questions, asking a person to repeat the question can be helpful. This technique gives you some more time to think of an answer. In addition, the questioner often gives extra cues in the repeated question that will help you know how to tackle the question. Try this tactic but don't overuse it. Asking for every question to be repeated may make you seem to appear slow. And if you don't know the answer to a question, we recommend admitting that and saying that you'll find the answer and get back to the person later. If you want to build your credibility, honesty is better than making up an answer or skirting the issue.

Chapter 11

Political Savvy for Interns — No Matter What Your Placement

In This Chapter
▶ Discovering the different types of power
▶ Assessing power in your intern supervisor
▶ Figuring out your appropriate political role
▶ Abiding by the golden rule of office politics

"*P*olitics is too important to be left to the politicians!"

Interns and other employees ignore this rule at their peril. If you're typical, you probably think of politics as running for elected office and having the outcome influenced by judges and vote counters trying to detect dimpled chads. But if you think of politics in terms of Harold Lasswell's classic definition of politics as "who gets what, when, and how," politics also occurs in corporations, unions, universities, community service agencies, churches, and any other place where you could be an intern/employee. The decision to hire or remove a church pastor or university president is political. A nonprofit housing agency engages in politics when it convinces a local government to allow low-income housing in that locality. Likewise, tycoon Donald Trump had to use considerable political influence to gain permission for his luxury high-rise apartment building that blocks the view of other luxury buildings on Manhattan's Eastside.

Why should you learn something about politics and power? Because they can influence where you can land an internship, whether you get juicy or dull assignments, and whether your internship leads to a job or further opportunities. And because issues of politics and power will follow you throughout your life and career.

Understanding Power: Why You Shouldn't Ignore It

Power has gotten a bad reputation because of its connection with might, manipulation, or Machiavelli (the advisor to 15th and 16th century Italian rulers known for his manipulative, cutthroat tactics). This distaste for notions of power has meant that many interns, and even experienced professionals, misunderstand power and how it affects their results. Power can also be linked with the ability to get things done. People with power get faster access to resources, to information, and to key decision makers, making them more successful in their work. So get over the notion that power is automatically dirty and evil and something to be disdained. You will need power — of various types — to accomplish your goals, even the most humanitarian ones.

Understanding sources of power and powerlessness

You should know the sources of power for two reasons. First, you need to know what power you have and what you lack so that you know where you stand in your organization. Second, you need to be able to tell whether other people, particularly your employer supervisor, have sufficient power to get you good assignments, protect you from infighting, and help you connect to a job. Pay particular attention to the following sources of power. This information is based on substantial research (and the school of hard knocks), so you can rely on it.

Expertise

What you know and can do for your employer makes you valuable and gives you some power. General or specific knowledge and skills, such as a talent for designing Web pages or knowledge of the company's history, may make someone more valuable and influential.

If you become an expert on Web page design, don't let a sense of power go to your head if every other intern and half of the permanent staff can also design Web pages. Expertise brings the most power if you're the only one who has the knowledge or skill — and if it would be hard to find someone else who can duplicate or replace your knowledge or skill. (The harder it would be to duplicate or replace your knowledge or skill, the more power you have.) Keep this in mind when deciding what tasks or functions you want to take on with your internship. Although doing what all the other interns are doing may be fun, that may not help differentiate your value to the employer. Of course, any knowledge or skill must be relevant if it is to be valuable and influential. For example, extensive knowledge of English literature may be considered worthless in a hospital internship but highly relevant for an intern in a publishing house.

Effort

Showing that you're a hard worker is important. The more you're viewed as giving your all for the good of the cause, the more power you have. Sluggards show that they don't care enough to work hard and tend to be written off as not counting for much. As with expertise, your effort must be relevant and reasonable to be viewed favorably. Hard work on an unimportant task or on efforts to undo your own mistake may well be considered misplaced effort. Don't expect misplaced effort, however strenuous, to increase your value or influence. Working long hours for effect may backfire. We have worked in positions where employees tried to outlast each other in seeing who would be the last to leave work. This tactic was supposed to show dedication and hard work, but it became apparent that much make-work occurred after 5 p.m. so that some of these employees could look busy and dedicated. This kind of tactic will likely be recognized for what it is — misplaced and manipulative effort. It also raises the question of whether such employees have to work so long because they're inefficient.

Collegiality

Don't confuse collegiality with congeniality — even though good colleagues *are* congenial to work with. Collegiality, or the art of being a good colleague, demands far more. Good colleagues not only are pleasant to each other but also take a personal interest in each other's well-being. They listen when a colleague has a problem or needs emotional support.

People support those who have been supportive to them when they needed reassurance, understanding, or forgiveness. You can't fake this personal interest and support — at least not for long. Your interest must be genuine, or it will be seen for what it is: an attempt to manipulate people's feelings for personal gain. Good colleagues are also loyal and honest with each other, although you certainly don't have to be loyal to the extent that you back colleagues even when they've done something illegal or hurtful.

Showing that you're a true colleague also means sharing some of the sacrifices as well as the benefits. This may mean that you occasionally must do some of the "dirty" jobs that need to be done. Interns shouldn't be stuck in only menial, low-benefit jobs, or they won't learn what they need to. On the other hand, interns who use their intern status to avoid sacrifices that every other employee is making, such as working late to cope with a crisis, won't be viewed as caring enough to show they belong and that they're team players.

Being a good colleague also means avoiding behavior that puts coworkers off. Being argumentative, sneaky, indifferent, a loner, or a know-it-all are not good ways to win friends and influence people. Research and experience show that people who are more comfortable and enjoyable to work with have more power. Collegiality involves knowing what the standards of behavior are for the organization in which you work and observing those standards. (See the discussion in Chapter 7 on fitting in.)

Connections and access

Another source of power involves the strength of your connections or your contacts. This strength comes in two ways: how strongly connected you are and the political strength your contact has. These contacts may be inside or outside the workplace, but a combination of both is better. A contact may be your high-level mentor at work, the head of another company, or a state legislator. Contacts may also be connections of your connections, such as an associate of one of your parents, professors, or friends. Here are some ground rules about connections:

- ✔ **Connections have to be real.** Merely claiming that you're "in tight" with the mayor without evidence of that relationship doesn't carry much weight.

- ✔ **Connections must be appropriate.** Strong ties to the president of your college or university may be influential if you're interning in another school but may count less if you're interning in an investment house (unless your connections can influence your school's investments). Your clergyperson may be appropriate for a reference about your character but inappropriate as a reference about your job-related skills.

- ✔ **Connections must be used sparingly and carefully.** If you constantly turn to your connections to bail you out or to trump someone else, you run the risk of turning off your connections and giving the impression that you have no other sources of power, such as expertise, effort, or collegiality. Call on your contacts when they'll do the most good, such as when you need help landing a job or promotion.

Communication

A source related to connections is access to communication. People who regularly receive information and can pass it along tend to have more power than those left out of the loop. Passing along information gleaned from one of your outside contacts, for example, may add to your image and influence inside your workplace. If that means betraying a confidence, you may decide that keeping good relations with your contact may outweigh the value of a few "points" for passing information. Because access to communication (getting yourself in the loop) is an important source of power and learning, look for this quality when choosing or accepting a given internship or specific job assignments. For example, assignments that require you to work alone most of the time won't give you much access to communication or much influence. Working on a team with experienced professionals is a more likely prospect for being in the loop.

Visibility

Your expertise, effort, connections, and communication value may not count for much if no one else recognizes your contribution because you lack visibility. You enhance your status and power within your workplace by being more visible. The catch is that you must be visible in positive, constructive ways, such as writing a useful report, being the office Web guru, or taking on more challenging assignments (and being able to deliver). Being visible in negative, counterproductive ways, such as grandstanding at a staff meeting or dressing unprofessionally, damages your credibility and influence even more than being invisible. Some people spend so much time trying to get noticed by the boss and others that they fail to do their job properly. This is the wrong way to become visible. See Chapter 7 for more on building professional credibility.

Rating your power: The Power Sources Checklist

Review the following Power Sources Checklist. The more of these sources you can honestly check, the more power you have in your job and organization.

Expertise

☐ I possess specific knowledge or skill that is important to my organization.

☐ I am the only one or one of the few in my organization with this knowledge or skill.

☐ It would be difficult to find someone else who knows what I know.

Effort

☐ I work hard at my job, and the key players know that.

☐ I avoid working too hard or working over my head just to prove myself.

Collegiality

☐ I take a personal interest in the people I work with and am supportive of their emotional needs.

☐ I avoid antagonizing the people with whom I work.

☐ I show that I care enough about my organization and colleagues to take on some of the "dirty" jobs and share in other sacrifices that need to be made.

☐ I consistently abide by the standards of behavior where I work.

Connections and access

☐ People I work with know that I have some influential connections.

☐ I avoid name-dropping for its own sake.

☐ I avoid overusing or misusing my connections.

Communication

☐ I regularly receive and pass along information valuable to my workplace.

☐ I am viewed in my workplace as a credible source of information.

Visibility

☐ I am visible to my supervisor and other key players in positive ways.

☐ I avoid being visible in negative ways.

From which sources do you draw your power? Expertise? Effort? Collegiality? Connections? Communication? Visibility? Generally speaking, interns just starting a career may not have a lot of connections (unless they're born a Bush, Gore, Kennedy, or Rockefeller) and may not be in a position to be a hub of communication. Beginning interns can shine, however, by showing effort and collegiality, and by drawing upon their knowledge, skill, and effort.

If you primarily checked items in the expertise and effort categories, you're typical of someone early in a career. In-career interns should ideally draw power from a wider range of sources. Because drawing upon different sources of power is healthier than depending solely on one source, that should be the goal of all interns. Connections can dry up or fall out of power. Relying only on 130-percent effort may wear you out or antagonize other people willing to work only a normal amount. If your power comes solely from the attention you give to collegial relationships, work performance may suffer. Attempts at visibility without solid effort, competence, sound communication, collegiality and other attributes are doomed to fail. People who constantly aim for the spotlight without having anything to back it up are known as grandstanders or empty suits. There's nothing inside. Here again, being well rounded has its advantages. Even if you can honestly check all the sources of power included here (and we omitted some, such as wealth and official, legal authority that don't usually apply to interns), you still need to be careful about how and when you use that power.

Thinking that you can now wheel and deal with people with vast experience in office, community, or organizational politics would miss our point completely. Remember that a little knowledge can be dangerous if you assume you know more than you do.

Increasing your power

Being aware of the sources from which you can gain power is helpful. But this knowledge alone doesn't change anything. You may only understand better why you have so little power. We explain these sources of power so that you can put them to practical use by drawing upon each source to increase your own power. Ways to increase your power in Active Intern Mode are detailed in the following sections.

Increasing expertise power

- Choose job assignments — or even entire internships — carefully to maximize your expertise power.

- Seek assignments that help you carve out a specialty that no one else has or few have. But don't be so linked with one specialty so that you're stuck in that role and restricted from advancement. You don't want your supervisors to think, "She's our only Web guru. We can't afford to move her into administrative assignments." Multiple kinds of expertise get you further.

- Seek assignments that are important to your employer rather than inconsequential ones.

Increasing power drawn from effort

- Put in honest effort when on the job. If you don't have enough real work to do, ask for some. Don't just read magazines or do homework. You don't want to look unprofessional.

- Avoid being the last one to arrive and the first to leave.

- Avoid making a show of putting in long hours just for the effect.

- Pick your spots. Concentrate your effort where it will have the greatest positive impact.

Increasing power drawn from collegiality

- Learn what is acceptable and unacceptable behavior in your organization by consulting intern manuals, attending orientations, or asking your supervisor. Put into practice what you learn.

- Listen supportively to fellow interns and other staff members. Listening is sometimes all someone needs to get through a problem.

- Show that you care enough about your work to share part of the workload as well as the benefits. For example, you may need to work overtime if the staff is shorthanded or take your turn calling to raise contributions.

Increasing connections and access power

- Make a list of contacts to call on for advice about your career or about specialized knowledge or skills. Some of these contacts will be come from your earlier list of people to contact about finding an internship. Others will be new. Include information about how you know them — a former professor or a family friend, for example. Indicate how they might prove helpful — for example, "knows lots about interviewing" or "has many contacts in banking." Also include each person's street address, phone numbers, and e-mail address. Draw upon these connections selectively as needed.

✔ Every week, seek out coworkers for lunch or a coffee break. Ask them about the job they do and their role in the organization. Most people will be flattered by your genuine interest and will regard you as more professional. You will also learn in the process, increasing your expertise power. At the end of each conversation, ask the person with whom else you should talk. Talk with these people to further expand your network of contacts. Interns are expected to ask questions and are usually tolerated or encouraged when they do. Take advantage of your status as an intern. Heaven knows that internships have some disadvantages as well.

✔ Network with people outside your immediate workplace. Doing so gives you contacts with a different perspective and expands your network. Gaining access beyond your immediate workplace broadens your access to information (up goes your communication power) and gives you more options for assignments and jobs.

Increasing communication power

✔ Faithfully follow the tips for connections and access in the preceding section. You will broaden the network of people you communicate with regularly.

✔ When you have useful information that can be passed along to your contacts, do so as long as no confidences are broken.

✔ Scan newspapers, magazines, Web sites, and other sources for useful information that you can pass along.

Increasing power drawn from visibility

✔ Give a great presentation at a staff meeting or write a solid report. Communication tasks tend to be more visible than many other things you do and can help you get noticed favorably.

✔ Take advantage of any organized opportunity for interns to share their progress or results with the staff. Prepare for these sessions so that your efforts get favorable recognition. But don't try to hog the spotlight or you're likely to turn off fellow interns and your superiors.

✔ If no organized intern clinic or other show-and-tell opportunity exists, suggest it. Doing so could increase your standing with fellow interns and with your supervisor and others — as long as you don't try to steal the whole show.

Assessing power in others

Assess the sources of power that others around you have so that you know their overall standing within the organization and can determine how they may be able to help you. Use the Power Sources Checklist but mark the items from the other person's perspective. You may need to get scuttlebutt from other interns or staff members to perform this task. Observation may also help gauge people's power.

Here's how to tell who has power:

- ✔ They get immediate access to the boss as needed.
- ✔ They get the resources requested, such as equipment or travel funds, to get the job done.
- ✔ They're regularly consulted by others on the staff and throughout the organization.
- ✔ They're in the key communication loop, getting all or most of the important messages.
- ✔ They're featured in the newsletter, Web page, annual report, or some other place as an example of a high performer, indicating they're skilled in drawing power from visibility.
- ✔ They rate high on the Power Sources Checklist as having multiple sources of power.

Now that you've rated your supervisor's power or the power of other colleagues, how can you use the information you've obtained? Colleagues whom you rate as having more expertise power can probably help you learn key knowledge or skill. People whom you rate high in collegiality can serve as role models for being a good colleague. People whom you recognize as having strong connections are in a better position to help *you* get connected. And so it goes. But if you're an ethical intern — and a true colleague — you will view people for more than what they can do for you or to you. You want to be recognized as a person, someone with feelings, aspirations, and interests. So do other people. (We have more on the golden rule of politics at the end of this chapter.) For now, please understand that power is a resource that can help you, others, and your entire organization perform better, if it's used effectively *and* ethically.

Power and the Choice of an Intern Supervisor

You will likely have more success as an intern if your intern supervisor has real power drawn from multiple sources. Some intern programs give interns the chance to select their supervisor, usually based on the choice of placement. If you get to choose your placement, pick the placement with the most powerful supervisor, all other conditions being equal and assuming that this supervisor isn't Attila the Hun. Basing your choice of supervisor partly on your perception of that person's power may seem like a crass thing to do. Remember, however, that power as we define it includes expertise, effort, collegiality, connections, communication, and visibility, in addition to any formal power a person may have. These are essentially good qualities that can be used to accomplish good purposes if used properly. If you have the choice of being rotated through several different intern placements within the same company or agency, for example, pick the first placement based on where you can get the best overall foundation and head start. And what gives you a good head start depends in sizable part on the power of your supervisor to help you learn, get good assignments, increase your connections, become more visible, and so on. If you aren't sure what specialty to pursue, go with the best supervisor.

A good intern supervisor must be committed to the concept of internships in general and to your professional development and success. People may have vast amounts of connections, expertise, official authority, visibility, and other forms of power but no commitment to helping others, only themselves. Some people become powerful by ruthless preoccupation with their own career and success. Avoid such people to the extent you can. They will use you for their own ends instead of empowering you to pursue your goals.

To find out which potential intern supervisors have power and what kinds of power they have, do the following before you start your internship:

✔ Read annual reports, newsletters, Web sites, and other sources to see whether key names surface. You may not see names of people, but you may discover that certain parts of the organization get more visibility and resources and are more closely connected with the most important tasks. The most powerful supervisors tend to be in these parts of the organization.

✔ Use the internship grapevine to glean whatever information you can. Past interns can tell you a lot, as can intern coordinators at your school.

✔ If the organization lists its successful interns, note which specialties they worked in. Intern successes indicate those areas that have the most powerful — and committed — supervisors.

After you start your internship, you can do the following to find out which supervisors have power:

✔ Notice the roles that different people play in internship orientations. People who are highly involved in internship orientations and other intern activities generally have the most commitment to interns and are the best supervisors. Employees active in orienting interns also tend to have the most power. Most companies or agencies send their stars to orient new interns, especially if interns may get hired later as permanent employees. On the other hand, if you discover the organization typically sends its second- or third-string employees to handle orientations so the stars aren't distracted from making investments, trying cases, or counseling clients, watch out! This is a big sign that this particular organization doesn't take internships seriously. Consider another organization for your internship if you learn this ahead of time. If you're already committed to the particular organization, see whether you can get placed in another division or unit and keep your options open for an internship in another organization.

✔ Observe how people are treated by their peers. Are they respected? Consulted? Avoided? Feared? Ignored? Ridiculed? Such observations can help you determine who has power and what kinds.

What if you find out that someone is powerless, underpowered, or, in the words of the new political correctness, power challenged? Does this mean you should treat that person as a pariah to be avoided? We think not, for two reasons. First, this person may gain power either while you're interning or afterward because of reasons such as a change in top leadership, new priorities, or a crisis. If you have treated this person respectfully and even helped him, he is likely to remember that, appreciate it, and help you later. In fact, because other people may have treated him shabbily, your respect and support will mean all the more to him. Second, and more important, treating everyone with respect is the right thing to do. Treat others as you want others to treat you. That's the golden rule of politics that we discuss in the section, "The Golden Rule of Office Politics," later in this chapter.

Understanding Your Political Role

In addition to learning about power, interns must also learn what political role their organization expects of them. The most common roles include apolitical, partisan for a cause, and partisan for a party or person.

Playing an apolitical role: The neutral professional

Most interns are expected to play an apolitical role. Their intern organization expects them to stay out of politics, whether it's office politics, community politics, or national politics. In most internships, performance on the job counts most, and being overtly partisan about a cause or candidate is considered inappropriate, perhaps even grounds for a reprimand. For example, promoting one's favorite political candidate would be out of place at Crow Canyon Archeological Center in Colorado, where interns are expected to do archeological fieldwork, lab research, and the like. In such overtly apolitical settings, your best political strategy is to be seen as apolitical. For example, even when you're trying to influence people to accept your proposal (basically a political act) you should appear apolitical, basing your arguments on the facts and merits of the case.

Being partisan for a cause: The crusader

Another category of internships requires interns to be partisan for a cause — their cause! Obviously, internships in advocacy, public service, or government organizations demand partisanship. Interns at the Children's Defense Fund, for example, are expected to be highly partisan in protecting the safety, health, and welfare of children and to work with governments, religious organizations, and others to advocate children's rights by changing policies and practices. For any cause you can name, there is probably a partisan organization supporting or opposing it. Examples of other partisan groups include the Sierra Club and the National Wildlife Federation, which advocate for environmental issues, the American Civil Liberties Union, and the Competitive Enterprise Institute. In public interest organizations, such as the National Municipal League, and government internships, such as the U.S. State Department Internship or the Georgia Governor's Intern Program, interns can also expect to be partisan for various causes.

Less obvious is the need for interns in many businesses, churches, arts organizations, and other placements to take a partisan role. In such cases, interns may end up advocating the product line they're helping develop, the church they're assigned to, or the civic theater where they handle public relations. Here, as always, interns need to find out just what kind of partisanship is permitted and how much.

Being partisan for party or person: The disciple

Partisan politics is acceptable and expected for internships with political parties or highly political advocacy organizations. The White House Intern Program and Democratic and Republic internships for Congressional staffs and state legislative staffs are examples. Interns in such settings typically work on political campaigns and advocate party positions on policy. Partisanship isn't limited to political parties or party candidates. Interns at *The Late Show with David Letterman* may be expected to be partisan for him over Jay Leno and vice versa.

Some organizations allow and even expect interns to take on more than one kind of political role. The National Rifle Association, for example, advocates the cause of gun ownership but often engages in partisan party politics to accomplish that cause. Always know what political role or roles you're expected to perform. Being highly partisan when neutrality is expected or being apolitical when partisanship is expected are both mistakes that will damage your credibility and standing as an intern. Here's how to find out what political roles are expected of you:

Thirteen political mistakes to avoid as an intern

Advice on how to assess and obtain power is useful, but power is only one facet of politics. Some of the quickest ways to get into trouble as an intern come from making political mistakes. Following are a baker's dozen political blunders that interns need to recognize and avoid.

1. Thinking you know more about politics than you really do.

2. Openly criticizing your supervisor (or other staff member) in front of others.

3. Going behind your supervisor's back to her boss to complain.

4. Attempting a power play to get your supervisor's job.

5 Divulging confidential information to outsiders, hoping to gain their favor.

6. Constantly talking politics and being highly partisan for a particular party when a more professional, apolitical stance is required.

7. Incessant name-dropping to impress your colleagues with your connections, especially if you can never use these connections.

8. Using outside connections to intervene inappropriately in an internal matter (for example, to bail you out when you've made a mistake).

9. Playing favorites when passing along information you receive — systematically communicating messages to some colleagues and shutting out others.

10. Acting aloof and uncaring toward your coworkers.

11. Constantly mobilizing interns (or others) in protest against the leadership of your organization.

12. Avoiding learning any skill or piece of knowledge that would single you out from the crowd.

13. Thinking you know more about politics than you really do. (It's worth repeating.)

- ✔ Look at intern guides or manuals.

- ✔ Ask your intern supervisor and other colleagues.

- ✔ Observe the reaction to other interns when they play a political role. Do they get sanctioned or rewarded when they get more partisan, for example?

The Golden Rule of Office Politics

The Golden Rule of Politics says to treat others as you would have others treat you. You don't want to be dismissed as powerless or worthless, so don't treat others that way. You want to be included in the communication loop, so include others in it. You welcome support from colleagues during a rough time, so be a colleague yourself. Some people may consider such advice as too sappy or too sentimental. Remember, however, that the Golden Rule has withstood the test of time, proving that it really is good advice. Being positive, open, helpful, supportive and, yes, even nice really does add to your power and to your performance on the job.

Chapter 12

Organizational Skills for Interns

This chapter covers some of the organizational skills most crucial to your success. These skills are relevant whether your internship is with a multinational corporation, a church, or a political party and whether your workplace is an office, a laboratory, the streets, or an archeological dig.

The Intern's Role in Delegation

Interns usually are delegated the tasks that no one else in the organization has enough time or expertise to perform. Interns can handle a range of tasks, such as cataloging items in a museum, designing an ad layout, collecting different kinds of spiders for an ecological study, taking patient information for a mobile health clinic, and writing routine responses to a legislator's mail.

Interns can also often provide an entirely new service that had never been offered before, such as creating Web pages or strategic plans. But most of the tasks that interns perform were probably done previously by someone, either the one delegating the task or someone else.

As an intern, you will be *delegated* tasks, not *delegating* tasks, most of the time. Even as you progress in your career, supervisors will be delegating tasks to you. Even presidents of companies or countries accept tasks from others. But in order to understand where you fit in the process of delegation, it helps to first understand what bosses — such as your supervisor — want to achieve when delegating. Consider both the good and bad reasons for delegating.

Reasons for delegating to interns

Valid reasons for delegating to you, the intern, include the following:

- ✔ Your boss has too much to do and needs to offload some of that work onto you, the intern, who can do it.

- ✔ A short deadline requires your boss to delegate part of the work to you.

- ✔ The employer can save money by delegating a task to you. Because, as an intern, you're typically paid less than your supervisor, delegating these less critical tasks to you or other interns frees supervisors to do other tasks more appropriate to their higher pay. For example, if you're paid $10 an hour to do three hours of routine correspondence, it costs your employer $30 of wages (not counting benefits) for that task. If your supervisor does that correspondence at her $30 an hour salary, it costs the employer $90 in straight wages — $60 more than your wages. You're thinking to yourself, "But both of us would be paid anyway regardless of who did that correspondence." True, but for that particular task, having you do it costs less. Your supervisor could then be doing other necessary tasks, such as answering non-routine mail or concocting a strategic plan.

- ✔ Delegating tasks or projects to you gives you the chance to gain some experience and learn from it, which is what you're supposed to be doing in your internship anyway.

When you recognize that an assignment delegated to you has a valid purpose, make the most of it. This is your chance (or one of them anyway) to shine and to show that you can do this and more. You can proceed without worrying too much about motives and instead concentrate on the work at hand. Bosses and supervisors, being human, sometimes have less valid reasons for delegating.

Here are some poor reasons for delegating to interns like you:

- ✔ **Your supervisor doesn't know how to do the task so he or she pawns it off on you.** Because the delegator doesn't know how to do the task, you probably can't expect much guidance on how to do it or what pitfalls to avoid. If you take on a task the delegator admits is something he can't do or you suspect he can't do, ask whom you can consult for guidance and help. Getting such an assignment may turn out to be good for you if that task is something you know how to do well. It gives you the chance to shine and to make the person who delegated the task to you depend on you for those tasks. For example, many interns these days are more comfortable with computer applications than many of their supervisors, especially the more chronologically advanced supervisors who predate the computer revolution.

- ✔ **Your supervisor knows how to do the task but finds it boring and uninteresting so pawns it off on you.** This situation is better for you than the previous one because the delegator is capable of helping you if needed. You may have to work at getting the delegator's attention and interest, however. The downside here is that the task your boss didn't like may well be one you don't like either. Many of these tasks come under the category of *scut work,* tasks that interns often have to do along with others but that they don't want to be their entire workload.

Performing some of the tasks your boss doesn't like doing and performing them well also makes your boss depend more on you for those tasks. As a result, you can increase your power (more on that topic in Chapter 11). But make it clear that although you're willing to do some of this scut work, you also expect some meatier assignments that you can learn more from.

✔ **Your supervisor invents tasks to give you something to do.** Some supervisors don't care whether their interns are doing anything because they didn't want them assigned in the first place and don't know what to do with them. Chapter 8 tells you how to handle that situation. But most supervisors do want their interns to be busy. They don't want interns to complain about having nothing to do, and they don't want their peers or bosses to think that they don't have enough work to share with interns. So most supervisors create busywork if they can't think of meaningful work to delegate. If this happens to you, respond like the active intern that you are. Be prepared to suggest other tasks that need doing and would give you and your boss greater payoff. For example, suppose that many of the letters you have to answer ask for routine information about the products or services your organization sells. If you design a Web page that answers most of these questions or create template responses for frequent questions, you eliminate some busywork, learn more, and make both you and your boss look good. Talk about a win-win solution!

✔ **Your supervisor delegates a task to you that he or she doesn't want to do because it's too risky.** The risk could be *physical* ("climb that tall tree to get specimens of bird nests"), *political* ("deny Senator Edwards's request using your name"), or *legal* ("go snooping over at our competitor's head-quarters to see what secrets you can dig up"). In any of these situations, we recommend the suggestions offered in Chapter 8. Put the delegator on the spot by asking, "What are you really asking me to do?" or "Why aren't you willing to do this?" If the delegator is too dense (or too desperate) to catch your reluctance, put your concern in stronger terms: "Is it safe or legal to do that? I really think we should get a higher opinion on that." If the delegator still doesn't back off, consult your academic intern advisor and/or mentor if you have one. (See Chapter 14 for more on mentors.)

How to accept and handle a delegated assignment

The manner in which your boss delegates an assignment to you is crucial, especially if your assignment is a big, long-term project. Even for smaller projects or tasks, how the task is delegated is important. Getting the necessary information and gaining the support and confidence of your supervisor — or whomever is delegating to you — gives you a great start on your assignment. On the other hand, if you revert to Passive Intern Mode and accept your assignment without assertively and actively probing to get all the information you need, you undermine your start and others' confidence in you. You'll be embarrassed if you have to come back to your supervisor an hour later to ask, "What exactly did you need from me?" or "When is it due?" Those details are part of the information you should have gotten when the assignment was first delegated. If you didn't pick up such key details, you either weren't listening carefully or failed to ask all the proper questions to get the necessary information. Remember, bosses are human and they don't always supply the necessary guidance. They may not have had the advantage of reading this book. They may not know how you should proceed with the delegation relationship. The following guidelines provide direction on both accepting and following through with delegation.

Gather info

When getting an assignment, obtain the following information:

- ✔ The kinds of results or work products expected. For example, are you supposed to produce a written report, a designed and tested Web site, a cataloged box of artifacts, or a completed financial analysis?

- ✔ The date the project or product is due. In some cases, you may have several due dates if the project or work product is to be completed and submitted in parts.

- ✔ The person, group, or organization your project or work product should be designed for.

- ✔ How this particular assignment fits with other assignments you have had and with assignments that other interns and employees are currently working on. If you don't know how this fits with the whole, you may miss important nuances or ways you could coordinate with other efforts. Find out especially whether this assignment should be handled differently from any previous, similar assignments that you or other staffers have done.

- ✔ The resources available for completing this assignment, such as information, equipment, and people you can and cannot consult.

- ✔ The constraints you must work under, such as a limited budget or restrictions on whom you may consult or divulge information to.

- ✔ The delegator's sense of the overall climate for this project (a favored darling of management or a risky experiment, for example), knowledge of any pitfalls that are likely to occur (such as getting iffy data or lack of cooperation from field offices), and suggestions for contingency plans for handling these pitfalls.

- ✔ The person who will evaluate your progress and results and in what ways (see Chapter 13 for more on internship evaluations).

Start your assignment as soon as possible

Some interns procrastinate about starting their assignment. They think because it was just assigned that they have plenty of time to do it. Or they agonize over the assignment for a few days before getting started. Avoid these tendencies! They'll put you behind schedule, increase your panic level, and heighten your stress. Instead, take a few hours to think about your assignment, making sure that you have the information listed in the section "Gather info." Then do something that makes you feel that your project is off and rolling. That might be making some calls or queries for further information, assembling the tools or equipment you need, or doing the first step on your project.

A good technique is to use part of your initial thinking time to figure ways to carve the entire project or assignment into smaller, more doable tasks. Then get going with those tasks.

Monitor your progress and share this information

Keep the person who delegated the assignment to you (and your supervisor if he isn't the same person as the delegator) informed of your progress toward completing the assignment. Doing so increases their comfort level working with you, enables them to give advice if needed, provides periodic feedback on how you're doing, and gives you more chances to prove yourself. Be sure that your progress reports really mean something and aren't just contrived wastes of your supervisor's time. Such an approach puts you in an unfavorable light.

Think through a problem before bringing it to your supervisor

Supervisors don't like dealing with problems that the intern could have resolved or at least made some progress toward solving. So avoid the knee-jerk reaction of immediately taking any problem that arises to your supervisor. Doing this shows you haven't made the effort to think through the problem and indicates a lack of respect for your supervisor's time and workload. Your supervisor may interpret this behavior as a lack of ability to solve your problems.

We don't want you to think that you have to solve every issue you bring to your supervisor. Some issues are too complex for any intern, no matter how good, to resolve. We do mean that you should always give an issue some serious thought so that you can discuss it intelligently with your supervisor, offering plausible solutions to try. Chapter 17 gives more guidelines on when and how you can bring questions to your supervisor.

Present your results

Obviously, if you're assigned the task of photocopying two articles and distributing them to everyone on the staff, you don't want to make a Broadway production out of it. (But do make sure that your supervisor gets the articles promptly.)

For larger projects, especially those that last throughout the internship, give more attention to how, when, and to whom you will present your magnum opus. The nature of the project, your supervisor's preferences, and other factors should guide you. If your project is to create a Web page for your nonprofit organization or small company, a whizz-bang show-and-tell presentation is probably in order. This type of presentation enables you to actually demonstrate the Web page's features and uses and allow others to try it and ask questions. If your assignment is a report on the condition of housing within your community, it may make more sense to submit your report in advance so that your supervisor (and possibly others) can read it and be able to discuss it with you at a later arranged time.

Formally presenting your work provides a sense of closure to your project or assignment and provides a built-in opportunity to get feedback on your results. That's what you're there for, after all: to learn and improve. Presenting your results in an appropriate way allows you to finish with a bang, not a whimper. If your supervisor or delegator doesn't arrange for such a presentation, be assertive and take the initiative to suggest it.

Problems with reverse delegation

Reverse delegation occurs when interns or other employees delegate upward to their bosses. If you simply dump a task back onto your boss, you commit reverse delegation. If you bring a problem to your boss that involves her in solving that problem, that too is reverse delegation. This is not the same as seeking help that enables you to finish your assignment. Two key reasons exist for avoiding reverse delegation:

- ✔ As an intern, you're there to gain experience and to learn. Kicking assignments back to your superiors doesn't help you learn anything except how annoyed they can get because you've made more work for them.

- ✔ You're there to help your employer. That's your part of the internship bargain. Part of helping your employer — often a big part — is taking some of the load off your supervisor, not adding more.

So whenever possible, try to avoid bringing tasks back to your supervisor. The adage "never say never" also applies to reverse delegation. In some situations, you should approach the delegator, even if it means more work for her. Here are some of those situations:

- ✔ You have conscientiously tried to do your delegated task or solve your work problem but can't do so without some extra advice or help. Here is where you can rightly go back to your supervisor or the delegator to ask for guidance or direct help. Unless you bite the bullet and ask for help, you may continue to flounder or, at the very least, struggle with your assignment. This puts at risk the organization's performance on the project or task, increases your frustration level, and jeopardizes later relations with your supervisor (when you try to explain why you didn't get the job done!).

✔ You sense that something is going wrong with the project or assignment you have been delegated. Your organizational radar screen may pick up signals that your project or task is running into dire problems — or "turning sour" or "heading south" if you like euphemisms. You can tell you're in this situation if coworkers point out problems or errors, you realize that your expected results are seriously off the mark, or you're regularly missing deadlines. This is more serious than simply being "stuck." Here, you get signals of impending disaster if nothing is done to intervene. Admitting there's a problem, especially if it's one you caused or couldn't handle, takes foresight and guts. Conveying bad news rarely endears you to people. Good bosses — ones you can learn from and are worthy of imitating — will appreciate your telling them about the problem before it's too late. They'll also appreciate how difficult it was for you to bring them this bad news and warning.

Planning Your Work and Managing Your Time

Managing time for interns is like being thrown from one side of a careening bus to the other. Interns often face the situation of either having little control over their own time or having too much control (not having enough assigned work and having too much time on their hands). Discovering how to manage time in both situations makes an internship easier and more productive.

Reacting to others who largely control your time

As an intern, you will spend much of your time reacting. You will be working on assignments or following instructions given by your supervisor or others. You will be attending training sessions scheduled for you. In other words, you won't have significant control over your time in most cases. Other people will be controlling your time. Welcome to the wonderful world of work! Most professionals, managers, and others are in the same boat. They, like you, have only partial control over their time. Their day is largely taken up by meetings called by someone else, responding to orders or requests from others, and taking care of other work over which they have only partial control.

Learning some valuable lessons early can give you a head start in coping with this condition. Unless you're the rare exception, you will spend much of your career reacting to demands that others place on your time. Here's some advice:

✔ When others make reasonable demands on your time (via assignments, discussions, training, and so on), don't waste time, energy, and goodwill by resisting, complaining, or procrastinating. If the demand *is* reasonable (and not illegal or unethical as discussed in Chapter 8), just go ahead and do it — as cheerfully, professionally, and expeditiously as possible. Save your time, energy, and enthusiasm for those assignments, seminars, or situations that count the most.

✔ Avoid unnecessary, unproductive activities. Because so much of your time is blocked in already, don't compound your problem by doing unessential and unproductive activities. Removing staples from reports because they don't line up exactly right and shooting the breeze with other interns or employees are examples of unessential and probably unproductive activities. Many interns waste enormous amounts of time chatting on the job. Of course, if these chats help build rapport with key employees or help you learn something related to their work or yours, the chats are productive. But be sure they really *are* useful conversations and not an excuse for wasting time. Some socializing is necessary to get along with your coworkers. But extended socializing wastes your time and theirs.

✔ React intelligently. Because so much of your time is spent reacting, make it work for you. Instead of grumping about being at a meeting to represent your unit, turn the situation into a positive one. Look on it as both a learning laboratory and a showcase for your skills. Meet people who can help you with your internship or career. Learn what you can about what makes a meeting successful — or disastrous. That knowledge will come in handy later on. If you're sent to the company or agency library to fetch a report for your supervisor, spend a few extra minutes judiciously scoping out resources that could help you with your projects. Even if you're reacting to someone else's demands on your time, you can still get some benefit. In every situation, ask yourself, "How can I gain something from this?" Then you are functioning in Active Intern Mode.

✔ Organize your workplace so that you have what you need where you can find it. When many interns are given an assignment, they waste too much time looking for paper, pencils, computer software, calculators, scissors, and other tools. Even if you share a workspace with others, organize your tools so that you can easily find them when you need them. For other items, such as toner cartridges for your printer, microscopes, recording equipment, and so on, know whom to ask when you need these tools or know where to find them.

✔ Plan what you will do each week and each day. Unless you plan your time (assessing priorities for each week and each day), what you'll get done is whatever happens to come your way or whatever pops into your head at the time. Failing to plan is planning to fail. With this passive model of time management (really time *mis*management), time goes by without much to show for it. In many cases, you have little control over your time anyway. If you don't plan to make good use of that time, you lose what little control you have.

✔ Hold a weekly conference with your supervisor either at the beginning of each week or at the end of each week to assess your progress, discuss what's coming up in the next week, and plan your work for that week.

Using a to-do list

Use a to-do list to plan your weeks and days. Most to-do lists number the items to be done — and that's all. These serve as reminders of what you listed should be done. But to-do lists all too often become laundry lists where the goal is to check off as many items as possible, no matter how unimportant. We suggest using a refinement like the one in Figure 12-1.

Instead of just showing a list of what you intend to do, this priority to-do list forces you to assess each activity in terms of urgency (how quickly a task needs to be done) and importance (how crucial a task is to the overall performance of your organization). Only by assessing both urgency and importance can you accurately weigh priorities. Many interns and other employees factor in only urgency. They work on tasks in the order they're due — the most urgent first to those farther off. The danger with this approach is that it may fill the time with many urgent but unimportant tasks, leaving the longer-range and often more important tasks undone. Having no priorities for doing tasks or doing the urgent tasks first risks having nothing of real importance to show for your internship.

In the example shown in Figure 12-1, you would whip that news summary off as expeditiously as possible. The staff needs it to stay informed of news relevant to your organization, but it's not going to make or break your long-term performance. Once the news summary is done, work on the visual aids for your boss's presentation. That has the most likely critical importance for your organization and for your standing with your boss. You can devote any time left over until the visuals are prepared and tested to your longer-range assignment of checking Web page links. Because this task is ongoing, you can check some links each day or set aside certain hours per week just for this task.

Using a to-do list like the one we recommend will take more time and effort than merely listing activities. You need to think about each potential item. Talking over your to-do list with your supervisor each week is a good way to clarify priorities. If you both agree that an item is low on both urgency and importance, it may not need to be done. If one of your items rates high on both urgency and importance, you may need extra help or a deadline extension if possible. Or you may need to shed some of your workload to concentrate on this priority task. Using a to-do list like the one in Figure 12-1 and talking it over with your supervisor helps avoid these problems. Otherwise, your supervisor may not be aware that you have too much to do and need extra help or time.

The priority to-do list also works the other way. Your supervisor can clearly see if you don't have anything to do or if all your tasks fall in the low importance range. Too many interns get used for routine busywork. Some of this is part of working, and we all do some of this. But too much busywork and not enough real work is not why you're interning. By showing your to-do list with no medium or high importance items, you may get some meatier assignments. Or your supervisor may need to explain why some of the tasks you thought were low importance really are more crucial.

To Do	Urgency	Importance
Proofread daily summary of news events	*Rating:* Low Medium <u>High</u> *Comments:* Staff needs by 9:30.	*Rating:* <u>Low</u> Medium High *Comments:* Useful to keep staff current but doesn't need to be perfect.
Prepare visual aids for boss's annual budget pitch to board next week	*Rating:* Low <u>Medium</u> High *Comments:* Not needed today but by end of week for boss's review for following week's meeting.	*Rating:* Low Medium <u>High</u> *Comments:* Crucial. If visuals aren't done or are sloppy or inaccurate, my boss looks bad, I look bad, and our funding is jeopardized.
Test the accuracy of links on our organization's web page.	*Rating:* <u>Low</u> Medium High *Comments:* This is an ongoing process over next two months.	*Rating:* Low <u>Medium</u> High *Comments:* Important to our overall image. Need to make web page user friendly since more of our activity is coming via the web.

Figure 12-1:
A Priority
To-Do list.

Idling or pro-acting when you aren't given much to do

In situations where you don't have enough to do, the alternative to idling is *pro-acting* — taking the initiative yourself to find meaningful work. This involves working assertively in AIM (Active Intern Mode) to take more responsibility for your internship. Visually demonstrating that fact with a priority to-do list could help if your supervisor realizes the situation and knows other, more important tasks to assign you. If your organization doesn't use a tool like the priority to-do list, then take the initiative to suggest it. In some cases, however, your supervisor may not see other tasks that need doing or may not care enough to develop some useful assignments that provide solid experience and help you learn. In these situations, you need to be proactive, actually seeking out worthwhile projects or tasks. How do you do this? Here are some suggestions:

✔ Think of what may be helpful in your own intern work that isn't currently available (a current roster of customers or an inventory of information resources, for example). Convince your supervisor that supplying these resources would be a good use of your time and that you would learn something in the process.

✔ Ask your supervisor and other colleagues what workplace processes or documents might be useful that aren't currently available because of insufficient time or staff. If you can convince your supervisor that some of these improvements would be useful and are within your capacity (for example, an integrated project schedule or assessment of competitors and allies), you will likely be told to go ahead.

✔ Do some research at the library, on the Web, and through your personal network to find what practices other organizations similar to yours are using.

✔ If all else fails and you can't generate more meaningful work for yourself, concentrate on your learning. Much learning in an internship comes through the projects and tasks you do. But if you don't have meaningful work, concentrate on other approaches to learning. Request to be sent to workshops, seminars, and so on, either within your organization or outside. Your supervisor may be so concerned about having nothing important for you to do that he's willing to send you to these learning opportunities. That way, you're out of your supervisor's hair, and he gets to ease his conscience. Accelerate your program of systematically meeting and talking with key people in your organization and profession, whether doing so over lunch or coffee, or in their offices, labs, studios, and so on. Ask them about what they do, how they do it, what they think you need to do and be able to do to succeed in their profession. You'll make a good impression on them (if you do it genuinely and tactfully), and they may become part of your professional network. This helps achieve your learning and networking goals.

Deciding on internship goals

Crucial to coping with the situations discussed in the preceding section is knowing what you want to accomplish during the time you spend in your internship. Whether you have little control over your time or too much time, the bottom line is your overall accomplishments. As we discuss in Chapter 2, you should regularly (once a week perhaps) review the goals you set out to accomplish with your internship. How are you doing? Consider the example shown in Table 12-1.

Table 12-1	Evaluating Your Internship Goals
Goals for Internship	*Progress on Goals*
Get work experience that I can put on my resume.	Goal will be met. I'll have an entry for my resume.
Complete a project that qualifies for academic credit.	Haven't been assigned anything yet that has enough depth to qualify for academic credit.
Learn what knowledge, skills, and abilities it takes to succeed in this profession.	Haven't gotten assignments yet that allow me to learn what the profession requires.
Build a network of at least three top professionals I can call on for references or advice.	Have one good contact but need others to diversify the advice I get and strengthen my references.

If you made this progress check, it should tell you a great deal. So far, you're basically punching your ticket to get an entry for your resume, and you've made one contact for a reference. These are useful accomplishments. But if this is all you accomplish, some of your major goals would be unmet, and the internship would be a failure (assuming your goals are accurate and are realistic for you). A progress check like this should tell you to shift into higher AIM (Active Intern Mode) in order to accomplish your goals. This book is filled with advice on how to do this. Here are the most basic steps to take:

✔ Talk over your progress check with your intern supervisor and academic intern advisor, either individually or separately. Many intern programs build in periodic assessments with both the supervisor and the advisor. If key goals are going unmet, how can you (collectively) remedy this situation?

✔ Develop proactive strategies for getting more out of your internship, along the lines of those included in this section. These strategies include actively seeking more challenging and worthwhile assignments, actively meeting and learning from professionals in the field, and actively working on building your knowledge and skills.

Managing your time relates to managing your stress. Work overload or underload can be frustrating and increase your stress. The next section deals with intern stress and how to cope with it.

Developing a Strategic Outlook

Another organizational skill that you should start cultivating during your internship is developing a strategic outlook. This means looking for the big picture, beginning to learn the perspective your bosses have, and learning to see the forest and not just the nearest trees. Having a strategic, overall perspective comes after considerable experience, so interns aren't generally required to have this perspective. But because you're obviously motivated to go far and use your internship to help you get there, it isn't too early to start thinking strategically. Strategy involves questions such as "Where does the organization want to be in five years?" and "How does this fit into where I want to be?" Tactics involve questions about "What specific steps does the organization need to take to get where it wants to be in three years?"

Thinking strategically usually involves the following:

✔ Seeing beyond your own job to issues and conditions in the entire organization and seeing how the pieces fit together.

✔ Looking beyond the boundaries of your organization to see what is happening within the political system, economy, and industry. (Industry can apply to more than just business. It can mean the health industry or the educational industry, for example.)

✔ Keeping track of issues and trends that affect your profession.

By learning to see issues with the perspective of your bosses and more experienced professionals, you start grooming yourself for those loftier levels. And you also accelerate your learning and entry into that profession. How do you acquire this broader strategic outlook? Here are some good ways to start:

✔ Ask your supervisor, mentor, and other bosses — and even their superiors — what issues are important to them. Tell them you want to learn to see the broader strategic view. They are usually flattered and will want to encourage your interest in a broader view. If your superiors are as smart as you hope they are, they'll recognize that having a broader perspective makes you a more valuable intern and a more valuable prospective employee. If you have a real mentor (see Chapter 14), this person is a natural choice to give you a broader outlook.

✔ Get around the organization to see what's happening in the different units. An intern rotation facilitates this broader, more diverse experience. If your internship doesn't have a rotation, remember that you can often negotiate one. If that doesn't pan out, follow our advice to meet people in different fields both inside and outside the organization, learning from them what you can.

✔ Find out what books, reports, journals, magazines, or newspapers are considered must reading in your organization and in your intended profession. Start reading what those at the strategic level are reading. Doing so will help you start thinking along the same lines. When you can participate in discussions about broader issues, your superiors will show even more interest in you. On the subject of organizational and managerial skills, such as those covered in this chapter, we recommend *Developing Management Skills,* 4th edition, by David A. Whetten and Kim S. Cameron (Addison-Wesley, 1998).

✔ Volunteer for any assignments outside your organization. Interview community residents, serve on an interagency committee, or participate on a business round table with interns from other organizations. Such activities will give you a broader perspective that you wouldn't have if you stayed at your desk.

✔ Participate in activities of your professional association. Attending conferences, participating in programs, and working on committees help you to gain a sense of professionalism and discover what that profession is all about.

Part V
Making the Transition to a Job or Career

The 5th Wave   By Rich Tennant

"I'm sure there will be a good job market when I graduate. I created a virus that will go off that year."

In this part . . .

We cover how you and your performance will be evaluated at the end of your internship. Because mentors can play such a crucial role to your success, we also cover the topic of mentoring in this part. Part V concludes with advice on how to make your internship a bridge to a career.

Chapter 13

Internship Evaluations: Assessing Interns and Internships

*L*ife is measured as much by its endings as by its beginnings. Without a successful conclusion, a fast start and good progress get you only so far with medical operations, hostage negotiations, romantic relationships — or internships. Shakespeare's phrase "all's well that ends well" may not be totally valid, but it does have a kernel of truth. After investing time and effort in your internship, you want to finish it in grand style and move onward and upward — or at least upward. Preparing for the ending of your internship is, therefore, as important as preparing for your first days. This chapter concentrates on evaluations emphasized toward the end of your internship.

Purposes of Evaluation: Why Do It?

One key aspect of an internship ending is to learn what has been learned. This involves a variety of formal and informal evaluations of the internship. One of these evaluations revolves around you and your work performance. Another looks at your internship as a learning experience. A third kind of evaluation considers your internship experience overall.

TIP

Why you may not get much feedback — and what to do about it

Too often, the annual/final performance evaluation is the only time you and your supervisor really sit down to discuss what you're doing right and wrong and how you can improve. Although that situation is far from ideal, it's better than nothing. As an assertive, active intern, one thing you can do early on is to arrange for regular performance evaluations on a monthly or even weekly basis. Some supervisors welcome this opportunity to meet with you, but be forewarned: Some supervisors can be very reluctant to do so.

The reasons for this reluctance vary. Some supervisors are actually shy and find meeting with you to be awkward. Some supervisors dislike confrontations and fear that negative feedback, although honest and warranted, will lead to unpleasant situations. Some supervisors just don't know how to give good feedback, either because they don't really know what you're doing, can't assess it accurately, haven't mastered the art of evaluating, or some other reason. So they try to avoid evaluations like they would oral surgery. There are more reasons why regular feedback may not happen, but you get the idea.

A number of solid reasons exist why organizations conduct regular performance evaluations of their workers:

✔ Performance evaluations are a critical part of the larger process of good management. Organizations, whether multinational corporations, rural school districts, or community theaters, can't tell whether they're achieving their goals unless they evaluate the results. Because people still are the main reasons organizations succeed — or fail — assessing employee performance is crucial to overall success.

✔ Performance evaluations provide a forum for not only reviewing your past performance but also, assuming that you're staying on, for establishing new performance goals. In an ideal setting, you receive regular and ongoing evaluations about your work. Realistically, however, these evaluations come but once a year — if at all.

Whether you're doing well or struggling, you probably want to know where you stand. Imagine taking a class but getting no feedback. You wouldn't know until the last day of class whether you were getting an A or an F. Not much fun, huh? Not very useful either. Working on strengthening your weak points or polishing your strong ones is hard if you're unaware what they are or if you, gasp, think that your weaknesses are strengths and your strengths are weaknesses. Without insightful evaluation, such misperceptions can happen.

✔ Performance evaluations can serve as a communications conduit between you and your supervisor. For instance, try this exercise with your supervisor (or your significant other for that matter). Write a list of what you consider your ten most important duties or activities at work (or at home). Now ask your supervisor or significant other) to do the same. Compare the two lists. How similar are they? You're lucky if even half the duties are the same.

What we think we're saying to others and what we think others are hearing us say can be totally off the mark, as we discuss in Chapter 10. Your success depends to some extent on good communication so that you're doing what your supervisor wants and doing it when he wants it. This little exercise can make sure that you are on the right path and will get a good formal evaluation.

✔ Your performance evaluations should serve as a written and permanent documentation of your record and accomplishments for the internship. Everyone gets some oral feedback, usually in response to the question "What did you do?" Although spoken feedback may be more common, it's no substitute for written assessments that you can use when trying to ask for, say, a raise or promotion or when trying to get another job.

Getting Timely and Useful Feedback through Informal Evaluations

Because evaluations have multiple purposes, sometimes these purposes conflict. The purpose of evaluations to provide information for making decisions about promotions, raises, or firing can conflict with the purpose of providing useful feedback to help you learn. Supervisors and interns alike often get apprehensive or even defensive during formal evaluations because grades — and even jobs — hang in the balance. As a result, sometimes it's hard to have an open, honest discussion about your strengths and shortcomings and how you can improve.

For this reason, try hard to arrange informal feedback sessions that are typically better for your learning. Informal sessions can and should provide you feedback as you go along, not just at the end, when it may be too late for you to change (at least for this internship). Informal assessments don't typically become part of your official record, as do formal, official evaluations. But be sure to clarify that your weekly feedback sessions, for example, are off the record. Fortunately, informal sessions tend to be less threatening to everybody involved and, therefore, are more likely to happen. Here are some ideas worth trying:

✔ Ask your supervisor to meet with you for about 45 minutes each week toward the end of the week to discuss your activities and results for that week and the tasks coming up the following week. Friday afternoons are often a good time to meet because many people are winding down for the weekend and not taking on major new tasks. Obviously, this time period works only if your supervisor (or you) doesn't leave early for the mountains or shore each Friday.

✔ If your supervisor can't or won't spend more than 30 minutes a week (or every other week) discussing your performance, focus each time on just one aspect. One week you could talk about your writing, and another week, you could discuss your computer analyses. Concentrating on only one area of performance at a time may also make it easier for you both to zero in on specifics. You don't have to cover so much territory.

✔ Ask your supervisor to return your work to you with comments and changes. That way, you can see exactly what was acceptable and what your supervisor thought had to be revised. This is good practice for different intern tasks. Get that immediate feedback on your written reports, graphic designs, Web site designs, lab analyses, video commercials, or whatever tasks your internship involves. If your supervisor balks at taking time to grade your work, point out that some useful feedback in the beginning will eliminate mistakes on your next efforts, saving both of you time in the long run. If you make this argument, take the feedback seriously so that the next efforts reduce or totally eliminate the errors you made before.

✔ Many times we all learn better from an example of what we're supposed to do than from instructions on how to do it. If you fall into this group, ask your supervisor to give you an example of a report, graphic design, or other work that she considers excellent. This gives you something tangible to model and a level of performance to shoot for. In the beginning, you may want to know what an acceptable level of performance is if excellent is not yet realistic. And you *will* need to ask how the task you're doing may need to vary from the model. For example, the model analytical report your supervisor shows you may be written the way she likes but may include data that will have to be updated.

✔ Make the settings for informal feedback sessions, well, informal. Meet in the cafeteria, the lounge, a training or seminar room, or other such place, as long as you have some privacy. Such an environment tends to make your sessions less threatening than if you meet in your supervisor's office. It also may cut down on the number of interruptions from phone calls and other employees popping in to your supervisor's office.

Maximizing your learning from informal feedback sessions does several things for you. First, it shows your supervisor that you're indeed serious about learning and improving your job performance. Second, such informal sessions can lead to a mentor-protégé relationship that provides substantial advantages (see Chapter 14). Finally, by learning and improving as you go along, you prepare yourself for any formal evaluations that occur.

Making the Most of Formal Evaluations

Even if you don't get regular, ongoing feedback, you will almost certainly have a formal intern evaluation. Because you're a proactive intern, try to talk about your final evaluation as early as possible. How will it be done? When? What information will be used? From what sources will this information come?

We include a typical supervisor's evaluation form to show you the kinds of qualities on which you're likely to be evaluated. Be sure, however, to get the one actually used for you and start working on those qualities.

An example of a supervisor's evaluation form

Please complete this form evaluating the work that the student has performed for you in fulfillment of an internship.

Name of intern:

_____

Approximate number of hours worked:

_____

Dates during which intern worked:

_____

A) Position objectives and major responsibilities. Please summarize the intern's specific job duties and responsibilities:

_____

_____

B) Accomplishments and improvements. Please describe specific accomplishment and/or improvements this intern has made while under your supervision:

_____

_____

C) Please evaluate your intern on the following traits by using the ratings 1 through 5:

Outstanding: 5

Very Good: 4

Average: 3

Mediocre: 2

Poor: 1

Doesn't Apply: DNA

1) Dependability ____

Supporting Comments:

_____

_____

2) Creativity ____

Supporting Comments:

_____

_____

3) Initiative

4) Professional Appearance

5) Self-confidence

6) Emotional maturity

7) Emotional stability

8) Verbal communication skills

9) Written communication skills

10) Professional skills

11) Pride in work

12) Speed

13) Accuracy

14) Promptness

15) Resourcefulness

16) Interest in job

17) Ability to learn

18) Ability to organize

19) Ability to work with others

20) Ability to work alone

21) Ability to work under pressure

22) Contributes to organization

23) Understands procedures

24) Follows procedures

25) Accepts and makes use of criticism

26) Judgment skills

27) Dependability

28) Promise of future success

D) What specific actions can you suggest to help the intern improve his or her future performance?

Supporting Comments:

_____

_____

_____

_____

Name: _____

Title: _____

Department: _____

Organization: _____

Signature: _____

Date: _____

E) Each intern evaluated is encouraged to add any comments to this evaluation. If additional space is needed, attach a separate sheet.

Supporting Comments:

_____

_____

I have seen and discussed the above with the supervisor who prepared it:

Intern Signature: _____

Signature of Supervisor: _____

Date: _____

1 copy to supervisor

1 copy for employing organization

1 copy to intern

1 copy to school intern coordinator

Making sure you get evaluated

Too many supervisors dislike doing evaluations — whether informal or formal — and thus do as little as they can, as infrequently as they can, as hurriedly as they can. You want to try and keep this from happening to you. How?

As early on as you can, try to get a few minutes of your supervisor's time so that you can both follow this process.

> ✔ Get specific, measurable objectives for your duties, where feasible. Ask your supervisor exactly what she wants from you and when those assignments are due. Ask about methods and quality of results. Are there specific methods you should use (or avoid) to complete your assignments?

Finally, ask about quality. How will you, and others, know whether you have done a good job? Being on time and within budget is important, but so is the quality of your work. You need to know how quality will be assessed. Remember that using previously completed, superior quality projects, reports, and so on as models can help define the quality standard you want to provide. So be sure to ask your supervisor if she can provide you with examples of such before you begin.

✔ As with informal evaluations, ask for ongoing feedback. See whether you can get some regular time for specific feedback, perhaps once a week. Work to get specifics about how you're doing and let your supervisor know about your successes and setbacks. Ask for your supervisor's advice and help. Think of your supervisor as your coach in a sports activity. Supervisors can't go out and play for you, but they can make sure that you know the rules, know something about the other players, develop skills for playing the game, and have the proper equipment and support you need to do your best.

✔ If the evaluation forms weren't supplied to you by your academic intern advisor or during orientation, ask for copies of these forms. Note whether they call for your supervisor to check off ratings, write narrative comments about your work, or do both. The kinds of forms used will tell you on what criteria you will be evaluated and how much feedback you may get. Note that in many cases interns may give the evaluation forms that their school provides them to their supervisors. Or these forms may be sent directly to intern supervisors by the school's or employer's internship coordinator, depending on procedures of your internship program. No matter what these procedures, make sure early on that you and your supervisor have the same, correct forms and that you both understand how they'll be used.

✔ Inquire about how your supervisor keeps track of your performance on an ongoing basis. It sounds so logical to expect a supervisor to keep track of your performance on a daily or weekly basis and use all this information when completing your formal evaluation. Logical as this practice sounds, it occurs somewhat rarely. More often than not, many supervisors don't collect data regularly. The result? When they finally do your evaluation, they have to rely on their memory of what you've done (with an emphasis on the most recent stuff because that's what comes to mind the easiest). Asking how your supervisor will record and keep track of your performance is a polite way of reminding him to do this more systematically instead of waiting until the end.

✔ Remind your supervisor well in advance that you need the formal, written evaluation to satisfy the requirements of your school or of the employer's internship program. An evaluation can form the basis for a letter of recommendation or referral later on. Try to get as much feedback as you can, at a time and in a setting that are conducive to such a discussion. For example, try to meet where the two of you can talk without interruptions. This is even more important for formal evaluations than for the informal ones.

✔ Get a balanced assessment of your performance. Intern supervisors (like parents, professors, and significant others) tend to emphasize only the bad things you have done while ignoring the good. Supervisors often say that they use the *exception principle,* meaning that they comment on only the exceptions (mistakes and shortcomings) because interns are supposed to be doing their work right in the first place. We think that the exception principle is bad for learning *and* work performance. Concentrating only on exceptions to perfection turns supervisors into nattering nabobs of negativity and turns you into a dispirited wreck. If the evaluation process you use doesn't focus on strengths and accomplishments — and if your supervisor fails to point out the good things — ask to hear about these positives. Let your supervisor know that you aren't just fishing for compliments (well maybe a little). Explain that unless you know what you've done right, you may not keep doing it.

Self-Evaluation by Interns: How Do You Rate Yourself?

You may think that one way to get good ratings is to rate yourself. Many programs require interns to evaluate their own work skills and results. This adds another, important perspective to evaluating your performance — your own. You have your own sense of what you know, what you can do, and your own work situation. Rating yourself doesn't guarantee a positive evaluation, assuming that you're totally honest with yourself. And unless you are honest with your self-evaluation, the results will be GIGO (garbage in, garbage out).

Look at the sample self-evaluation form that follows. Even if your internship program doesn't require or distribute such self-evaluations, you would do well to use this one or one like it. Completing such a self-evaluation weekly keeps you actively engaged in assessing your own improvement on the job. Build this into your weekly to do list. Doing this conscientiously gives you good preparation for the final evaluation. Regular self-evaluation also should help you in your daily performance because it covers what you need to know about your organization, your work habits and skills, and the quality and quantity of your work.

A sample self-evaluation form

Complete a copy of this self-evaluation after your first week and weekly thereafter until your final evaluation.

Part 1: Self-Rating of Work Knowledge and Skills

For the following ten questions, evaluate yourself on a scale of 1 to 5, with one meaning very little and 5 meaning very well.

1. How well do you understand your organization's goals and values?

2. How well do you support your organization's goals and values?

3. How well do you understand your organization's structures and processes?

4. How well do you understand your department's/unit's structure?

5. How well do you understand your organization's standards and procedures?

6. How well do you follow your organization's standards and procedures?

7. How well do you understand your roles and responsibilities and how they fit into the larger work processes of your organization?

8. How well do you communicate and interact with your peers?

9. How well do you communicate and interact with your supervisors?

10. How well do you understand your supervisor's goals and values?

Part 2: Descriptions of Work-Related Knowledge and Skills

1. Describe your organization's goals and values (be specific).

2. Describe your organization's structure.

3. Describe your department's/area's structure.

4. Describe your greatest strength in communicating with others on the job. What can you do to make things better? Answer this question once for each audience you communicate with such as other interns, regular employees, supervisors, and so on.

5. Describe your greatest weaknesses in communication with others on the job. What can you do to make things better? Again, answer this question once for each type of audience you communicate with such as other interns, regular employees, supervisors, and so on.

Part 3: Rating of Work Performance

Think about the various skills, projects, tasks, and so on that you have worked on recently. For each of these, rate your performance in terms of quality of work, quantity of work, and meeting your scheduled commitments.

Low quality 1 2 3 4 5 High quality

Low quantity 1 2 3 4 5 High quantity

Failed to meet any commitments 1 2 3 4 5 Met all commitments

Skill/task/project	*Quality*	*Productivity*	*Commitments*
_____	____	____	____
_____	____	____	____
_____	____	____	____

Notice that Part 1 of the sample self-evaluation asks you to rate what you know on key points, while Part 2 actually asks you to describe what you know. If your results are consistent on both these parts, you're probably being honest with yourself. If you rate yourself high on Part 1 but can't write a convincing answer on Part 2, you're probably overrating your knowledge. If your ratings are lower than your written answers indicate, you're probably being too hard on yourself. A self-evaluation like this one can be a useful tool to use during your weekly informal feedback sessions because it helps structure what you and your supervisor discuss. Comparing your first self-evaluation and your last gives a good idea of your progress during your internship.

As you develop relationships with other interns, you can be a resource for each other as well. Consider meeting once a week to talk a bit about your own experiences overall and to seek each others' feedback based on your own observations, things you may have heard, and so on.

Evaluating Your Learning Experience

Don't you forget and don't let your supervisor forget that internships are for learning as well as working. It is true that you offer your organization a bright mind and a strong back at low or no pay. In this way, the organization gets high-quality work output for low cash costs. At the same time, you're also working in this environment to learn about the work itself and about the career field in general.

If the work side of the equation gets to be too onerous, you may become little more than a disenchanted drudge. This wasn't what you signed up for, was it? At the same time, if you immerse yourself too much in the learning side of things without the chance for the doing, you may as well be back in the classroom. Think of this as the yin and the yang of your internship. You need to keep these forces in balance for your internship to be a success.

You will also find that you must adopt an assertive, active stance in your own life on the job or risk losing all. In the classroom, all too often you are handed a syllabus, told what you're expected to do and when, and then tested to see whether you picked up any knowledge. All this is well and good, but it's a very passive model. You just show up, do what you're told and, voilà, you complete the class. (If you have enough initiative to buy this book, you probably know that good students in the classroom are active rather than passive learners.)

Your internship won't succeed (nor will you) if you operate in PSM (Passive Student Mode). You will be entering a jungle without a guide. You won't have a prepared syllabus of what you are to learn or instructors eagerly waiting to teach it to you. Many interns liken it to being up a creek without a paddle. You can't passively sit and wait, or the current will carry you away. Chapters 7 through 12 can guide you in assertive, active interning (AIM, Active Intern Mode) so that you arrive at your destination as successfully as possible.

You need to evaluate yourself and be evaluated on both your work *and* your learning over the course of your internship. Documenting intern learning is usually a prerequisite for those of you who take an internship to receive academic credit. As with a class, you're supposed to be learning and growing during your internship. What have you learned, how have you grown, and how can you tell?

Just as you need to discuss your final work evaluation with your organizational supervisor early in your internship, you likewise need to discuss your final academic/learning evaluation with your academic advisor as early as possible. You should receive a set of guidelines for self-evaluation of your learning. If you don't get some guidelines, ask for them.

These guidelines are also referred to as a learning contract. (The concept and sample of the learning contract are introduced in Chapter 2.) By reviewing the goals you set in your learning contract, you get a good sense of whether you have met your learning objectives for the internship.

Keeping a journal is a good idea because doing so helps you to think about and focus on what you do and learn day by day. Many learning contracts require a journal. If the contract includes a formal requirement for keeping a journal, find out ahead of time exactly what format is required and follow it. If your advisor can't come up with any specifics, ask for a sample of a good journal from a prior intern so that you have some sort of model to follow. You don't want to be told (by your advisor or supervisor) to just do it any way, only to later find that there really was a preferred journal style, which, of course, is different from what you did.

Getting Useful Feedback for Learning and Working

Whether it applies to your learning or your work, your evaluations should be seen as tools to help you — like a visit to the dentist. Evaluations (as well as dentist appointments) are for your own good and should be approached with a good attitude. Remember that feedback, both positive and negative, is the only way you can continue what you're doing well and improve in other areas.

No news (or feedback, to be precise) is bad feedback! Useful feedback also needs to be *specific* feedback. Although you feel good when you're told, "Keep up the good work," how useful is that to helping you improve? Keep up *what* good work exactly? Even a comment such as "Don't do that again" isn't very useful. You don't know whether it's what you did, how you did it, where you did it, or when you did it (or some combination thereof) that is problematic.

If you don't get specifics, assert yourself and ask for them. For example, you could say, "Thanks for the feedback. I really appreciate it. At the same time, it would help me a lot if you could be more specific. What was it about my work that pleased you the most? What could I have done differently to be even better?"

Consider this example of bad feedback.

John's supervisor tells him that he is pleased with his "hard work to keep costs down and efficiency up." John's supervisor was, of course, referring to John's having found a less expensive supplier for many of the department's supplies because the company's overall budget was down a bit this year. John, however, thought his supervisor was referring to the hours John had put in on finding new types of computer software packages that the office could purchase to revamp many of its procedures.

Thus emboldened, John proceeds to spend even more time on the software search and keeps bringing to his supervisor more and more requests for new software to purchase. John's supervisor continues to turn down these requests to spend more and more money and grows frustrated with John's continued insistence on this type of spending. John, too, is growing frustrated that he's doing more and more of "what he was told" while his boss keeps criticizing him for it. Guess what John's next evaluation is going to be like?

The only way to avoid such problems is to assertively work for frequent, specific feedback. Armed with that information, you can do your best to see that both your work and your learning are meeting the specific expectations of your supervisor and your advisor (and hopefully you, too). See Chapter 15 for more advice on learning from both praise and criticism.

Evaluation Issues for Interns

Problems with evaluations are not all in the domain of supervisors. Interns, too, may have a general tendency to avoid their work, their coworkers, and even their supervisor during the last days of an internship while trying to avoid the dreaded final evaluation. Or interns may be counting down the minutes, relieved that the internship is about to conclude and eager to get the evaluation over, no matter how it comes out. What was once a remote inevitability is now an in-your-face event that can be hard for interns to cope with.

Try thinking about the evaluation from a different perspective. Each day your internship lasts is part of a process that you always knew had a first day and a last day. The end is not some sudden event occurring out of nowhere. Thinking this way can also be a motivator because, by focusing on your ending, you're seeing your work in terms of a finite period. A deadline, so to speak, is more likely to get people working harder than an infinite amount of time stretching out before them.

Be prepared

Begin thinking about your evaluation as early as possible. By trying to find out all you can about what's going to happen, along with when and how, you can be prepared for your evaluations. Yes, your internship evaluations will occur about the same time that your term papers are due and finals are scheduled. Forewarned is forearmed (another good cliché, eh?), so the more prepared you are ahead of time, the better things may go. You may even be able to schedule some events at a more advantageous time for you.

Being emotionally prepared for evaluations is just as important as being prepared intellectually. Going through any type of evaluation process is stressful. You're also likely to find that you don't agree with everything that is said about you. After all, who knows you better? Yourself, with all your years of knowledge on the subject, or your supervisor who has had only a few months to get to know you?

Sometimes it's a matter of perspective. For instance, what standard are you being measured against? Is your supervisor comparing you and your work to that of a first-timer just learning or against the other interns you work with or perhaps even against regular employees with long-term experience? These are the kinds of questions and issues you want to work out with your supervisor in advance. Unfortunately, not all supervisors are created equal, and you may run into one who has such a full plate of her own that she has little regard or support for your training needs.

Consider the supervisor's role

Personalities (yours and your supervisor's) can play a role in your evaluation. Although you probably always got along perfectly with every teacher and boss you have ever had, you should at least consider the possibility that the two of you may not get along as well as you would like and how this could affect your evaluations.

Sometimes, you may have the opportunity to actively take part in your evaluation. That is, some supervisors allow and even encourage interns to contribute their own input to the evaluation. This can happen in several different ways. For example, you may be asked to write your own self-evaluation of what you have learned or accomplished. Your coworkers may be asked for their thoughts about you. You may be offered the chance to expand upon or clarify any pieces of your evaluation. You may even have the chance to review your evaluation alone before you meet with your supervisor so that you can have a chance to think about what has been said about you, both good and not-so-good.

Some supervisors see the whole process as a positive learning and growth experience and try to convey the same to you. Others see the whole thing as a waste of their time at best and a major pain at worst. You can imagine what you'll hear about evaluations from coworkers in this type of environment. Either way, do your best, stand up for yourself, and roll with the punches. You don't control either the overall evaluation process or the ways in which your particular supervisor chooses to implement it. You can but do your best.

Evaluating the Internship and Organization

During the termination phase of your internship, you will also likely get into the evaluation act to assess your internship experience. Back when you began your internship, you should have established some goals you wanted to achieve from this upcoming opportunity. What did you want to get out of all this? What did you want to learn? What skills did you want to acquire? What situations did you want to sample? Well, what happened?

No one truly knows better than you do the answers to those questions. One formal way to help you with this assessment is to keep some sort of journal during your internship. Some schools require a journal as a part of your academic credit for your internship. Even if a journal isn't required, it can be a good way to reflect on where you're trying to go, where you are now, and what is left to be done in order to get there.

If you're part of an academic program's internship, you may well be asked to formally evaluate your organization. Your academic intern advisor and your school want to know what your world was like and whether this was a good situation for future students to experience.

You may be asked to complete some type of fill-in-the-blank form or write some type of report critiquing various aspects of the organization, your supervisor, your advisor, and your internship overall. You need to be prepared for such a possibility ahead of time.

Here are some questions that may help you pull your thoughts together in this matter:

- What were your initial expectations?
- What specific goals and objectives did you have? Were these written down in clear and concise terms that you, your advisor, and your supervisor saw and understood?
- What went right?
- What went wrong?
- What other information or assistance would have helped you?
- How satisfied were you at the end of the first month or so? Why?
- What problems arose, and how were they handled?
- What changes would have made things better for you (and for those who come after you)?
- Were you properly prepared for and ready for the tasks and duties that were assigned to you?
- What kind of interpersonal contacts and relationships developed? That is, how did you get along with others, such as coworkers and your boss?
- How would you evaluate your supervisor as your work supervisor?
- How would you assess your supervisor in helping you learn?
- What kind of feedback did you get? When? How? Was it what you needed?
- Were you able to ask for and get help when you needed it?
- What were the best things about your experiences?
- What were the worst things about your experiences?
- Did your internship better prepare you for your future? Specifically how and why?
- Overall, what is your evaluation of this particular internship?
- What could be done to improve this opportunity for future interns?

✔ What weren't you told/didn't know to ask till later that would have helped you out early on?

✔ Finally, would you recommend this internship opportunity to others? Why or why not?

When conducting your evaluation of the internship and employer, actively collect data on these questions as you go along, systematically keep track of the data, use all the data when doing your evaluation, and spend plenty of time creating and producing an insightful evaluation that helps the employer improve the internship and once again demonstrates your superior performance.

Chapter 14

The Mentor-Protégé Relationship: Making Your Internship Pay Off

• •

In This Chapter

▶ Defining mentors and protégés

▶ Picking a good mentor

▶ Recognizing bad mentors

▶ Establishing a solid mentor-protégé relationship

• •

The most crucial assessment of whether an internship has succeeded is whether the internship gives you expanded knowledge and skills and broader career opportunities. If those two payoffs don't occur, a high rating and top grade are pretty meaningless. Think about it! Few people will care throughout your career what grade or evaluation report (the little payoffs) you got in your internships. But most people will care about what you've learned, what you've achieved, and how far you went (the big payoffs). Mentors and mentoring are crucial to getting the big payoffs. This chapter provides some basic knowledge about the care and feeding of mentors and your role as a protégé. The chapter defines mentors and protégés, offers guidance on choosing a good mentor, describes rules of fair play between mentors and protégés, and shows how mentors can be links to a career.

What Are Mentors? Who's a Protégé?

A mentor is someone, usually someone with much greater knowledge, skill, and experience, who helps a protégé, typically someone younger and less experienced, develop professionally and personally. In this regard, mentors play the same role that master artists or artisans have played by historically training apprentices. Mentors are the torchbearers passing on the torch of knowledge and professionalism to others. Traditionally, mentors were a generation (or two) older than their proteges. Think of Merlin mentoring King Arthur or Obi-Wan Kenobi mentoring Luke Skywalker. That age difference holds true today in most cases, but advances in knowledge and changes in society sometimes result in mentors being younger than their protégés. Isn't change wonderful?

Itzhak Perlman, the world-famous violinist, had a mentor who helped him become established as a concert soloist. That mentor was Isaac Stern, an equally accomplished and renowned violinist who has helped many young musicians. In turn, Mr. Perlman mentors some of the newer generation of violinists, imparting musicianship, advice, and access to opportunities, as Isaac Stern did for him. That's what good mentors do. They teach, coach, counsel, model role behavior, and even befriend their protégés. Protégés are the learners who try to absorb as much as they can from watching and hearing their mentors as they perform their craft, be it legal cross-examination, graphic design, newscasting, systems engineering, crisis management, lecturing, or playing the violin.

A mentor can do a lot for you if you interest him or her enough to take you on as a protégé. A mentor can help you solve work problems; give you advice about what jobs to take, what schools to attend, and what fields are promising; write recommendations on your behalf; facilitate access to opportunities; plug you into a broader network; and even offer personal advice.

A mentor-protégé relationship, if it is to be successful for the long term, must be reciprocal. The benefits must go both ways, or this relationship, as with any other relationship, will sour. If you're a protégé, you must do your part by conscientiously learning from your mentor, fulfilling the promise your mentor saw in you to warrant all the time and effort on your behalf, letting the mentor know you appreciate these efforts, and helping your mentor, where possible. The mentor-protégé relationship requires active involvement on your part in order to work. You can't sit back passively and wait for a mentor to find you and carry the relationship. More on this later. Now that you know how beneficial a mentor-protégé relationship can be, what do you look for in a mentor?

A Good Mentor Is Hard to Find

We take that back: A good mentor is hard to find only if you don't know what to look for and where to look. The follow sections give you the info you need to make the search a little easier. But don't be frustrated if you don't find a mentor during your internship. The mentor-protégé relationship is more common when the protégé is more advanced in career and more likely to work closely with a mentor. We include this chapter, however, to give you a head start in preparing for the mentoring relationship and in finding a true mentor as an intern. It does happen.

Looking at the qualities of a good mentor

Good mentors are a fairly rare species, so most interns never benefit from the invaluable experience of learning from a mentor. We want you to have that experience and advantage, so here's what to look for in a mentor:

✔ **Good mentors possess significant expertise and professional skill.** These talents make them worth observing and learning from. It's hard to learn much from people who have little mastery themselves.

✔ **Good mentors are willing to share their expertise and skill with others.** Some experts hoard their knowledge to protect their power position, a topic we discuss in Chapter 11. Avoid choosing one of these hotshots as a mentor, no matter how famous or powerful the person is. Such mentors are out only for their success, not yours or anyone else's. You may be able to learn something from them, but rely on someone else for your mentor.

✔ **Good mentors have considerable power drawn from different sources.** The most effective mentors have significant professional power and influence derived from multiple sources, such as expertise, effort, collegiality, connections/access, communication, and visibility. They have most or all of these sources. Protégés tap into these power sources, just as we advise interns to do in Chapter 11. People who lack most or all of these sources of power make poor intern supervisors and even poorer mentors.

✔ **Good mentors are trusted and respected within the profession and organization.** They're good colleagues in the truest sense, giving them two strong advantages from a protégé's viewpoint. One, you can trust your mentor to give sound advice, to look out for your interests, and to protect you when necessary. As a temporary and largely unknown intern, you may be in a vulnerable position, so you must be able to trust your mentor. Two, some of your mentor's trust and respect rubs off on you, the protégé. If you're capable enough and motivated enough to be mentored by "the maestro," then the maestro's peers and other protégés will trust and respect you. But you'll have to continue to earn that trust and respect as you progress in your career.

✔ **Good mentors are passionate about their profession and deeply committed to it.** Because these people are on fire with excitement about what they do and how it benefits others, you're more likely to catch their passion and take on that sense of commitment. A sense of passion for what they're doing is generally what makes highly successful people tick. This sense of passion separates highly successful people from others.

✔ **Good mentors have a sense of vision about their profession and where it is headed.** Effective mentors not only are passionate about their profession but understand their profession — where it has been, where it is now, and where it's headed. As a result, they have a unique perspective from which to advise you on your career and to socialize you into the profession.

✔ **Good mentors are willing and able to give protégés career advice.**
Valuable mentors not only have a sense of the profession but are willing
to advise protégés on career moves and strategy, further educational
skills and knowledge, and so forth. They're also good resources when
problems come up on a particular job or educational program. All this
takes time and requires commitment to you. Look for people who are
likely to invest considerable time and effort in you, your career, and
your happiness. How do you know who's likely to make this investment
in you? Look for people who have successfully mentored others.

✔ **Good mentors challenge protégés to attain greater performance.**
Mentors worthy of the name encourage and even prod their protégés to
move beyond current levels of performance so that they don't get stale
or complacent. Mentors need to do this to help the protégé to greater
fulfillment and to protect their reputation, because protégés are a
reflection of their mentor.

✔ **Good mentors protect their protégés from harmful interference or
criticism.** You're getting the idea that mentors instruct, counsel, and
promote protégés. They also protect them from harmful interference or
attack. Protégés, especially intern protégés, are vulnerable. Some
protection may be needed to keep them from getting pushed around,
thwarted, and having their ego destroyed. Mentors typically help protect protégés in such situations. The operative phrase here is protection
from "harmful" interference or criticism. Mentors wouldn't be acting in
the best long-term interests of their protégés if they protected their
protégés from deserved, constructive criticism. Without such criticism,
people are unlikely to improve.

✔ **Good mentors keep their protégés from becoming too dependent upon
them.** Protégés typically depend on their mentors for advice, connections,
and even protection. The power relationship is unbalanced by its very
nature, although in the best relationships protégés gain more power and
are able to reciprocate to aid their mentors. The most effective mentors
encourage their protégés to become independent professionals in their
own right, not just extensions of their mentors. They do this by introducing
their protégés to other professionals. Doing so widens their networks and
decreases dependence on their mentors. Effective mentors also cut the
apron strings if their protégés ask too often for advice or avoid making a
move without the mentor's blessing. Watch out for would-be mentors who
try to keep you isolated and dependent so that they can use you for their
own ends — or their ego trips.

(These criteria draw upon *Communicating for Results in Government: A Strategic
Approach for Public Managers,* by James L. Garnett (Jossey-Bass, 1992).)

Finding good mentors

Now that you know what qualities to look for, how do you find people with
these attributes?

✔ Look for people whom other professionals turn to for advice and instruction. Employees, especially savvy long-timers, are unlikely to keep turning to colleagues who can't or won't give them good advice or help with their work. So find out whom others, especially those in the know, turn to.

Be aware that not all employees' or interns' needs are the same. Some people are effective mentors to people well into their career but don't relate well to younger, less-experienced employees or interns. We are reminded of the adage "Watch where truck drivers stop to eat and go there." That may be sound advice *if* you have the tastes and cast-iron stomach of a truck driver. The same caution applies to mentors. Find a mentor who can help people at your level and with your needs. The best mentors are those who are willing and able to help people at all stages in their career. This gives them the added perspective of dealing with a broad range of work- and career-related issues. If you find such a gem, you probably won't have to change mentors during your career. Some protégés outgrow their mentor's capacity to help them because their mentor can help only those who have fairly routine, beginning-of-career issues and problems.

✔ Look for senior staff who actively participate in orientations, workshops, intern discussions, and so on. This type of involvement shows a commitment to helping others develop their professional potential. Beware of intern groupies, however. These older professionals may just want to be around younger interns who look up to them and hang on their every word. For them, it's an ego trip, not real mentoring. Their peers don't respect them, so they try to get attention and respect from interns. You should respect them, but you don't have to depend upon them as mentors.

✔ Look for people who have a consistent track record of producing successful, independent protégés. Don't be fooled by someone who has one star protégé who goes on to great success. That star may have been good enough to succeed despite the mentor's efforts. Look for people who have consistently produced successful interns who had different levels of ability and interest and who themselves now mentor others. Such a mentor increases your odds that this mentor relationship will work for you. For any potential mentors, find out where their protégés have gone and what they've accomplished by asking the potential mentors, consulting the grapevine, and searching organizational newsletters. Some intern programs track their "alumni," making this a valuable source.

✔ Look for people who have taken on protégés before and who may even have one or two now but still aren't too busy with their own work or with other protégés to give you attention. The most effective mentors won't be able to help you much if they're too busy to see you, answer your calls, write references, and the like. They may be swamped with too many prior commitments to other protégés to squeeze you in. If you spot overload, don't ask. The mentor may be too polite or unrealistic to say no. Then you both would regret it.

Helping a mentor find you

The best way to find a mentor is often helping the mentor find you. Is this a riddle or sound advice? We think the latter. By showing that you are worthy of being someone's protégé, you can attract a mentor. If you were a mentor, what would you look for in a protégé? Try thinking from that perspective. Here are ways to make you worth a mentor's long-term investment:

✔ Show enthusiasm for working and learning. You're more enjoyable and rewarding to work with if you're enthusiastic. Interns who constantly act bored probably won't attract a mentor. Would *you* want to put much effort into helping someone who acts bored?

✔ Work hard at your job and at improving your performance. Mentors want to work with people who will accomplish something, producing a return on their investment. By working hard and showing what you've accomplished in the tasks you're given, you show that you're likely to achieve in the years ahead. Interns who fail to work up to their potential will have a hard time enticing a mentor unless they find someone who enjoys taking on tough cases. (Or has a bet going, as Henry Higgins did as motivation to transform his protégé Eliza Doolittle in *My Fair Lady*.)

✔ Actively but intelligently seek advice and help from potential mentors. After you finish your scouting report on the potential mentors in your workplace, seek their advice and help. Doing so shows them that you value their advice, you're motivated enough to seek outside help, and you're willing to take the risk of showing that you need help or advice. Actively seeking advice also provides a good test of your potential mentors. Which ones brush you off, barely listen to you, give inane advice, or pour their troubles out to you? Cross them off your potentials list! The ones who listen carefully and supply useful help or advice are worth considering further.

Don't ask frivolous questions or dump all your problems on prospective mentors. If you ask about things you're expected to know or about irrelevant topics, mentors will regard your questions as a waste of their time. Be sure that your questions are genuine. If you really need to know how boards of directors function, ask. But don't come up with artificial questions just to have something to ask. Good mentors easily recognize and discount such queries.

✔ Take advantage of opportunities to learn and to develop professionally. Good mentors are more likely to be involved in professional development of others. By actively participating in orientations, seminars, intern discussions, and so on, you're more likely to find a mentor and be noticed by that mentor as someone who shows promise. But avoid grandstanding at orientation sessions to attract attention. You may attract attention all right, but not the kind you want.

✔ Be a good colleague yourself. It takes a good colleague to attract good colleagues. Be pleasant and understanding and show that you care about your colleagues and your organization. Such behavior provides a source of power, and, more importantly, is contagious and attracts others. Mentors have problems and needs too! In fact, they generally have far more work-related problems to handle than do interns because of their higher level of responsibility. For this reason, you need to be a good colleague to them by sensing when they're too busy or distracted to talk, by caring about them and their welfare, and by offering to take on some of their more routine tasks if you sense that they're overloaded.

✔ Make an effort to meet people in your workplace and beyond. Seek out people on an unofficial basis for breakfast, lunch, coffee breaks, and after-hour discussions to get to know them and pick their brains about what they do and how they do it. Active networking broadens your knowledge and increases the odds of finding a mentor.

✔ Accept assignments that involve people in other parts of the organization or outside your organization. Not all the good mentors are in your particular unit. Because good mentors are rare, maybe your unit doesn't have a good mentor. By actively seeking and accepting assignments that put you in contact with more people, you increase your chances of finding this rare species. (Note that this kind of boundary-spanning activity also increases your breadth of experience as well as your visibility to potential mentors — and potential employers.) In fact, the mentor-protégé relationship usually works better if the mentor is not your immediate supervisor or someone in your immediate workgroup, because that tends to complicate the relationship.

Spotting and Avoiding a Bad Mentor

Astute reader that you are, you no doubt have been reading between the lines above, figuring out how to spot a bad mentor: someone you want to avoid like the proverbial plague. Bad mentors lack most or all of the qualities identified earlier in this chapter. They may have expertise but aren't willing to share it, so they lack power and commitment to others. Their commitment is to themselves and to their success, and don't you forget it!

Bad mentors also may be genuinely committed to helping others but have no other qualifications for mentoring. In particular, look out for the following characters:

✔ **Bleeding hearts:** Their motives for helping you are good, but they have no other qualities for mentoring. Bleeding hearts need to help people and feel important but lack the expertise, power, experience, connections, and other qualities to provide that help. They aren't a threat, but they can waste your time and sap your energy. With bleeding hearts, be polite and supporting, as a good colleague should be. As an intern, however, you can't really take on a "project" that requires you to mentor someone like a bleeding heart. Be nice but don't start hearing their confessions or trying to rehabilitate their careers.

✔ **Users:** They may have some power or other qualities, but their intent toward you is selfish. They want to use you for their purposes — their work, their ambitions, their ego trips. They may promise some payoff (a fantastic reference or future job offer) but rarely deliver. Users can often be spotted because they use the word "I" much more than "you" or even "we." You may be able to learn something from them but at a high cost. You would do better to find a real mentor.

✔ **Predators:** These mentors are the worst and are to be avoided even more than users. Predators' intent toward you is harmful. From you they seek financial, psychological, or even sexual gain.

Here are some ways to avoid these and other disastrous mentors:

✔ Know in your own mind the qualities you want and don't want in a mentor.

✔ Be prepared and act confident. If you're seen as having your act together, you'll attract the constructive mentors and discourage predators and users who thrive on vulnerable interns.

✔ Avoid situations where you could be cornered alone by someone. This includes such places as the cafeteria or lounge when nobody else is around.

✔ Take advantage of the typically prolific and usually accurate office grapevine to get the scuttlebutt on the current employees to stay away from.

✔ Likewise, use the intern grapevine, talking with interns who have already finished their placements in your workplace or who are there when you arrive. The intern coordinator at your workplace or intern advisor at school can often supply names of interns to consult. And while you're at it, talk with them, too.

Making the Mentor–Protégé Relationship Work

By actively searching for a mentor and actively making yourself more worth mentoring, you increase your chances of establishing a mentor-protégé relationship. How is this relationship established? Does it require a proposal as with marriage? "Will you take me to be your lifelong protégé to advise, help, and protect till death do us part?" Sometimes one partner formally or informally asks the other. Students may ask a professor, for example, to be their thesis advisor, knowing that role has aspects of mentoring and often evolves into a full mentoring relationship. An intern might ask an experienced professional if he can work with her for the next rotation, anticipating that his scouting reports are correct and that she would be a good mentor. Likewise, potential mentors might ask interns to work for them or with them. The "I do" can be prompted from either direction. Quite often the relationship just falls into place without either saying "I do" in a formal way. You just start talking together and working together, and the relationship evolves — just as it does with many other kinds of relationships.

Are intern supervisors good mentors?

Some intern supervisors make good mentors, but many don't. Effective mentoring requires different skills from supervising. An intern supervisor, even a good one, may not be a good mentor for you. Your intern supervisor may have considerable power via expertise and connections but may be too busy to help you. Because you're directly accountable to your supervisor, asking your supervisor some of the questions you ask of a mentor may be awkward or politically stupid. Such questions may reveal your shortcomings or failures.

Because supervisors are responsible for you and your work, it's harder for them to preserve their authority relationship with you and maintain a professional, mentoring relationship at the same time. It can be done, but it's more difficult. Suppose that you consult your mentor/supervisor about problems you're having with your present internship or about the possibility of taking a different internship. Will the supervisor respond wearing her supervisor hat or her mentor hat? Supervisors, remember, must think foremost as a supervisor. That's the nature of that role and what their superiors expect of them.

So what's the bottom line? Don't discount your supervisor out-of-hand as a potential mentor. Good supervisors do many of the things good mentors do: coach, encourage, give constructive feedback, protect their subordinates from unjustified attack, and so forth. But don't immediately assume that your supervisor, however capable, is also the right mentor for you. The extra strains and constraints from having dual — and sometimes conflicting — roles as both supervisor and mentor may prevent your supervisor from also serving as your mentor.

Having a mentor who is your supervisor's boss also complicates both sets of relationships. If you've always enjoyed playing with fire, this set-up may be right for you. Imagine the dilemma this puts your supervisor in if you're seen as her boss's protégé? Can she treat you the same as the other interns reporting to her? Can she reprimand you without repercussion? Right now you may be thinking, "So this is bad? What's the catch?" The catch is that you probably will have considerably more contact with your supervisor, and your supervisor likely has more direct control over you, including your assignments, your evaluation, and so on. If your supervisor feels threatened or undermined by your mentor relationship with her boss, she may take it out on you. Doing so would be human nature. At its best, however, this situation would probably make working together more difficult. At its worst, you could be caught in a power struggle between your supervisor and her boss. Enough said. We're not saying to always avoid having a mentor who is your supervisor's boss, just that it is fraught with complications and potential dangers.

Factoring gender into the mentoring relationship

Women have been disadvantaged historically in mentoring because comparatively few women were promoted to high enough positions to have the resources, influence, and experience to mentor other women. Being left out of the old boys network and having relatively few women to help as mentors, young women often had to find men to mentor them. Most of the time, this arrangement probably worked well. But occasionally innuendoes surrounded the nature of these relationships, especially ones involving an older, influential man and a younger woman. When nothing was going on (which was usually the case) and sometimes when there was, the mentor relationship often suffered because of gossip and tensions.

Classic examples of how a mentoring relationship complicated by a social relationship had adverse consequences come from business and from government. In the business example, Mary Cunningham, 28, vice-president for corporate affairs of the Bendix Corporation, was forced to resign because of "inappropriate public behavior" with her mentor (and supervisor), CEO William Agee. This didn't do his career any good either. In government, everyone remembers White House intern Monica Lewinsky and her relationship with her mentor, President Bill Clinton. The mentor was almost forced to resign, and the effects on the country will be felt for decades.

Fortunately, far more women now hold positions of responsibility and influence, enabling them to be good mentors for other women — and for men. Some women feel more comfortable with another woman as mentor. Others do not. Eyebrows are sometimes raised when men are mentored by senior, more influential women. This mentoring relationship may be a healthy sign of the greater upward mobility of women these days, but the suspicions generated are also unfortunate. Good mentors are hard enough to find without making gender a complicating issue. Our position is that you should weigh other factors, such as expertise, commitment, trust, vision, and influence, more heavily than gender. But you still must take into account the sensitivity surrounding the gender issue.

Chapter 15

Using Your Internship to Launch a Job — and a Career

In This Chapter

▶ Discovering ways to learn on the job

▶ Moving up

▶ Building your career

"Nothing succeeds like success." That's advice you've probably read or heard. Like many of those sayings that have burned themselves into people's consciousness, this one has a lot of truth to it. The way to greater future successes is to build upon smaller past and present successes. That's true of most things, including careers. Yes, a few people make it big with their first try, but most people who are now successful or even famous started at or near the bottom and built on each success — and failure.

This entire book is aimed toward helping you make a success out of your internships. (Remember that these days doing more than one internship is becoming common.) Make the most of each internship *as you are in it* and then move on. Don't make the mistake of ignoring the here and now and always be looking ahead: "This internship is the pits. I'll do the minimum today and spend my time hooking up to a really great job tomorrow."

This chapter focuses on making that link from your internships now to a professional job and career tomorrow. But the best way to make a future link is to build the current link you have in hand as strongly as possible so that it connects securely to the next link. That's the way to build a solid fence, and that's the way to build a solid career. If you work hard, learn whatever you can, sharpen your skills, and establish a good reputation in your current internship, linking to the next valuable internship and to a full-time job becomes that much easier. Following that pattern is key to building a successful career. But if you fail to work hard, learn, and improve your reputation, making the break into a professional job and career becomes that much harder.

Pointers for Learning on the Job

"Experience is a great teacher" is another saying that makes sense. Even though we're both teachers, your authors are the first to admit that the firsthand experience of an internship teaches many things we can't teach in the classroom, or at least not as effectively. Throughout this book, we advocate AIM, or Active Intern Mode. That is nowhere as important as with your learning on the job. To learn the most from your internship — and that's the main reason you're there — you need to be an active learner, constantly learning current information, mastering new skills, and getting to know different people. Doing so will help you make the most of your learning on the job, whether it's your first internship or your ultimate position.

In school you learn by reading, listening, observing, and experiencing. These methods are also your learning tools for on-the-job learning. You need to make some adjustments in how you use these tools, though.

Reading isn't just for school

To succeed in school, you read your assigned textbooks, other materials on the assigned list, and if you're extra diligent, books and articles from the recommended list. On the job, you aren't given a reading list unless handed one during orientation. It's up to you to find out what is important to read and to fit that into a hectic work schedule. Interns rarely have a designated "reading period." You have to make time for that yourself, meaning that your job-related reading is much more up to you. You have to decide what to read, when to read it, and how. Here are some pointers on finding out what to read:

- ✔ Ask your colleagues, especially the more experienced ones, what they read to stay current in the field.

- ✔ Notice what people are reading or have ready to read in their offices. Doing so may give you a more accurate picture than what colleagues *say* they're reading.

- ✔ If your workplace has a reception area, browse through the reading matter left for clients or others who are waiting. The kinds of magazines, newspapers, reports, newsletters, and so on left in the reception area often reflect the employer's priorities and tastes in reading. Use your judgment, as always. The reception area may be filled with old magazines or papers that the receptionist (or somebody else) had lying around at home. If you find that this is the case, don't waste time reading those publications. Suggest, diplomatically as always, that profession-related reading material would give a better image of your organization and offer to help round some up.

✔ Look at book reviews or lists of best reading in your field. Find these in professional or trade journals published by the leading professional societies in your field.

✔ Find out what your contacts made through professional society activities think is important to read.

✔ Read the books or sources we refer to in *Internships For Dummies* or that are referred to in other things you have read. If you find a book or article valuable, you're likely to benefit from reading what those authors use or recommend. Suggestions for reading occur at various points in this book, especially in Chapters 4, 5, and 15.

Listen and ye shall learn

We learn more by listening than by talking. Some people say that's why we have two ears but only one mouth. In fact, learning something new by talking is almost impossible. (For more information about listening, turn to Chapter 10.) Here are a couple tips on *when* and *where* to listen:

✔ Of course, listen actively during formal meetings, training sessions, presentations, and the like. You're expected to listen carefully at such times, even if much of what is said is dry or unimportant. Listening carefully during these official situations allows you to pick up that occasional pearl of wisdom, and it trains you to listen effectively at all times. You're building your listening muscles.

✔ Don't forget to listen actively during unofficial occasions and in informal settings. Some of the most useful learning by listening occurs during unofficial situations, such as during lunches, breaks, and after-hours get-togethers, and in informal settings, such as hallways, elevators, restaurants, and bars. People often say what they really think in such places and times. These are really good opportunities to listen for feelings and attitudes. And even though such settings don't generally lend themselves to listening for substantive content, some of the most intellectual learning occurs at these times.

Being a good listener is a key to success in most areas of your professional and personal lives. If you need to brush up on how to listen well, this may be a good topic for your first reading foray.

Find and follow models

When we advise you to find and follow models, we don't mean the ones who make the covers of fashion magazines. We mean that you should find professional role models, people who are the kind of professional and person you aspire to become. These people model the knowledge, skills, behaviors, and values that make them a true success.

Career models, like other models, come in different shapes and sizes:

- **Perfect Tens:** The Perfect Ten is the ideal model: no flaws, only positive qualities. In the world of work, Perfect Tens are as hard to find as in fashion or entertainment. Few people, even those at the top of their profession, do everything flawlessly. If you find one of these — or even models who come close — learn as much as you can from them about how to communicate, how to motivate, how to build trust, how to cope with change, and the like. If you're really fortunate and deserving and followed our advice about finding a mentor in Chapter 14, a Perfect Ten or Near-Perfect Nine may become your mentor. Mentoring relationships maximize your learning in your current position and throughout your career.

- **Anti-Models:** You've seen advertisements or magazine stories that show makeover pictures of someone. These pictures show what the person looked like before and after fantastic things were done to the model's hair, teeth, face, or other body part. The message in these commercials is that you don't want to be like *this* model but like the new, improved version. Such anti-models also exist in working life. They are the opposite of the Perfect Tens. These are the people you have worked with or will work with who can teach you many valuable lessons about what *not* to do and how *not* to behave. In other words, they teach by example — bad example! But you can learn a lot from them, including how *not* to make a presentation, how *not* to offer criticism, and so on.

- **Specialty Models:** Specialty fashion models have some terrific features (face, figure, legs, hair, or even feet, for example) that look great even though the rest of the body may be far less than perfect. You see various parts of these models in commercials for products such as shampoo, lipstick, hair grower, or toenail polish. Such specialty models exist, too, in the world of work. In fact, most of your learning models fit into this category. Some people speak brilliantly, but you wouldn't want to write like them. Other people can serve as examples of how to manage conflict, but don't follow their example in keeping track of spending. The trick here is to recognize what these people do best and follow their example on that. At the same time, you have to recognize their flaws and learn how to avoid imitating those flaws in yourself.

With all these types of learning models, carefully watch and listen to what they do or say (or don't do or say) and make mental notes to yourself about what works and what doesn't.

When making use of learning models, make adjustments for differences in your personality, experience level, or position. Simply copying someone else's good traits doesn't always work. Just because your boss can blow people away with the force of her personality doesn't mean you should try to emulate that. Your personality is different. You may be able to use some of her approach to dealing with people, but in a lower-keyed way. One of Jim's former bosses was masterful at handling a political crisis, pulling agreements together at the last minute. However much Jim admired his boss's crisis-handling skill, Jim realized that he lacked his boss's high-level position, extensive experience, and forceful personality to copy this behavior. Instead, Jim worked on learning how to prevent situations from reaching a crisis. You, too, need to adjust what your role model does so that it translates well to your personality, experience, and level of skill. Over time, you can work toward developing your confidence, experience, and skill level so that you can be a learning model for others.

Engage in your profession

You can learn a great deal from your professional society's publications, conferences, workshops, and other formal means of learning. The people you meet and the contacts you make are a key benefit of being an active member of your professional groups. The informal learning through all your professional contacts, everywhere, is valuable to your success.

Professional associations are often the best places to find learning models because they attract that sort of person — people who want to build their knowledge and skill, work on important issues, and meet other such people, like you. Your contacts made via professional society meetings, conferences, and so on can share their knowledge, their skill, their insights, and their understanding. Having contacts who aren't in the same workplace as you is always helpful. These "outsiders" can often give a different and more valid perspective on your situation because they're emotionally removed from it. And you can often share things with them that you would never dare share with your coworkers.

Where can you find appropriate professional societies or associations? Some of you will get started in belonging in high school, others in college, and others as you start a career. If you never got connected in school and aren't sure how to find the right associations for you, don't forget the *Encyclopedia of Associations* that we introduced in Chapter 5. This reference is a gold mine that contains information on most associations listing associations by topic and containing valuable information such as number of members, types of professional activities, and dates and locations of conferences.

Learn from your own mistakes

You can learn from other people's mistakes, but the most valuable mistakes to learn from are your own. That's because you're more likely to be motivated to do better next time. In addition, you have the most insight about the situation in which the mistake occurred and the perpetrator of the mistake: you. To learn effectively from your own mistakes, you need to change your attitude toward mistakes and failure and learn how to take criticism well.

Changing your attitude toward failure

Let's face it! Not everyone has the savvy and guts to learn from their own mistakes. Many people automatically and immediately bury their mistakes. They don't want to think about them again. Thinking about it is either too painful or too much like a jinx, or it breeds failure. They reason that if success breeds success, doesn't failure breed failure? In a way it does if we dwell on the fact that we failed somehow but don't try to learn from our mistakes in order to improve.

It helps to put failure in perspective. In baseball, if you get a hit only 30 percent of every time you're at bat, you'll be a multimillionaire and sports idol. That's failing seven times out of ten if you look at it that way. But your coaches, teammates, and fans still consider you a success.

Keep in mind that inventors and business entrepreneurs fail far more often than they succeed. The most successful ones keep trying and keep learning from their mistakes. The story goes that the great inventor Thomas Edison had been trying to find the right elements for the light bulb. After trying a thousand different elements that didn't work, someone asked him if he thought all this failure had been a waste. "Hardly," Edison is reported to have boasted, "I have discovered a thousand things that don't work." This is the same Edison who patented 1,093 inventions during his lifetime, including the motion picture projector, phonograph, and alkaline battery, as well as the electric light bulb. Think of how our lives are richer because Tom Edison knew how to turn his failures into successes.

Taking criticism the right way

Nobody we know likes to be criticized. Maybe some masochists do, but they're rare. If you're normal (and we assume you are), taking criticism is probably something you avoid if you can and endure if you must. Denying fault and ignoring criticism are also normal. Both tendencies compound the problem. Consider the two scenarios depicted in Tables 15-1 and 15-2, which take place between you the intern and your supervisor (or anyone else who has the nerve to criticize you). The criticism is that you have done school homework on the job instead of doing work assignments. You would never do that, but pretend and learn.

Table 15-1	The Adversarial Approach	
Step Involved	*How You Act*	*Consequences*
1. Set the tone.	Stiffen up. Take defensive (or aggressive) posture	Supervisor is put off and becomes defensive or more critical.
2. Deny complaint.	"That's not true! I always do my work assignments right away."	Supervisor has to escalate complaint to try to get you to accept criticism. "But the secretaries have seen you doing your schoolwork on the job."
3. Dwell on criticisms.	"I don't do homework on the job, and I get my work done. That's all there is to it."	Focus stays on complaints, and supervisor may have to repeat or escalate complaints to convince you.
4. Counterattack.	"Well, if I had enough real work to do, I wouldn't have to study to keep from being bored."	Supervisor gets defensive because his competence is threatened. Working relationship between you and your supervisor are strained.
5. Business as usual.	"I don't see that I did anything wrong. There's no need to change."	Supervisor becomes more determined to make the charge stick and looks for repeat offenses.

Table 15-2	The Problem-Solving Approach	
Step Involved	*How You Act*	*Consequences*
1. Set the tone.	Have open, receptive posture and expression. Show interest in what the supervisor is saying.	Supervisor relaxes, sensing this won't be so bad. Takes a lower-keyed approach rather than a heavy one.
2. Seek information.	"What am I not doing for my internship that I'm supposed to be doing?" Were there specific assignments I missed?"	Supervisor can shift from role of critic to that of coach, helping you assess your performance.

(continued)

Table 15-2 *(continued)*

Step Involved	How You Act	Consequences
3. Agree with some part of the complaint.	"I have done some homework on the job, but I really thought I was caught up on my assignments. There may have been some work to do that I didn't know about right away." (Note: There is always some part of a complaint you can agree with even if you only agree with the complaint in principle: "I agree that interns should put their job work first when on the job.")	Supervisor impressed with your mature attitude and willingness to accept some criticism. Relaxes further and pursues a cooperative rather than adversarial approach.
4. Seek ways to improve.	"Would it work better if I consulted you or your assistant to see if anything else needed doing before I did my schoolwork?"	Supervisor senses your motivation to be a good intern and your problem-solving ability. Supervisor is more likely to accept your suggestions and to suggest other options. "Would it help if I gave you a weeklong assignment schedule instead of getting tasks one at a time? You could work further ahead when you have time."
5. Try new ways and see how they work.	"Thanks, that longer-term to-do list helps me work ahead and plan my time better. This way, I can spend more time on tasks and do them better."	"You have been doing your assignments on time or ahead of schedule. I am pleased with the way you cooperate and show initiative. How would you like to have some juicier projects on that to-do list?"

You can see the difference between the two approaches! Denying all criticism and fighting back won't get you very far — except maybe out the door if it persists. Of course, you may try to be a true problem solver but be torpedoed by a supervisor or other critic who takes the adversarial approach. Your sticking with the problem-solving approach will help because your willingness to cooperate will throw adversarial supervisors off base. They won't be used to that and probably will soften in their approach. You can also show your supervisor this book so he can see how criticism should be handled. Then you can work on this together.

Learn from your successes 'cause you can't take them for granted

Don't faint, but learning from your successes may be even trickier than learning from your mistakes. When you make a mistake, you're more likely to try to figure out what went wrong and how to fix it. But when you do something that turns out successfully, do you also stop to figure out *why* it worked so well? "What a stupid question," you're probably thinking. "Of course it was successful because of my brilliance!" It may be. We hope you're right. But it may also have been successful for other reasons. When you do something by yourself that turns out well or when you're part of a team effort that succeeds, take a few minutes after the praise dies down to reflect on that success.

✔ Was this successful because of my competence, or was it more due to luck? Did the stars just align the right way and things fell neatly into place in spite of what I did? Some less-than-stellar efforts work because of accidental circumstances. Look to see whether that was true in your situation.

✔ Did this succeed because of my skilled performance, or was it well received because expectations for interns in general (or me in particular) were too low? Supervisors and others should try to encourage you and even praise you. But sometimes they may overdo it. They may heap praise on you to motivate you to work harder and smarter because you haven't done so well and they want to keep your spirits up. This technique helps your confidence, but it may give you a false sense of how well you're really doing. If you want to avoid getting overconfident — and impress your supervisor — ask, "I know this worked out well, but how can I improve this for next time?" Wording it this way avoids putting your supervisor on the spot by implying that she wasn't telling you the truth. And it gets at what you really want: some more useful feedback on how you did and how you can improve.

✔ Was this a success because of my efforts, or did somebody else make it succeed? If you really look hard, was somebody else responsible for your success or the success of the team project? Did somebody steer you the right way early on when you were floundering? Did someone else edit your report so that it looked more professional than it would have been with your effort alone? Did another member of your team get the team back on track after your best attempts to sidetrack it? If you think and look hard and your success really was from your effort, great! Keep in mind, too, that getting help from other people is natural and useful. Don't worry about that! As an intern in AIM, you should be actively seeking advice and help from others. That's how you learn. That's how the overall results improve. For example, good advice from other people, including interns, and careful editing significantly improved the book you're now reading. What is important is recognizing the help you receive from others. First, doing so makes you more aware of what you needed help on. You can then work harder on improving those things yourself. Second, recognizing that others helped you also reminds you whom to acknowledge publicly and thank for their part in the successful outcome. This is what good leaders do, and it's a terrific habit to acquire early.

Connecting to a Full-Time Job or Better Internship

If you do what we have recommended thus far, you're in a good position to take the next step: connecting to a full-time job or better internship. "Yes," you probably think, "A full-time job with higher pay and possibly benefits is definitely a step up. But why should I even consider another internship? Wouldn't that just be a holding action until I can land a real job?"

Consider another internship

Obviously if no "regular" job is in the bag, another internship could give you extra experience and contacts. But under certain conditions, another internship may even be a better choice for you than a full-time job:

- **Condition 1:** The internship option gives you the chance to learn far more than the job option. (For example, you get the chance to intern with one or more of the leaders in your field on an exciting and promising project.) This kind of experience is likely to be worth its weight in gold in both added learning and extra income in the long run. Doing the job for some of the professionally well-known "stars" in your field could unlock doors for you throughout your career.

- **Condition 2:** You honestly don't think that you're ready for a full-time job in your profession. Especially in some highly specialized fields, it is common to take a further apprenticeship, fellowship, or other placement after finishing school in order to gain further experience, knowledge, confidence, and contacts. Even in less specialized fields, working into a regular professional position more gradually may make sense for you. Maybe a critical aspect of a profession wasn't really covered in the first internship or in classes. Not all students have the same level of academic preparation or maturity level. There is no harm in doing another internship to get yourself ready for the big time. In fact, you may be worse off if you rush into a professional job only to find out that you weren't really ready to handle it. The loss of confidence and reputation could set you back further than if you had taken longer to work into that level. Here again, don't make this call on your own. If you have doubts, consult your mentor, advisor, family, and others about whether you're ready to move on.

✔ **Condition 3:** You may have personal reasons why another internship makes sense. You may be planning on going to graduate or professional school in a few months and don't really want to take a job and quit soon after. The internship may make it easier for you to help out with a sick family member. Just be sure that the personal reasons are really valid and outweigh the advantages of taking a regular job.

Move up

Here are some tips on connecting to a better internship or job. Some of these have been offered before, but we summarize them here.

✔ Wind up your internship with a bang. Doing so gives it some closure and also strengthens your launch pad for your next job. At or near the close of your internship, present your main project to your supervisor and possibly other colleagues. You can do so both orally and in writing or in whatever way makes sense depending on your project. If such an opportunity isn't built into your internship, take the initiative to request it. If some kind of main professional project isn't part of your internship, ask for your supervisor's approval to do one. This project and the experience of presenting it provide a launching pad for your next move — whether in the same organization or another one. A project that concludes with a presentation increases your knowledge and skills and gives you a tangible product to show prospective employers. Presenting your work and letting your colleagues know how much you have appreciated their advice and support go a long way toward keeping them interested in you and helpful to you. Look for some sort of capstone experience that demonstrates what you have learned and can accomplish. You also want a project that separates you from all the others who just showed up and put in the time.

✔ Keep your mentor informed about your plans and consult your mentor before you make a move. Your mentor from school or work may have job leads or advice to help you. Even if your mentor has no good leads or advice at the time, let your mentor know what kind of job or internship you'd like. Doing so puts your aims on your mentor's radar screen and may motivate her to seriously think of options or actively scout opportunities for you.

✔ If you don't have a true mentor, consult your school intern advisor and work supervisor, who should know you and your work performance pretty well. They can supply leads and advice. Consult your work supervisor only if you've done a solid job for your employer and established good rapport. Your supervisor isn't obligated to help you just because you were an intern. Your supervisor will know the score.

If your employer has vacancies for which you may qualify, talk over your interest and your chances with your supervisor. If there are no job vacancies in the unit where you intern (as may happen in many cases), let your supervisor know that you're very interested in staying on in some capacity. He may be able to find or make a position for you. If there are no openings where you work and no chance of creating any for you, your supervisor may have contacts in other organizations that could lead to a job. If you've really done the job for your employer, your supervisor or someone else will take enough interest in you to help you get placed.

✔ Take on projects or assignments that get you around your organization and ideally beyond your organization. This wider visibility increases your chances of being hired because it lets more people see what you have to offer. More visibility can lead to offers from your same organization or from different organizations. This assumes that you've heeded our advice about doing a good job in your home unit. A key career rule is to cover home base. Don't make the mistake one of our friends once made of working so hard to make himself visible to the top brass in his organization that he alienated his own supervisor and lost his job.

✔ Take advantage of the career and job placement resources at your school. Your school's career center should be one of your first and most frequent stops in making the link between internship and full-time job or better internship. Your center will likely have career counseling, job and internship databases, career diagnostics to help you learn your career interests, and other resources.

Principles for Building Your Career

Internships are ideal times to think about your career. Internships typically occur at the beginning of your career, when you're just starting to get your act together, or later on, when you're making a transition into another field (really another career). For this reason, we want to share some pearls of wisdom about building your career that we've gleaned from reading, listening, experiencing, and observing.

Career principle 1: Make the most of the job you have

The first principle for a successful career is to make the most of the job you have. Solid careers are built one job at a time and one success at a time. If you succeed at what you're doing now, you'll be all that more attractive to another employer. In professional sports, teams typically bid for players who have had a good year in terms of their scoring, defense, and other criteria.

Few teams flock to hire players who have had poor seasons unless those players have a track record of success and the poor season can be blamed on an injury or family crisis.

The same goes for you. If you do good work at your current job, you prepare yourself for the next job, probably one with higher challenges and higher rewards. But if you make a mess of the job you currently have, you reduce your chances of getting the next job or a better job at better pay.

Career principle 2: Don't assume your good work will automatically be rewarded

In her highly useful book, *Skills for Success,* Adele Scheele cautions about believing that, in the working world, virtue will always be rewarded. In fact you probably know someone who has done good work — on a team, in the classroom, or in an office — but hasn't really gotten enough recognition for all that good work. Scheele points out that far too many workers haven't learned that doing the job well isn't enough. The right people also have to recognize that you're doing a good job.

That's where a little self-promotion is needed. We say "a little" because promoting yourself can get carried too far. We've known employees who were so busy promoting themselves that they didn't have time or make time to do the job they were supposed to do. They were constantly trying to make other people think they were the best thing since sliced cheese: constantly dropping in to chat with the boss, sending memos on every topic they could think of, and hogging the spotlight in training workshops. Guess what? These tactics of unrelenting self-promotion almost always backfired. Bosses got tired of having their time wasted by bragging and unnecessary memos. And most of all, they got tired of all talk but no performance to back it up. Be sure to avoid overdoing it.

Career principle 3: Get connected and stay connected

Making contacts starts with your first internship and should continue and build throughout your career. Your goal should be to keep in contact with some people in each job you have throughout your career. And don't forget the interesting, caring people you meet outside the job. Some of your best contacts will come from outside the job. These contacts make up your active network: the people you can call upon for advice, instruction, or other kinds of help. People in your active network can also call upon you.

Some of the people in your network will be central — your mentors, role models, advisors, and others you turn to over the years. Other members of your network may be newer contacts and people you interact with only occasionally as the need or interest arises.

The care and feeding of your network involves the following: You need to understand the nature of your relationship. You need to do your part to make the relationship work. It can't be one-sided, so that you (or the other person) are the only one to get advice, acquire information, or get help. The stakes may not be as high as with mentors, who are more important to you than most members of your network, but treating people professionally and fairly makes sense in the long run, even if you have only occasional contact with them. Think of how you want to be treated.

How do you stay linked with your network? Here are some pointers:

- ✔ Let your network know what you're doing, especially if you change jobs or careers.
- ✔ Share some of your latest results or creativity with your network.
- ✔ Don't burn your bridges with members of your network. Avoid alienating your contacts, losing track of them, letting them lose track of you, or doing anything else that removes these people from your useful network.

Career principle 4: Stay alert to the need for change

Spencer Johnson's amusing and enlightening story, *Who Moved My Cheese?*, tells about two mice and two tiny humans and their hunt for cheese. The cheese represents whatever we value most: money, a beautiful home, success, fame, happiness, or other treasures. In the story, the mice and the little people find a huge supply of cheese. The humans get so used to the cheese being there that they think of it as "their cheese," something they are entitled to. They get so complacent about the cheese always being there that they don't see that the cheese is gradually disappearing. When the cheese is gone completely, the humans complain, "Who moved my cheese?" The humans got so set in their ways that they kept coming back to the same place, hoping the cheese would somehow be there as before. One of the humans took a long time before realizing that he would have to change his behavior because the cheese would never be in that same place again. He sets out to look in new areas and finds new cheese, but we don't know if the other human ever made the adjustment to changing conditions. It's a useful story with many lessons. We recommend it.

The key lesson in the story is clear. Change happens whether we want it to or not. We need to be alert to change and adjust to it if we are to achieve and maintain what we value. Constantly relying on the same old ways, even if they have succeeded before, won't necessarily work in changing conditions.

That's another reason for trying to learn from successes as well as failures. What has succeeded brilliantly for you in the past may be linked to a particular set of conditions (for example, colleagues who know and trust you, support from your supervisor, or projects that draw on your strengths). If you see conditions changing from what you came to rely on before, you may need to adjust your approach.

How do you know if change is coming or has already happened?

- ✔ Stay current with your field by being active in professional associations. Conferences, seminars, and even receptions for professionals in your field are good sources of clues about changes in the field.

- ✔ Regularly read leading newspapers and journals. The kinds of topics that are covered give you a cue as to what is "hot" and important in general and in your field. Of course, notice what the content tells you about what kinds and how much change is occurring.

- ✔ Tap your mentor and other key advisors about what they foresee coming in the field. Don't simply talk with them. Also observe what adjustments they're making to cope with change. This will give you cues about how to adjust.

- ✔ Learn from your successes and failures. See what should have been different and adapt accordingly.

Career principle 5: Be willing to take risks

Some risks seem foolish to us. Flying a decrepit airplane is one of them. Trying to one-up your boss in public is another. Yet some risks are not only worth taking but are probably necessary if you want to deal with change successfully. Unless you take risks once in a while, you're likely to get overconfident and complacent. Then your motivation and performance suffer. You tend to look for the cheese in the same place and in the same way, not adjusting to changing conditions. Staying at the same level is difficult. People tend to either improve or regress. If other people are getting better, staying at the same level puts you behind. Here are some tips on risk taking:

- ✔ Reach out to people you don't know but you think would be interesting or helpful to know. This is what author Adele Scheele calls the skill of *risking-linking*. By linking with people you don't know, you take a risk. But often that risk pays off in making a new linkage, increasing your professional network, and enabling new opportunities for cooperating with this new contact.

- ✔ When possible, get feedback from part of your existing network about people whom you're thinking of linking to. Before you do some risking-linking, your own contacts may be able to tell you something about your potential contacts that could warn you or reassure you. If someone has a reputation for having a glossy image but being a sleazebag underneath, you need to know that before allying yourself with that person. Likewise, a favorable report gives you more confidence that your instincts were right. This person would be a good contact.

✔ When considering taking the risk on a new opportunity, consider, as conscientiously as you can, the potential benefits and costs of taking this risk. If you as an intern take the risk of leaving a solid, successful company or agency to take a full-time job with a new one, what are the potential benefits and costs? If the new job doesn't pan out, can you come back to your internship? Were you about maxed out on learning from your existing internship anyway? Would this move get you into a new field likely to grow and prosper? You may even want to set up a kind of balance sheet to weigh the potential benefits and costs of taking the risk.

Career principle 6: Follow your heart as well as your head

Most of the career advice we've given so far applies to your head. But successful careers are built on more than thinking. Think about the people at the top of their professions, whether they're musicians, athletes, teachers, scientists, actors, or managers. One thing stands out: They love what they're doing! They're passionate about their craft. Many of them would do what they do for far less money because they love their work. The paradox is that because they have such a passion for what they do, they make the extra effort to excel and then become worth all they're paid. These "stars" so thoroughly enjoy what they do that their enthusiasm is contagious, spreading to their colleagues and other people who watch their career. This effect makes them even more successful.

Our advice to you is the same that we give our students and friends: Follow your heart! Do what you passionately enjoy even if it may be riskier and more difficult in the short run. If you burn to be a history teacher because history fascinates you but you detest accounting, then you're more likely to be a successful history teacher even if accounting jobs are more plentiful or better paying right now. In the long run, you're more likely to work harder and be more successful in what you love to do most. If your passion is accounting, go *that* route. But whatever career path you take, stay alert to change and the need to change. You are likely to change *careers* more often than your grandparents changed *jobs*. Mind-boggling, isn't it? But exciting, too!

Should you follow *only* your heart? No. Involve your head, too. If your passion is sports, for example, but you lack the size, speed, and reflexes to compete with 21 year-olds, you may need to pursue your passion as a sports trainer, analyst, or reporter. Let both your head and your heart guide your career. But pay the most attention to your heart!

Part VI
For Advisors, Supervisors, and Employers

The 5th Wave — By Rich Tennant

"THE SHORT ANSWER TO YOUR REQUEST FOR A RAISE IS 'NO.' THE LONG ANSWER IS 'NO, AND GET OUT OF MY OFFICE.'"

In this part . . .

For you college and university intern advisors, on-the-job intern supervisors, and employers, we offer advice on how to handle these key roles in the world of internships. We cover some of the important issues and tasks that you need to deal with so that you maximize the benefits of having an internship program — for both your organization and the interns.

Chapter 16

Being a Successful School Intern Advisor

· ·

In This Chapter

▶ Determining program guidelines

▶ Identifying internship placements

▶ Establishing school policies for advisors

▶ Overseeing interns on the job

· ·

This chapter is written as a guide for all the educational faculty and staff members who are charged with acting as advisors to students during their internships. Intern advisors act more behind the scenes than do interns and supervisors, but it is a key role in successful internships. School-affiliated advisors are more likely to be involved in the internship program on an ongoing basis, giving them many opportunities to shape and guide the internship program. Even though we target this chapter toward the advising role, we don't address advisors in the second-person "you" as we do for interns, who are our primary readers. We thought it might be too confusing — for us, too. We do occasionally use the "your" form when referring to "your school." This applies to both advisors and interns.

Intern advisors, like internship programs overall, tend to operate at two levels: schoolwide for students of all backgrounds and by department for students within a specific major or program. At the schoolwide level, almost all schools have a full-time career center that helps students with a number of career issues, including internships. These centers generally have full-time staff members to help students and graduates. A school-wide internship coordinator may be part of the career center staff, be connected with academic affairs, or even be part of student affairs. Not all schools have internship coordinators for the entire school or even a schoolwide internship program.

Most schools offer at least some internships at the department or academic program level. At the departmental level, things are a bit different. Programs and majors that are primarily comprised of full-time, day students (and of course those with legally mandated internships such as nursing or teaching) tend to have one or more full-time faculty or staff who handle internships.

Programs that have generally part-time students, especially those who are evening and/or in-service working people, tend not to have a full-time internship staff. In such cases, the existing faculty and staff tend to share the role of advising or even rotate as advisors. These people in particular can use some help and guidance on how to serve as a successful advisor to a student intern.

Establishing or Reviewing Internship Program Guidelines

One of the very first things intern advisors need to do is to review and learn about the school and department guidelines regarding interns and internships. And of course, if these guidelines don't exist, advisors need to help get them in place as soon as possible. What kinds of guidelines are we talking about? Guidelines typically are needed on intern eligibility, how to enroll, the amount of credit given, whether internships are required or optional, how long they last, evaluation criteria and procedures, whether interns are paid, and legal issues.

Eligibility: Who can get in?

Schools typically use a number of criteria to determine which students are eligible to take an internship.

- ✔ **Class standing:** Does a student have to complete a certain number of years or units before doing an internship? Most schools don't permit internships until a student is a junior, even sometimes a senior. Graduate students may be restricted to taking an internship toward the end of their program, or they may be allowed to take internships earlier. What is your school's policy? What if a 32-year-old sophomore has been working in the field for the past decade? Would your school consider that student ready to do an internship with a different organization or in a different field? If not, why not?

- ✔ **Field of study:** Are internships open to students only with a particular major or field of study, or are they open to other students as well? For example, can students who minor in that field take an internship, or are internships restricted to majors only? Some academic departments allow only their own majors or minors to take an internship in their department. Other departments provide internships for any student on campus regardless of the field of study.

- ✔ **Course prerequisites:** Does a student need to complete one or more specific courses before being eligible to do an internship? If so, does the program have a way to make sure that students have completed these courses beforehand? A growing number of internship programs require for-credit internship seminars or courses. In some cases, these courses precede the internship and are intended to prepare students for their placement experience. In other cases, students take the internship-related course at the same time as they serve their internship placement. This arrangement allows discussion of issues that arise during the placements and enables students to seek help with specific projects or problems that arise during their placement. Some schools require students to take a course before *and* during their internship. Other schools don't require a full academic course for internship preparation but do require or offer a noncredit workshop to help prepare interns. These can range from three hours to several weeks. Establish a system that makes the most sense for your school. Some schools, such as Pepperdine University and Slippery Rock, even have two-course sequences to prepare interns.

✔ **Academic standing/student readiness:** What about grade point average and the like? Would students with a D grade point average be eligible, or do they need a C or higher? Do students need letters of recommendation from faculty? Are any other kind of formal screening processes in place to ensure that any students sent out as interns are really ready for the task and will be a credit to themselves, their school, and their department?

For example, graduate students seeking a Presidential Management Internship have to be nominated by their graduate program, and programs are limited to how many students they can nominate. Screening may be done by a faculty committee or by a program administrator. Further screening occurs by the U.S. Government via a national competition that requires candidates to be evaluated on their professional and academic record, writing ability, speaking skills, problem solving, and interpersonal communication. At Jim's master of public administration program at Rutgers-Camden, Jim oversees preparation of his program's candidates. Because of the careful screening and pre-competition preparation via information, advice, and skills practice, about two-thirds of the students nominated have earned Presidential Management Internships in a national competition.

Intern advisors, their programs, and their schools are judged on the quality of their student interns just as much as on the quality of their graduates.

Enrollment procedures: How do students get into the system?

Most students who intern typically do so through the mechanism of enrolling in a specific course. What courses does your school have for this purpose? In some schools, the course that involves the internship is called (guess what?) Internship, Field Work, Practicum, Externship, or something similar. In other cases, the internship is part of a regular course, such as Small Business,

Community Politics, or Seminar in Health Care Management. If more than one internship course is required (or allowed), it typically shows in the course title, for example, Internship II.

Who teaches the internship courses? What is the relationship between the course instructor and the intern advisor? Some schools may have one course with all interns enrolled in that course, but they divide the advising roles among several people. Other schools may have multiple sections of the same course, with multiple instructors each teaching and supervising just a handful of students. Again, each school and program needs to find out what works best for it and its students.

Credits: How much for how much effort?

How many credits do students earn for completing an internship? Are there a minimum number of units granted for an internship? A maximum? What about in-betweeners? For instance, if your school only offers internship credit in fixed 3-unit segments, what about a student who has a wonderful internship opportunity but it is for far fewer hours or weeks than usual? Can your system handle such a scenario? Some schools offer a variable number of units, say from 1 to 6 units based on the number of hours worked. This arrangement also allows more flexibility in internships because some opportunities may not offer as many days or hours as others. With most internship programs academic credit is earned not just by "putting in time" but by demonstrating learning and work experience through a journal, research report, lab project, or some other tangible product.

Speaking of credits, what credit or benefit does the intern advisor receive for this duty? We have found a direct correlation between support, recognition, and rewards for faculty and staff intern advisors and level of effort. Schools that just dump this responsibility as an overload without providing any type of economic or workload compensation generally get minimal advising. This system isn't good for the advisors or for the students who need an advisor who has the time and support to help them.

Mandatory or voluntary internships?

Are internships voluntary or mandatory? Some career fields, such as nursing, social work, health administration, and teaching, require supervised internships in order to graduate and get licensed. Most career fields are not so structured. For example, in law, business administration, and public administration, internships aren't required by the profession but may be required by particular schools. What about your field? If you have a mandatory internship, what supports are present to make sure that each student has viable internship opportunities available? Few things are more unpleasant than a situation in which students are required to complete an internship and at the same time left on their own to locate and secure an internship. If you mandate a student internship, you should have the resources in place to support that requirement. After all, you wouldn't mandate a particular course and then not budget for it to be offered in your schedule, would you?

Hours and duration: How long should it last?

What is the relationship between the credits awarded and the number of hours that the intern works? Who is responsible for keeping track of how long and when the intern is working? Generally, it appears to work better for on-the-job intern supervisors to keep track of time worked and to sign a time sheet (if necessary). This system makes interns more accountable to their work supervisors and relieves school advisors from trying to keep track of hours by remote control, which is a frustrating and inaccurate process.

In some programs, an intern must work a certain number of hours per credit received, say 40 hours per credit. In other cases, there may be a link between the number of hours worked and the grade received, with the more hours worked, the higher the grade. This is a less common method because it doesn't give enough weight to the *quality* of work.

The timing and scheduling of internships also deserve thought. Academic institutions run on fixed calendars with specific starting and ending dates. Employers don't use such calendars and may need interns based on an entirely different project schedule. Can your school be flexible about the starting and stopping dates and the overall duration of an internship?

How do you evaluate the intern?

If interns take a course for academic credit, how will they be evaluated? Based on what standards? Some schools link the number of hours worked to the final grade. Other schools make these types of courses straight pass-fail options. If students do take a course for a grade, explicit criteria are needed.

Interns need regular feedback and an overall evaluation by the employer supervisor (see Chapter 13 for more on evaluations). Feedback and evaluations can and should be a part of the grading criteria. Consequently, advisors must be in regular contact with the supervisor so they know how the student interns are doing and how the supervisor is evaluating them. Most internship programs require some form of written evaluation of the intern, usually performed by the work supervisor. Sometimes an intern self-evaluation is also done. Chapter 13 gives examples of different types of evaluations and discusses them`.

Most schools require that interns complete some form of internship journal and/or paper. Is this a part of their criteria for a grade? What about the time involved? Is the time spent in meetings and preparing such papers and writings considered a part of their internship hours? Or do internship hours include only time spent on the job? Why?

How many internships are allowed?

Some students don't want to complete any more internships than necessary. Others may have a single experience that is transformational and may lead directly to a job. Still others may find that they enjoy the opportunities and benefits that internships offer and wish to complete several. What are your school's guidelines?

If a student wants to complete more than some minimum number of internships, are they allowed to? What if they wish to do so even if they can't receive any additional academic credits for doing so? Are provisions available for allowing students to take noncredit internships or internships as an overload? There are also limits on the advisor's time and energies. Should students be limited to one (or two) internships to enable advisors to spend enough time with each intern?

Advisors also need to consider the whole-versus-parts question. If students are required to complete 100 hours of work for their internship, is it acceptable for them to work 50 hours for employer A and the other 50 for employer B? In some cases, the extra placement may give a different and richer experience. In other cases, allowing two placements in one term may stretch interns so thin that they don't really learn much in either placement. The most sensible arrangement may well depend on the specific situation and the specific intern.

Money: To pay or not to pay?

What are your guidelines regarding payment? Some schools prohibit paid internships. Other schools require that interns be paid. For example, it is standard practice for cooperative placements (co-ops) to be paid, some handsomely. Still other schools may require graduate students to be paid, but undergraduates may or may not be paid.

Does your program have any standards for how much a student intern should be paid? Most schools require at least minimum wage, of course, and some internships pay quite well indeed.

Think too about *how* interns are paid. We recommend that you read Chapter 18 for more information on the matter of pay and employment status of interns.

One example that we provide in Chapter 18 illustrates how one school works with employers to avoid any legal employment complications regarding interns. The employers don't hire or pay interns. Instead, the employer contracts with the school for a fixed number of hours of student research assistants' time, the same as they would with a temp agency. In this way, students are employed by the school and simply perform their intern duties at the employer's workplace. We have also worked in situations where employers set up an internship scholarship fund at a school. Interns were then paid out of this fund. Because this was done as a scholarship, some complications were avoided about intern status as employees.

The law: Some legal issues

Your school should have formal legal knowledge of current federal and state laws regarding students as interns. Because interns are quasi-employees, their status will be affected by both state and federal labor laws. If student interns are injured in the workplace, who is responsible and how much? What does the law say about interns regarding pay? If interns are paid by their organizations, are they entitled to unemployment when the internship is over? What is the school's liability? What is the advisor's liability?

If these kinds of matters haven't been taken care of, address them before anything unfortunate occurs. If these kinds of issues haven't been resolved before, the legal departments and risk management units of both the school and the employer need to work out these legal details — before, not after, a problem arises.

Finding Opportunities for Interns

How are internship opportunities uncovered at your school? Who has the responsibility for helping students find internship opportunities? A schoolwide internship coordinator and staff? An intern advisor? The student?

If finding and developing internship opportunities are part of the intern advisor's duties, what resources are available? What about training and support from the school? Some advisors naturally or intentionally develop a large network of contacts in the outside world who can often provide leads to internship opportunities and post-graduation job searches. Establishing contacts, however, does require time and effort.

Does your school have (or need) limits on where internships are located? Obviously, many internship opportunities will be close to school because many of the school's contacts will be local. Many internship opportunities are available worldwide, however. How does your school and program deal with students who may be away from campus for months at a time? Is your curriculum program geared for such situations, or does it assume the student will still be around and taking other classes at the same time?

Internship opportunities open up in many ways. Employers may approach schools to recruit interns. In other cases, coordinators, advisors, or students from the school have to contact employers.

Fielding and reviewing queries from employers

In some cases, employers contact schools directly to recruit student interns. This can be a good source and provide a long-lasting relationship between the school and the employer. At the same time, the intern coordinator or advisor must ensure that the employer is reaching out in good faith. Some unscrupulous people and firms aren't looking to offer good internship opportunities but instead are reaching out for free or cheap labor. Advisors — and students — must be on their guard.

You also need to consider the guidelines for reviewing and approving internship opportunities. Not all opportunities are created equal, and not all opportunities are good ones from the student's point of view. Your school needs a process to evaluate new opportunities as they arise. For example, schools (and students) need to know the following:

✔ Who will supervise the intern?

✔ Is this person on site?

✔ How direct will the supervision be?

✔ What are the duties and responsibilities of interns?

✔ How well do these duties match students' needs and abilities?

✔ What is the value of this internship for student learning?

✔ What are the terms and conditions of the internship (hours, pay, benefits, and so on)?

✔ What is the history of working with this organization in the past? Have previous interns had a good experience? Have there been problems in the past?

Reaching out to employers to place interns

Intern advisors, coordinators, and faculty members need to prospect for internship opportunities. Advisors must take the initiative to contact organizations to see whether they would be willing to offer internship opportunities to students.

Mass mailings or calling

One way to recruit internship placements is to use mass mailings (or mass calling) of leading employers. For example, here is a sample letter an advisor might send.

> Ms. Mary Ann Stapleton
> Stapleton and Stapleton, Inc.
> 555 Constitution Avenue
> Denver, CO 81111
>
> Dear Ms. Stapleton,
>
> We here at Whatsamatta U are in the process of establishing internships for our statistics students.
>
> We are seeking firms such as yours that could benefit from the energy and talents of our students while providing them an opportunity to observe and learn firsthand the various routines and duties of professional statisticians. Our students can become interns during their junior and senior years after completing substantial coursework in the field. Our students will have completed a minimum of four upper-level courses in the field and are screened for academic achievement and personal maturity.
>
> Student interns typically work from three to fifteen hours per week during the course of a semester. The attached list shows the kinds of work-related projects our students could help you with.
>
> If you would be interested in finding out more about our internship program, please call me or complete the enclosed card and return it to me. I will respond as promptly as I can.
>
> Sincerely yours,
>
> Dr. Marge Inovera,
> Associate Professor of Statistics and Intern Advisor
>
> Enclosure: Examples of Applied Statistic Projects for Interns

Internship programs may also wish to produce brochures or flyers that can be sent to various organizations and distributed at various professional and business meetings and conferences.

Reaching out to business and professional organizations

One of the best ways to market your program and your students is through personal contacts established with professional and business organizations. Membership in these types of groups can prove very fertile in making contacts and exploring possibilities for you and your students.

Conducting internship fairs

Internship fairs, which are similar to job fairs, are another way to match interns and opportunities. At an internship fair, the various individuals and programs responsible for internships on campus combine and invite organizations that are ongoing providers of internships, along with those who have any existing positions, to a central location on campus where prospective interns can come, meet, and mingle.

Compensation and Support for Intern Advisors

Schools need a policy that deals with the questions of institutional support for faculty advisors. Some basic questions that must be resolved include issues of teaching load. How does serving as an intern advisor count in relation to the expected teaching load? If an advisor has a section of interns, does it count the same as a section of another course? What if a faculty member is "just" the advisor for a particular number of students? Is this role factored into the teaching load, or is it simply seen as part of the overall advising duties? Do intern advisors receive some sort of overload pay or release time? If there is no recognized pay or support for the duties of internship advisor, it's a good bet that the school doesn't value internship opportunities. As a basis for comparison, see how internships are handled by faculty in nursing or education, fields in which students must complete supervised internships as part of their licensure and graduation.

Looking at the bigger picture, where does the work of an intern advisor fit into the questions of tenure and promotion? Although being an intern advisor is a most worthwhile and personally rewarding task, there is considerable risk if this time-consuming role is not valued for career advancement by the intern advisor's department or school. At worst, could it interfere with the advisor's getting tenured or promoted? At best, could it be that the advisor is trapped doing an unappreciated and thankless task? This is one reason why intern advisors in many schools are paid permanent staff rather than faculty members trying to get tenured and promoted.

Faculty members also need to consider their overall role in the department or school. If they begin to develop and bloom as the internship advisor, the likelihood is that both students and the institution itself will begin to see them in that light. As a result, they may become the permanent intern advisor or career counselor, and the other faculty members won't share these duties. This job can become a burden that a faculty member may not wish to assume and can also isolate that person from other faculty on campus and in the department who are off doing the "actual teaching and research." If this is how your school wishes to operate, then the position is best filled by a dedicated, full-time staff person, not by a regular member of the faculty.

Advising Interns

Ideally, advisors should meet with their interns on a regular basis, at least every other week, either by phone or face to face. Some advisors maintain regular email interaction with interns, which gives both advisor and intern a record of issues raised and progress reports that can go into a record or journal. Advisors should also be in regular contact with their interns' work supervisor at least at the beginning and near the end of the internship, but ideally every few weeks. The amount of contact with interns and supervisors may vary depending on the situation. New placements and new supervisors tend to need more attention.

Helping students secure an internship

Advisors help interns on matters such as preparing resumes, writing cover letters, and interviewing. They also should help interns find the best resources, such as *Internships For Dummies.* Advisors guide students in locating opportunities and applying for those placements and offer advice about which offer students should accept. A wise advisor lets the student make the final decision but helps the student to ask the right questions and consider important issues.

Advising students on learning through work

After the internship begins, advisors need to make it clear that they're available to help during the actual internship.

Set parameters on what students should expect of advisors. We find it useful to establish some guidelines on what kind of help is reasonable and constructive. Here are some key parameters:

✔ The advisor's role is to help interns learn on the job, not to do their work for them.

- ✔ Good advisors help students prepare for their work but also allow them to make mistakes and to fail on their own if that is in the student's best interests. Chapter 15 contains more about learning from success and failure.

- ✔ The advisor functions best if kept informed about what is happening on the internship — before a crisis occurs.

- ✔ Of course, if a crisis is imminent, the advisor *must* be informed. Examples of crises include a total breakdown in relations between intern and supervisor; charges against either the intern or supervisor concerning harassment, discrimination, or impropriety; and hazardous or risky working conditions.

- ✔ Advisors need to set clear guidelines about when, where, and how they can be reached, as well as under what circumstances. Make sure that you're as easily accessible as possible. A student with an urgent problem or question could easily turn into a student in the middle of a disaster by your next regular office hours.

Advising as the internship progresses

Although there are never enough hours in the day nor days in the week, an advisor's job isn't done once an internship begins. When an intern is simultaneously doing an internship and taking an academic course, ongoing contact and advising are relatively simple. When this is not the case, advisors should arrange for a regular process of ongoing check-ins by their students.

Some students are quite forthcoming about their situation, including discussing problems or asking questions. Other students may be less willing to open up. Advisors must never assume that silence on the part of an intern equates to a lack of problems or issues. No news is *not* always good news.

Advisors also need to consider the supervision of their interns' organizational supervisors and the organization itself. For instance, will advisors conduct one or more site visits? Will these be before, during, or after students intern in that organization? Whenever possible, advisors should seek to develop a strong and positive relationship with the interns' supervisors. The best internships occur when there is a strong, communicative relationship among all three major players. And, like it or not, the job of structuring and maintaining this relationship typically falls upon the advisor. The intern doesn't have the authority and experience to do this. And the intern's supervisor has his hands full doing the regular work duties and supervising the intern.

Chapter 17

Being a Successful Employer Supervisor of an Intern

• •

In This Chapter

▶ Supervising interns

▶ Coping with common internship problems

▶ Preparing employees for interns

• •

*T*his chapter is written as a guide for workplace supervisors of interns.

We should start by telling you what this chapter is *not*. This chapter is not about how to be a good supervisor to regular employees. We assume that intern supervisors already know how to be effective in general supervision of others. Otherwise, they shouldn't have been selected for this additional responsibility and opportunity. Being the supervisor of an intern is not the same as supervising other full- or part-time employees; it is more than that and a major responsibility in and of itself. It is also a major opportunity because internship experiences are often pivotal in the lives of the interns both at a personal and career level. This chapter is about how to be a success in the role of intern supervisor.

An internship involves at least a two-way relationship, a relationship between the intern and the organization (and most especially the intern supervisor). Most often, an internship is a three-way relationship involving the intern, the organization where the intern works, and the school which the intern attends. In either case, intern supervisors on the job must begin by recognizing the uniqueness of this relationship and by ensuring full and open lines of communication with the intern and the intern's academic advisor.

If you're fortunate, your intern will be a student and have a good academic advisor with whom you can work. Especially with your first intern, the advisor can help orient you to what is going on, explain the various processes and procedures, and even supply you with any needed forms.

The Basics of Internships

If you haven't done so yet, we strongly recommend that intern supervisors take the time now to go back and read Chapters 1, 2, 7, 8, and 9, which deal with what an internship is and with some of the crucial issues that arise. Also read Chapter 18, which looks at the internship from the employing organization's perspective. An internship is not simply about a person coming to a job, working, and getting some form of remuneration in the form of school credit or cash or both. First and foremost, an internship is a learning experience. The fundamental purpose of an internship is to provide a situation in which interns can see and experience the practical side of what they've been learning in the classroom. From this, they learn new skills and abilities and discover what it takes to be successful in the working world itself. They also get to see various career options so that they take the most appropriate path possible. None of these things will happen if the key player in the organization — that's the supervisor — is not up to snuff. In fact, a disastrous internship experience can sidetrack and even derail a promising young person from a given career field altogether.

Intern supervisors need to understand and handle basic functions in the internship process if they are to perform their role competently. Here are the most basic functions of intern supervision presented in about the order in which they occur in the internship process.

Step 1: Handling the legal and official paperwork

Before an intern arrives on the scene or during the intern's first day or two, intern supervisors need to take care of some important paperwork: the internship agreement and the learning contract.

The internship agreement

As discussed in Chapter 2, the internship agreement (or whatever it's called) is between the employer and school and contains the legal, official details of the internship. This information typically includes the names of the school, the intern, and the employer; the duration of the internship; legal liability; amount and procedure for payment; and other key details.

The supervisor, along with the overall intern coordinator — if there is one — and legal department, need to make sure that the agreement is correct. This is the employer's contract with the school, union, or whatever organization is supplying interns. If an ongoing internship program is in place, the internship agreement may have already been approved. If terms of the agreement change because of funding cycles, number of interns to be supplied, or other conditions, a new agreement may be needed.

The learning contract

Learning contracts are the agreements among the employer, intern, and school about what the intern should do and learn in this placement. See the sample learning contract in Chapter 2. A key first step for supervisors in dealing with the new intern face to face is to sit down and work out a good solid learning contract. Think of a learning contract as a detailed and written guideline about who is going to do what, when, and to what effect. The intern's academic advisor should have already helped the intern start completing this contract. But alas, not all advisors are of equal experience or motivation. If there is no contract, create one.

As illustrated in Chapter 2, a learning contract begins with the traditional job description and a detailed layout of the intern's duties and responsibilities. Included are specifics such as starting and stopping dates, hours to be worked, credits being earned, and wages (if any).

Part two of the contract talks about what the intern is supposed to be learning while on the job and what he or she will be doing to see that their learning is occurring. For example, interns should have required feedback sessions with both the supervisor and the advisor. Most interns are required to keep both a regular journal and write a summary report at the end of their internship. The contract should also include information about how and when both you and the advisor will evaluate the intern.

Step 2: Orientation

One thing that distinguishes the best organizations is their attention to detail, including the details of how to bring a new worker on board. A good, solid orientation is a key in turning a new worker into a fully productive member of the organization. A new intern needs this as much as (if not more than) any other new worker. So we start by getting your new intern worker plugged into the formal orientation process.

Chapter 7 covers internship orientations from the intern's perspective. It covers the general content of an orientation and what interns should do if no orientation exists.

Covering the basics

Supervisors should review their general orientation process by asking two questions: Are things in the orientation inappropriate or unnecessary for interns? Are there things missing in the orientation for regular workers that should be here for interns? For example, interns probably don't need hours of information about employee benefits and retirement options. On the other hand, a more detailed history of the organization and its workings may be very helpful.

Consider the following orientation checklist. These points generally need to be covered whether the orientation is done as a group or individually. Employers and supervisors may not need to cover all of these points, but then again, they may have more of their own to include.

Who

- ✔ Who is my supervisor?
- ✔ Who are my coworkers?
- ✔ Who are my fellow interns?
- ✔ Whom else do I report to?
- ✔ Who will be evaluating me?

What

- ✔ What are my duties?
- ✔ What are my hours?
- ✔ What are the rules about conduct, safety, and so on?
- ✔ What am I supposed to learn?
- ✔ What should I call my supervisor and other employees? Should I use last names or first names? Titles (that is, Mr., Mrs., Dr., and so forth)?

Where

- ✔ Where will I be working?
- ✔ Where is my desk or workspace?
- ✔ Where can I keep my coat and personal things?
- ✔ Where are the bathrooms?
- ✔ Where can I get something to eat?
- ✔ Where do I park?

When

- ✔ When do I start?
- ✔ When will I be evaluated?
- ✔ When do I get paid?
- ✔ When does the internship officially end?

How

> ✔ How will I be evaluated?
>
> ✔ How often will we be meeting?
>
> ✔ How do you prefer me to interact with my supervisor?
>
> ✔ How do you prefer me to interact with other employees?

Make sure that intern orientations cover all the basics a new employee needs, including the generic information from human resources materials, employee manuals and guides, safety procedures and training information, orientation materials, videos, tours, and the like. Because interns sometimes enter an organization though an alternative path, they don't always get included in the normal new employee orientation.

The same issues need to be covered at the department or work level. Interns need to learn who their immediate coworkers are; what the processes and procedures they will need to follow in their specific work unit are; organizational rules, procedures, and protocols that apply to them; and organizational terms, vocabulary, and slang/jargon. Even try to include such content as the organization's culture and climate, such as the "how we do things here" tips that can help interns fit in as quickly and easily as possible.

Although not a part of the intern's orientation, you need to address one other matter now. You should have spoken with and/or met with the intern's academic advisor. Because an internship experience is a three-way relationship when a student is the intern, it is important that you begin developing a relationship with this third player *before* the internship begins. Reading Chapter 16 will give you a good picture of what the academic supervisor's role is and how the two of you can and should work together.

Orienting interns to their coworkers

Whether your orientation system is long and detailed, short but sweet, or nonexistent, interns need to fully understand through orientation their relationships to other workers. Employers and intern supervisors may have to orient the other workers to this issue as well. Regular employees often tend to see student interns as a new source of labor for their personal needs and errands. Stop this before it begins. In fact, we advise thoroughly explaining the intern's role to regular employees before the intern arrives. Make sure that employees understand the purpose of an internship and are aware that the employer takes the internships seriously, particularly if interns are new to that workplace. This discussion about the do's and don'ts of working with interns may go over better if done informally so that interns aren't seen as newly imposed problems for employees to handle. Informal discussions allow employees to be more open about their concerns.

Some employers and supervisors hold the view that they do not and should not see or treat an intern any differently than they do any other employee. Although this thinking is laudable because interns are less likely to be mistreated or segregated in some way, we think it is a crucial error. If an intern is nothing more nor less than a short-term temporary worker, then there is really no reason to have an internship program at all. Temporary workers are about getting the work done. Internships are about helping the interns to learn and develop — while on the job and while getting the work done.

Also consider the question of multiple interns. If your organization will host more than one intern, how will they interact? It is a good idea to provide all interns a chance to meet and socialize and share their experiences. Interns often learn a lot from each other as well as from their supervisors and other regular employees. Having multiple interns (or intern "classes") may also provide the opportunity to have interns oriented together rather than one at a time.

Step 3: Let the games begin

Interns go through a very interesting process. They've been searching and applying for positions, been interviewed by others, and have dealt with the entire selection process. They've even been through the processing that moves them from outsiders to insiders in an organization. For many of them, this may have been the first time they've ever been through these steps. A little numb, shell-shocked, and even a bit overwhelmed, they now report for their first day's work.

Supervisors need to plan for how they'll handle this moment. Life today, especially at work, seems to be an ever faster process of doing more with less. Everyone is so busy trying to cope and even catch up that they rarely have the time to plan and prepare. But in order to succeed, intern supervisors must be prepared by having a plan. They must plan the initial meeting with interns and decide how interaction is to occur and how the evaluation process will work.

A good intern supervisor is more than just a good work supervisor. The main task of work supervisors is to see that the work gets done correctly, on time, and within budget. The main goal of intern supervisors is to help interns make the most of their learning opportunities. Intern supervisors are more than bosses. They're also coaches, teachers, advisors, role models, and sometimes mentors.

All of this ties back into the learning contract that we talk about earlier in this chapter and in Chapter 2. The learning contract spells out what the intern should be experiencing and learning during his or her placement. With traditional workers, supervisors are measured primarily by worker performance and secondarily by the growth and development of workers. For intern supervisors, these measures are reversed.

Being a supervisor and a mentor

To adapt an old phrase, "the many who can, do; the few who understand, teach." A supervisor's first goal as a mentor is to be a teacher and to create learning opportunities that are challenging and stimulating without being overwhelming and impossible. Here are some pointers for doing this:

- Think through carefully what projects and tasks you will assign to interns. Is there a payoff in experience and learning, or is it just busywork?

- Plan what you will say when you delegate each task. (Consult Chapter 12 on delegating skills.)

- Break major projects up into smaller, more doable parts or help interns do this themselves.

- Actually show interns how you start and complete the kind of task they will be assigned.

- Deliberately seek opportunities for interns to learn (meetings, workshops, community visits, customer visits, and so on).

- If interns will be writing on behalf of their supervisor, show them what kind of writing is expected.

- Share any pet peeves so that interns don't have to find these out the hard way.

As interns perform, supervisors should regularly monitor them and their progress. Yearly performance evaluations may be enough for regular workers (although it's really not), but interns need a much more regular and useful system of feedback. They will likely need feedback on a wide variety of measures beyond just their work output. We suggest different forms of feedback in Chapter 13. Supervisors must work to help empower interns to have personal and professional successes.

A good coach and teacher talks not only about failures but also about successes. Supervisors should help interns analyze what problems or choices they faced, what decisions they made, and the possible outcomes from each step in the process. In this way, interns can learn right from wrong and discover how to solve problems and make decisions in the future.

A good coach and teacher accepts that occasional trial and error and even failure are part of the learning process. It is almost always easier for supervisors just to do something themselves the first time. They know how to do it quickly and correctly after all. But the primary goal here is not to get things done but to help interns learn how to do the work themselves. And that doesn't happen if interns aren't encouraged to do things themselves and to understand their own thoughts and actions.

Being a good communicator

One constant theme in being an effective intern supervisor is the importance of communication skills. Many bosses are able to function even though they may communicate little or focus their communications only on the negative. Good coaches can't succeed like this, however. Intern supervisors must communicate positively and encouragingly to interns and listen for what interns are saying (and even for what they aren't saying).

Supervisors also have to interact with the other team player in this arrangement, the academic advisor. Some advisors are as talented and motivated as you are. Some of them aren't. If possible, establish a good working relationship with the intern's advisor because doing so will benefit all involved. Such a partnership is a two-way street. If the advisor hasn't reached out to you, make the first move and reach out to the advisor. Try to meet advisors halfway and to work together to do the best possible job for the interns.

Step 4: After the game is over

All good things, including internships, usually end. Supervisors should think about how the internship will end. Will it go out with a bang or a whimper? On a high note or a low note? One of the best ways to end on an upbeat note involves a good solid final evaluation and discussion of where interns started and how they have progressed during the internship.

Also consider the relationship between supervisor and intern after the internship ends. Is it okay for interns to keep in touch? If so, how? What about things like letters of recommendations? Will this be arranged before the internship ends? Will supervisors be willing to continue writing letters on behalf of interns? If internships end with the intern being there one day and gone the last, there can be no proper closure for that stage of the relationship. Nor can there be any groundwork for the future. Anticipate these issues before the internship ends and be prepared for them.

Final Thoughts: Bumps along the Road

We end this chapter with final thoughts and reflections on some of the more common problems that interns and their supervisors encounter during their time together.

Bump 1: The tortoise or the hare

When assigning a task to interns, a supervisor may think, "Well, that should keep them busy for a couple of days," only to have the interns reappear, the task completed in half the time. Or a supervisor may find that a two-day assignment drags into three days, four days, or more.

The best bet in these situations is to not only assign a task but to give an approximate amount of time the task is expected to take. In this way, supervisors can help interns get a feel for what their pace should be. If interns are running behind, they know they need to come to you. What if interns finish sooner than scheduled? A good strategy is to always have a couple of backup projects that are to be done on a time-available basis. That way, if interns find themselves with time on their hands, they already know what useful tasks they can do in the meantime.

Bump 2: The Tar baby or greased pig

Sometimes interns aren't prepared for working on their own (or even with others) on a given project. They may have a tendency to be constantly coming back to the supervisor for guidance, feedback, approval, and so on. In short, they're stuck to the supervisor as to a tar baby in the Uncle Remus tales. In contrast, some interns have a hard time knowing how far to go with their assignments or how often to check in, and supervisors can't seem to find these interns when they need to, even to see what they're doing. Such interns are like the proverbial greased pigs at the county fair. They're slippery. Now you see them; now you don't.

Along with a timeline for a given task, supervisors should consider pre-arranging a contact routine. Before turning interns loose, supervisors should create a system for guidance and feedback. Create an intermediary, a contact, whom the intern can go to with questions before they come to you. To make their questions more useful to them, require interns to have one possible answer or solution to each question or problem before they ask it. Set aside specific times during the day (or week) for regular feedback and questions.

Bump 3: How interns see the world

Here are some common misperceptions that interns may bring to the employing organization. Most of these can be cleared up beforehand through a good solid orientation. If they aren't dealt with directly, however, they can creep into every day intern behavior, creating all sorts of problems along the way:

✔ I operate on student time. In school I can generally come late or leave early if I need or want to, so why not here?

✔ I am only an intern. I should be grateful, therefore, for whatever comes my way and should put up with anything as a part of my gratitude just to be here.

✔ Intern is spelled VIP. Being one of the chosen few, I am entitled to certain special privileges and special treatment.

✔ I'm God's gift to the office. Oh boy, now I finally get to show what I can do! It's hard to be humble when you know as much as I do.

✔ I'm a door mouse personified. I'm just a lowly intern. What can I possibly do or say that would help?

Bump 4: How supervisors see the world

Supervisors and coworkers are also liable to have some skewed ideas about what it means to have an intern around. Here are a few examples:

✔ Interns are just like everyone else. Interns should already know how to do things, or know they don't know, and know how to learn as quickly as possible. After all, being on the job is exactly the same as being in a classroom.

✔ I am a warm and cuddly person. My interns will automatically feel comfortable in my presence and will comfortably come to me with any and all questions and concerns.

✔ Interns are expert judges of what they need to do and learn, as well as what they should have learned from what they just did.

✔ This is the kind of opportunity I never had, so those interns should realize how lucky they are just to be here. Therefore, they should always be eager and enthusiastic, never tired or anxious or nervous.

Because of these potential misperceptions, here are some of the key things regular employees need to understand about interns in their workplace.

✔ Interns are there to learn from regular employees — not to take their jobs.

✔ Interns are a valuable resource and not to be used primarily as menial labor. To help spread this message, distribute the intern's resume or a summary of their qualifications. After seeing that, employees may be inclined to take interns more seriously — but only if they aren't afraid of losing their jobs.

✔ Interns can and should take their turns doing routine tasks (along with everybody else), but they shouldn't be confined to routine work.

- ✔ Interns are primarily there to learn how to do the work and how to become a professional. Staff members act as teachers and coaches in this learning process, and they can benefit both from what they can learn from interns and also from teaching interns key parts of the job.

- ✔ This is a great opportunity for regular staff to be on their best professional behavior so that they can serve as good role models for interns.

- ✔ Interns need a few weeks to get oriented, so be patient.

- ✔ The work/professional relationship is the most important relationship. Employees should be polite to interns but should not lean over backwards to be liked. On the job, being respected is more important than being liked.

Even though we recommend that employers or supervisors simply tell employees what they need to know about the intern's role, employees may come up with these same ideas on their own during a focused discussion session facilitated by an employer or supervisor. An employer or supervisor might ask, for example, "Because we'll be getting a new intern (or group of interns) next week, what are your understandings and expectations about internships and how they should work?" This type of dialogue helps raise some potential concerns that employees may have and also lets them make some of the key points, such as "Interns are here to learn about this kind of work."

Being a successful intern supervisor is a little like being a tree farmer. Some results show right away, but in general, the full fruit of their labors isn't known for years to come. If supervisors want to know how they're dong, their best bet is to keep the communication channels open during and after the internship. Few things are more rewarding to any mentor or teacher, in a school or a work environment, than to have an intern let you know years later what a major difference you made in their lives.

Chapter 18

Creating a Successful Internship Program

This chapter serves as a guide to the organizations who want to explore, and we hope create, their own successful internship program. It is hardly a difficult process, but, like anything else, making it work takes proper planning and implementation. Many organizational leaders have thought about internships and even taken some haphazard steps in this direction, usually without much success.

What typically happens in these organizations is that someone brings up the idea of having some interns. After kicking the idea around, everyone agrees that it seems like a win-win situation, so the okay is given to start an internship. Then what? Someone gets assigned the task of running the program. So the person in charge makes a few quick calls to local colleges to let them know this employer is looking for interns. And who knows, a student or two may even call.

Now tell us, what organization could have rolled out any other new product or service in this way and had any kind of real success? Having a successful internship program isn't brain surgery, but it doesn't just happen either. It requires the same kind of thoughtful planning and implementation that any other successful venture does.

Why Have Interns?

Interns aren't the only ones to benefit from internships. Employers may also discover the advantages of having interns.

✔ First and foremost, internships are learning experiences — for both parties. Regular employees can often learn much from interns, who can provide different knowledge, skills, and perspectives without the costs of hiring new employees.

✔ Interns can also serve as a low-cost source of additional people power for an organization. There is no shame in an organization needing and wanting recently educated, eager, low-cost help. Because many organizations lack enough employees or enough trained employees to handle certain projects or tasks, employers often turn to interns. This creates valuable opportunities for work experience and learning. Interns shouldn't be seen, however, as a virtual replacement for needed regular workers. Such an attitude puts too heavy a burden on interns to carry the load and makes scarcer the number of regular employees from whom interns can learn.

✔ Using interns in an organization provides a system for screening potential employees. Many firms, agencies, and other kinds of organizations find that individuals who have proven to be top-performing interns also eventually make top-performing employees. Interns already know the ropes and routine in that organization. They probably know something about the kind of work to be done and have established working relationships with a number of employees. An internship is like a probationary period for a prospective employee without most of the tension and pressure. Even if an intern doesn't end up working for that same organization, a positive experience with that organization makes them a walking, talking advertisement for that company or agency.

✔ Interns who are part of academic institutions help employers to form links with these schools and with all the school's resources as well. Some business firms, government agencies, and nonprofit organizations use internships to form a broader, long-lasting relationship with schools that bridge out into training, research, degree programs, and the like.

Some internships may involve individuals who aren't students, setting up a direct relationship between the employer and the intern. Some employers prefer this arrangement so that they don't have to deal with schools at all. In some ways, this preference is understandable, and we certainly encourage any organization to be open to internship opportunities outside of only academically related ones.

At the same time, don't sell schools short. When organizations have an intern who is also a student, they gain more than they may think. In addition to gaining possible new partners and resources, employers also gain the potential advantage of having the school as a partner in developing their (intern) employees. Because many school internship programs have ongoing instruction and monitoring, interns frequently are participants in a variety of ongoing training sessions and workshops through their school. These types of programs only increase their value to employers.

Working with schools also gives employers a partner in dealing with interns. This partnership can help employers manage the overall internship program, prepare employees to serve as effective intern supervisors, and deal with internship issues as they arise. If an intern receives some form of academic credit for her experiences, this credit can also help serve as an extra motivator. Affiliation with schools also helps to ensure that standards will be maintained: that the internship experience will truly be a mutually beneficial arrangement and not an exploitative one. Employers may even receive some financial and legal benefits as well. For example, employers may be able to deduct all or a portion of the costs associated with their internship program and interns, and of course, employers will likely be paying for any work their interns do at less than market rates.

Step 1: Conduct an Internship Readiness Review

Interns can bring many benefits, such as new ideas and extra help, to an organization. To get these benefits, organizations must be sure that they're ready to launch a successful internship program. If not, they may end up getting more problems than benefits.

Organizations considering starting an internship program should start with a review of relevant, existing conditions and resources. We call this an Internship Readiness Review. Step 1 in the process requires employers to review systematically each of the following areas to make sure that they're ready for an internship program of their own.

Getting support from decision makers

Any project is only as good as its supporters. Does creating and operating an internship program have the support and backing of the organization's top people? Having interns is not a costly or time-consuming endeavor per se, but like anything else, it does involve using some resources and introducing some change. Neither is likely to happen or work out well without good support from above and below.

Finding committed and able people to work with interns

A successful internship program requires various key people, including an internship program coordinator and intern supervisors.

If an organization is hosting more than one intern at a time or expects to have interns on an ongoing basis, then it only makes sense to have an internship program coordinator, someone who oversees the organization's overall internship program as part of regular job duties. This coordinator is the go-to person for the schools, interns, and organization's intern supervisors.

The organization's intern supervisors are the real keys to making internships successful. Who is going to select the staff who will serve as supervisors? Which people have the right stuff to be good intern supervisors? Because an internship is a learning experience, being a supervisor requires someone with the time, energy, and willingness to provide the kind of guidance and mentoring needed. Even then, will the organization provide supervisors with the support they need to develop and maximize both the intern and the intern's contributions to the firm? Will the organization perceive serving as an intern supervisor as a valuable service or an ignored burden?

Identifying where interns are needed

Employers should be thinking about where interns are most needed. They need to decide where, on what projects, and in what areas an intern would be of the most value to the employer (and to the intern). Employers also need to determine whether a good potential supervisor is available in the locations targeted as places where interns are needed. If there is no real need for extra help and at the level an intern can provide, the internship may end up being busywork and a waste of time.

What about timing? Are there particular times of the year when interns would be more or less valuable? Or could they be used year-round as available? Is the work process oriented (for example, manufacturing or product testing), or is it more project oriented, meaning that interns could take on specific projects or parts of projects over time?

There is no single right or best answer to these kinds of questions. Employers don't even need to have a specific plan in mind. What they do need is regard for interns as potentially valuable resources and — even more importantly — as people with dreams, ambitions, and feelings like the rest of us.

Some organizations do quite well by having interns rotate across departments in a rather systematic way on a regular schedule. Others are more free-flowing, allowing interns to work on tasks and projects as they arise. Either approach can work as long as the emphasis is on providing interns with a diverse, rich learning experience. And either approach can fail if interns are an afterthought.

Considering the cost

What financial resources are available for the internship program? First and foremost is the question of whether to pay interns. Although employers usually have no legal obligation to pay interns, in many fields (such as finance, engineering, and information technology), good people are at a premium. Employers may have to pay to get good interns. In other cases, interns may get no pay, but they do receive travel and tuition expenses. Employers also need to know what the competition pays to remain competitive on intern pay and benefits. Potential expenses include the following:

- Pay, benefits, or expenses for interns (may include tuition)
- Salary or extra pay for the internship coordinator
- Extra pay or perks for intern supervisors
- Orientation and other training costs
- Printing of brochures, handbooks, or other materials
- Field trips, tours, and other enrichment activities for interns

Deciding whether interns fit in

What are the employing organization's goals and objectives? What are the goals for an internship program? How well do these mesh? Is the organization goal-ready for interns? Some organizations, for instance, consider people as interchangeable parts to be used up until a cheaper part can be obtained. An internship program wouldn't fit well in such a climate. Interns would likely be used as lower-cost or no-cost labor to replace regular employees. Such a situation invites frustration and resentment all around.

How about the organization's recruiting strategy? Is the employer looking for raw talent and energy to pitch in, or is it looking for specific skills and abilities? Does the overall recruiting strategy view interns as potential future employees, or is that a minor consideration? If you have more than one intern in more than one position, then all of these hiring issues may be relevant.

Step 2: Deciding Whether to Proceed

Step 2 in the process is to make a specific go or no-go decision. After looking at all the factors in the internship readiness review, the organization needs to decide whether having an intern program makes sense. Such a decision is best arrived at after lots of discussion and consultation with all those involved.

Remember that "one size fits all" doesn't apply to an internship program. Organizations can go full tilt or ease into internships. Options include the following:

- ✔ **Trial run (small-scale effort):** Organizations that choose this option place one or two interns at a time in selected departments depending on need and supervisors' interest and ability. Other features of this option are a limited or informal orientation, primarily on-the-job training, and reliance on the school's evaluation system.

- ✔ **Gung-ho (comprehensive internship program):** Organizations launch a multi-intern, multi-department program with an overall internship program coordinator, assign and train supervisors, conduct orientation and training sessions, and have their own evaluation system — the works!

This decision isn't an either/or choice. Different degrees of size, scope, expense, and quality fall in between these extremes. Many employers take the incremental approach: starting small but carefully, and then building and refining their internship program over time.

Step 3: Getting the Internship Program Up and Running

After deciding to proceed, employers must take several important steps to get the internship up and running. These steps include doing some research on internships, developing descriptions of what the intern position entails, getting the infrastructure in place, and recruiting interns.

Doing some research

Even if organizations haven't done this when considering whether to attempt an internship program, they should do some homework of their own before trying to get any interns. Here are a couple suggestions:

- ✔ **Find out what other employers in their region and industry are doing regarding internships.** Where do they get their interns? What do interns do? How and how much are they paid? What types of orientations and other training sessions are used? This homework can be done via visits, interviews, phone calls, Internet searches, library searches, and the like.

> ✔ **Do some scouting around on the schools or other sources that may likely supply interns.** What kinds of students do they have (younger/older, undergraduate/graduate, liberal arts/specialized)? What academic programs are offered? Are internships required? Are there other ways to pay for interns, such as federal work study? Do schools have an internship agreement or learning contract to draw upon? Do they have any position descriptions? Are controls in place to make sure that interns get prepared, get advice, and get evaluated?

Notice that we advise doing general information gathering before making a specific request for interns. These scouting trips give organizations a lay of the land and help them get their act together before plunging in.

Developing a position description

A next step is to create a semiformal type of position description. Here is one of the first places that academic partners can help. If employers are working with one or more schools, employers should consult them. Some schools have a central office for career services or experiential education that oversees all internships. Although virtually all schools have a career center, some internships are handled by individual departments. So an employer looking for someone with writing skills should check with the communication, journalism, or English departments. Nearly all business, health, and public administration programs have strong internship programs that send students to business, government, and nonprofit organizations. Programs in social work, counseling, architecture, and computer science typically have internships of some type.

The local school liaisons may well be able to supply employers with sample job descriptions from other internships. They can also help with internship contracts, evaluations, and other issues as needed. Don't think of internships as some sort of new and strange ground. Several professions and organizations deal with these matters on a routine basis. For example, student nurses are required to perform a series of nursing internships in order to graduate and receive their licenses to practice. The same holds true for several allied health professions. Student teachers also perform one or more teaching internships as part of the required curriculum.

Position descriptions for interns require a different focus than regular job descriptions. Specifically, because internships are educational experiences first and foremost, the primary focus of the position descriptions should be on . . .

✔ What interns will do during their internship (types of projects, tasks, activities)

✔ What interns will learn during their internship (knowledge and skills acquired)

An important but secondary focus should be on . . .

- ✔ Qualifications needed for interns (skills and knowledge the employer wants)
- ✔ Hours and work routine (days and hours required, location of workplace)
- ✔ Compensation (pay, benefits, tuition, expenses paid)

When employers have contacted us to get an intern, we advise them to put together a good description that includes this kind of information. It makes it so much easier to get students or others interested in that internship. These days, sending it out via e-mail makes it easier to circulate to prospective interns — as does posting it on a Web site.

Getting the infrastructure in place for interns

We strongly recommend that employers get their house in order before even recruiting interns. By doing that, employers don't have to scurry around when interns are already there, and having the pieces in place helps recruit interns. Interns, especially the informed, active interns most worth having, are attracted to organizations that are well prepared to take interns. The following sections explain how employers can get their house in order.

Deciding who will have overall responsibility for the internship program

Employers need to figure out which employee will be in charge of the internship program. A new internship coordinator? The personnel department? The training department? CEO? Assistant to the CEO? The size of the organization, the number of interns, and the priority given to interns are factors to consider when appointing someone to oversee the internship program. In small firms or nonprofits, the CEO may be the ideal person to coordinate this effort. In larger organizations, someone else may need to be identified, or a new position may need to be created.

Recruiting and training supervisors

Employers must identify employees who have the experience, ability, and willingness to supervise interns. All intern supervisors need some training, even employees who have supervised interns before. They can help the new supervisors.

Developing an orientation program

The day that your interns appear on the scene isn't the time to start thinking about how to orient them. Employers should have an orientation plan in place before they arrive. Remember that orientation refers to more than just the initial session in the first day or two. Orientation means the internship-long effort to acclimate interns to the organization and the profession.

Making arrangements to get interns compensated

It often takes several weeks to get interns on the payroll, pay their tuition bills, or handle other forms of compensation. So the systems must be in place ahead of time. Nothing demoralizes an intern more than waiting several months to get any money while their bills are mounting.

Sometimes pay comes directly from the employer. In other cases, employers may avoid legal or union problems if the interns are paid by their school. Consider this example. An organization, let's call it Acme Enterprises, entered into an arrangement with Mid-State University for the university to supply a variety of interns. The interns thus were employed by the university, not by Acme. The University received the "wages" from Acme and paid interns in the form of scholarships. Acme never had to put interns on the payroll, collect unemployment insurance, or do some other things legally required for employees. These are some of the same advantages that occur when employers use temp agencies to supply workers. The interns in this case were not only "working" for the University; they were also enrolled in the appropriate course to receive credit for their internship experience. One down-side: Making such arrangements with universities can take even longer lead-time than handling payroll and other logistics in-house.

Making sure the legal issues are addressed

Legal issues may arise with interns just as they can with any other workers. Employers should consult their attorney early on to make sure that they're on sound legal ground on issues such as employment status and liability if interns come to work for their organization.

We're not attorneys, and we don't presume to act in that capacity. Employers should consult their attorneys on these matters just as they would in creating any new class of workers. We can, however, discuss some general guidelines. Employers should assume that all labor laws that apply to full- or part-time employees also apply to interns, whether they're paid or not. For some silly reason, some employers seem to regard student interns working on their property as something less than or different from other employees. Just because they're interns doesn't mean that they should be abused, harassed, placed at risk, or discriminated against. This advice should all sound like reasonable, common sense. But both reason and common sense can be hard to find in some work settings. If employers hear anyone start a sentence with, "Well, they are only interns," this should raise a red flag that something is wrong.

Although employers don't have to pay interns, if they do, they should follow the same guidelines that the Fair Labor Standards Act applies for other employees. For example, if an employer provides training to regular workers for a given task, they should provide the training for interns too. Likewise, it is just as proper for interns to complete the same confidentiality agreements that regular workers complete.

Recruiting interns: Finding them and getting them to apply

Our advice in the last chapter on recruiting applies here, but the perspective is reversed. The following sections present recruiting from the employer's point of view.

Recruiting through schools

Most interns come via school programs. Although it would be nice if all schools followed a single recruiting pattern, they don't. The best bet for employers is to follow a two-pronged approach. First, they should contact the staff at the school's career center, which is designed to help students reach decisions about their future careers and prepare them for the job market. Career center employees can work with employers in establishing and operating an internship program.

At the same time, employers should look at their position descriptions and consider which academic majors are likely to have those qualifications. The second prong of the approach then should be to make direct contact with each of the academic schools or departments identified. Departments or schools, such as schools of engineering, business, law, nursing, and social work, also have their own internship options, and they too can help with a program. While targeting the obvious majors and fields, employers should still be flexible and creative in their intern recruitment. Some of the most successful business leaders, for example, have come from liberal arts backgrounds.

Yet a third recruiting option is for employers to get on the invitation list for any intern fairs to be held on campus and submit their placements to the school's internship listings, both the paper and the electronic versions.

How many schools should employers work with? Well, it depends. It depends on the size of the employing organization and the number of interns wanted. It also depends on the organization's location, how many schools are in the vicinity, and the kinds of internships being offered.

Small organizations with a few intern positions may be quite satisfied to work with just a few schools in their general vicinity, especially if theirs is an unpaid internship. On the other hand, many larger employers — for example, Disney World in Florida — operate a college internship program that recruits thousands of interns from nearly every state and many foreign countries.

Recruiting through trade and professional associations

Employers may find it helpful to make a list of professional and trade associations. These groups are eager to help their student members, and they usually have both national and local chapters through which employers can advertise.

Recruiting via internship directories and Web sites

Print and electronic versions of internship directories provide contact information for employers offering internships. When posting internship opportunities, employers should target more than one directory or listing service but should use only directories or clearinghouses likely to produce the kinds of interns needed. For example, employers seeking interns in business and economics should contact AIESEC (www.aiesec.org), which runs exchange programs in those fields in over 80 countries. But they would be less likely to find business interns via International Association for the Exchange of Students for Technical Experience (www.iaeste.org), which covers 70 countries but focuses on engineering and technical internships. Dozens of Web sites like these offer employers the chance to post their internships. For most on-line clearinghouses or directories there is no cost to employer, but checking the terms for each site is advisable. To get started, see Chapter 5 for useful Web sites.

Recruiting via word of mouth

Word of mouth is a most popular and often most effective recruiting source. Employers should put out the word wherever possible by letting everyone — current workers, suppliers, social organizations, you name it — know that they're looking for interns. Some of the best interns may be related to or live near an organization's employees. The more people who learn about intern opportunities, the more that potential interns are likely to apply.

Selecting interns

The last step in the process of launching an internship program should be a familiar one for employers: selecting the new people (interns). Some basic steps in any good selection process also apply to picking interns.

Reviewing qualifications

Employers should review academic records but focus on more than courses and grades. Other experiences, including extra-curricular activities, volunteering, part-time jobs, and other experience that is relevant to the internship, are also important. Whoever makes the hiring decisions for the employers (a committee or one individual) should also assess whatever work samples (reports, designs, videos, computer programs, and so on) are required of applicants. These can often tell more about potential interns than their grade average.

Considering references

We advise employers to require references for their intern candidates because they provide insight into the candidates' character and abilities. Even if candidates pick references likely to boast about them the most, references are often revealing. A reference, for example, that doesn't go into any specifics about the candidate generally reflects a lack of enthusiasm or lack of contact with the candidate. References that are inappropriate (someone's mother, for example) show a lack of maturity and savvy about how things work. Employers should call the candidate's references and other people (with permission of the candidate) to get a more candid opinion. We're always amazed that so few employers (even when hiring full-time professionals) bother to call references to verify what's in the written reference.

Interviewing intern candidates

When interviewing interns, employers should maintain the same high level of professionalism that they do when interviewing people for other positions. Pointers on interviewing that we give in Chapter 6 apply to both prospective interns and interviewers.

The biggest difference between interviewing for a traditional position and interviewing for an internship is that both sides are usually less familiar with internships overall. For that reason, interviewers must find out as much as they can, before the interview, about the employer's internship position, procedures, the school's requirements about credits, and so on. Time frames are also an issue here. Student interns often must work within a given academic calendar, so interviewers need to know these dates and act in a reasonable and timely manner. Another difference is that candidates for internships typically have less experience in interviewing than do candidates for regular positions. As a result, interviewers need to be more tolerant and more encouraging than usual. But interviewers still should expect professional behavior on the part of intern candidates and coach them on that, if appropriate. Otherwise, interviews should be nearly identical to those with other employees.

Step 4: Operating an Ongoing Internship Program

Once an internship program is launched and up and running, employers need to keep it running smoothly and effectively. Ongoing operation of an internship program typically involves checking and fine-tuning the internal parts of the program and maintaining good relationships with interns and the schools that sent them.

Monitoring and upgrading internal components

Keeping the internal machinery of an internship running smoothly involves continuous attention to the internal ingredients: overall coordination, supervision, orientation and training, and evaluation. Here are some of the tasks:

- Continually checking to see whether the program is well coordinated and taking steps if it isn't.

- Checking the evaluations of supervisors and talking with them about the internship experience. What should be done differently? Some supervisors may need to be replaced or get further training.

- Assessing orientation and training of interns (and supervisors), upgrading and fine-tuning where needed.

- Continually evaluating the evaluation system to make sure that it's working. This means not only revising the evaluation *process* when necessary but also assessing overall intern *performance*. If interns consistently aren't producing the quantity and quality of work expected, the evaluation process may be lax or misguided. Or expectations may be too high.

Maintaining an ongoing relationship with school partners

Employers who are part of a working arrangement with a school need to maintain an ongoing relationship with several types of partners.

Overall school internship coordinators

Many schools have an Office of Career Services, an Office for Experiential Education, an Office for Service Learning, or even an Office of Intern Services (we hope not an Office of Intern Affairs!) that coordinates all the internship programs. Employers should discover who this central actor is (if there is one) and establish regular contact not only with that person but also will all the academic partners. Doing so helps prevent problems and increases the likelihood that good interns will come the employer's way.

Deans, department heads, and key faculty members

Employers should maintain ties with faculty members in fields related to their business. For example, corporations should maintain ties with the deans of business Schools, and law firms should stay in touch with law school deans.

This networking advice applies also to assistant deans, program directors, and others who may actually have more control over internship programs. If specific faculty members are prominent in your field, they may be in the best position to refer outstanding interns. Employers shouldn't confine their contact to academic administrators.

School intern advisors

Students who complete internships for academic credit typically do so under the direction of a school intern advisor. This person is normally a full-time faculty or staff member of the school. Usually they are selected and prepared for these responsibilities, but not always.

The main role of the intern advisor is to watch over the student and be the bridge between the student and the employer. The faculty intern advisor works with the employer (usually through the intern supervisor) and the student to develop the learning contract. This contract outlines what interns are supposed to do, what they are to learn from their efforts, and how they will be evaluated.

Daily job-related issues are primarily handled by the organizational intern supervisor, who is the employee serving as the intern's on-the-job supervisor. Thus the supervisor also needs to be a key player in this three-way relationship.

In the real world, some faculty advisors are strong, and others are weak. Some people take these responsibilities very seriously and work hard to interact with employers, work supervisors, and students on an ongoing basis. Others, as a result of lack of training, know-how, time, or incentive, act in absentia. Employers may not see or hear from them throughout the internship. Employers need to know what is expected of academic intern advisors and what can be realistically expected from the advisors to their interns.

Employers must make sure ahead of time that they're aware of the specifics of their student's internship arrangements, including knowing who the student advisor is, what the academic responsibilities of a student intern are, and what pertinent documents and forms, such as the internship agreement and the learning contract, are needed. To understand the role of the academic advisor and intern supervisor more fully, please read Chapter 17.

Keeping in contact with intern supervisors on the job

The other side of the intern coin is the supervision that the intern gets from the organization itself. One of the most common problems that arises in an internship situation is that organizational supervisors are improperly trained or briefed for their role in the process. Orientation for intern supervisors is often a quick five-minute meeting when supervisors are introduced to the new interns who will be working with them for the next few weeks (or months).

Organizational intern supervisors need to be a full part of the process. They need to know who the faculty advisor is and to understand what the school and the advisor expect from both the student and the supervisor. Supervisors also need to know about what is expected in terms of working with and evaluating interns. Chapter 17 can help prepare employees to be successful intern supervisors.

Working with interns on the job

The more employers treat interns like any other employees, the better off things will be — if the employer has what author Peter Senge calls a learning organization. In his book, *The Fifth Discipline: The Art and Practice of the Learning Organization,* Senge describes a *learning organization* as one in which learning is a priority from top to bottom. Constant learning is seen as essential to coping with constant change. The reverse of this is those organizations that just plop new workers down at their desks after a five-minute walk around the building! The emphasis in those organizations lies in workers doing their jobs — not on learning and upgrading their capabilities.

New workers (and new interns) need competent orientations and training in order to be effective. Some employers go to great lengths to do so. "Mickey D's" has McDonald's University, and Disney has Disney U to help new workers become familiar with the history and culture of their organizations as well as the more mundane matters of day-to-day work.

Interns in particular may need a bit of orientation to the real work world. For a few, this may be their first real on-the-job experience, and they may need a bit of adjustment. Current workers may need their own orientation about the role of these new interns and how to treat (and not treat) them. Chapters 7 and 17 give more details on intern orientations.

Interns, like other new workers, need to receive some basic training for day-to-day survival and functioning. They need to be socialized so that they feel like they're a part of the organization. They need to know what's expected of them and how they will work to accomplish these goals. In short, they (along with all other employees) need to be treated like intelligent, useful members of the organizational team.

Interns should be told sooner rather than later (even in the interview) whether the organization tries to use internships as early screening and recruiting opportunities for future workers. Interviewers could say, for example, "Many of our successful interns later go on to full-time positions with our organization" or "While we generally do not hire our own interns, our successful interns are highly sought by others in our field."

The internship experience can help interns to develop their own career goals and strategies. Good feedback about their work and assurance of the employer's future support is vital for interns to set realistic goals for employment, however. For instance, how highly (or lowly) does the intern rate? Can the intern expect a letter of reference from the employer? Can the intern count on the employer to offer help in networking for future positions? The answers do not have to be yes, but interns should not be left wondering or be left assuming that silence actually means future support in getting employed once the internship is over.

Finally, employers need to consider how to get feedback from interns. Many firms fail to get feedback from their current or former workers about the organization overall or about their supervisors in particular. This is a true waste of a priceless opportunity to get answers to general questions like these: Is the internship program meeting its goals? Who are your better supervisors and what makes them so well regarded? What problems exist in the program, and what improvements might be made? Employers won't know if they don't ask. Employers can get feedback through interns' written evaluations during the internship and exit interviews at the end of the internship. Chapter 13 gives far more guidance on evaluations of interns and by interns and lists specific questions employers can ask interns.

Working with intern supervisors

Because intern supervisors generally are delegated the day-to-day contact with interns, they, too, need to be properly oriented and trained so that they can function successfully with their new responsibility. Employers should select organizational supervisors on the basis of their special roles as teachers and mentors — and not merely because they're the least busy people in the office. The proper expression of the old saying is, "The many who can, do; the few who understand *and* can explain, should teach."

Intern supervisors are the keys not only to interns' successful experience during their internship but also perhaps to their overall growth and development. Supervisors who fail to communicate or provide feedback, fail to challenge or support their interns, and perhaps even resent their role as supervisor can wreck not only an internship opportunity but an entire career. By checking periodically with intern supervisors, employers signal that internships are important and keep supervisors on the ball. Chapter 17 covers the basics of being an intern supervisor. Employers should join supervisors in preparing for the end of the internship experience to make sure that interns finish with a bang, not a whimper. See Chapter 15 for more on how to do that.

Parting Advice for Employers

Hosting interns means far more than grabbing cheap or free labor. Internships have become the "farm systems" for many highly successful organizations in the business, government, and nonprofit sectors. Internships often attract the best and brightest students, give them a taste of that workplace, and, if the experience is positive, motivate interns to stay on in a longer-term capacity. Internships build goodwill for the employer, link to other resources, and help keep the organization learning and growing. If internships and interns are taken seriously, the rewards are many. But if done haphazardly or badly, internships can be an aggravation and waste of resources.

Employers *and* interns the most at stake in this process. But employers have more control over the internship process than do interns. Employers, therefore, should operate in active mode — like interns — instead of sitting back and assuming that everything will work right. We aren't advising employers to meddle in an internship program well run by their designated employees. But we emphasize that strong, enlightened support from the top makes a world of difference to the morale and performance of supervisors, interns, and employees.

Part VII
The Part of Tens

The 5th Wave   By Rich Tennant

"Our indirect pay package includes your choice of company car or company skateboard."

In this part . . .

Every *For Dummies* book ends with top-ten lists. We give you the ten habits that shape and define a successful intern. We also point out ten mistakes to avoid as an intern.

Chapter 19

Ten Internship Mistakes to Avoid

In This Chapter

▶ Avoiding mistakes before getting an internship
▶ Balancing an internship with other parts of your life

Throughout *Internships For Dummies,* we give you pointers on what to do and how to do it. That's the essence of a how-to book like this one. But recognizing the most common mistakes interns make can be just as important as getting pointers about the best way to do things. Recognizing the potential landmines ahead of time helps you to avoid those landmines, saving you untold problems and frustration. Spotting and avoiding the ten mistakes we talk about here can put you on your way to internship success.

Having no specific goals for your internship

A first mistake interns make is having no specific goals for their internship. Such interns either take an internship because their school requires it or because they think it is the thing to do. Their friends are "doing internships." But without doing any soul-searching to identify what they need to accomplish through an internship, such passive interns are likely to drift through their internship. They may gain some experience and learning along the way but have no idea whether they are getting out of it what they should because they have no goals. Interns with no goals (or fuzzy goals) are more likely to end up with an internship that is inappropriate for them and to get minimum benefit from that internship.

Waiting for internship opportunities to fall in your lap

The number of terrific internships grows each year. But so does the number of qualified applicants for these prized plums. And employers can be more selective about whom they pick as interns, especially if interns tend to be hired as full-time employees. Offers won't come unless you have actually applied, and that takes effort. Students (or others) who wait for that special opportunity to fall out of the sky have a long wait coming. Remember that an internship is really a job. You wouldn't expect to get a job offer without searching for opportunities, applying for them, interviewing, and considering the offer. Passive interns wait for others to give them breaks instead of making those breaks happen. They sit around waiting for their few leads to strike gold. And, if they get an offer, passive interns take the first internship that comes their way — even if it doesn't fit their needs and goals.

Ignoring your school's internship policies and intern advisor

Another set of intern miscues involves ignoring school internship policies and advisors. Failing to register for the correct course may mean you don't get credit for all the work you put in as an intern. Failing to sign the proper paperwork might cause legal problems later on and give the wrong impression before you barely get started. Failing to know what your school requires you to do, to complete those requirements, and to submit that work on time may result in just that — failing. The same holds true for ignoring advisors. Your school advisor can be a strong ally who offers advice on how to succeed, intervenes on your behalf if absolutely necessary, and writes a recommendation for you. But that won't happen if you never contact your intern advisor or ignore any advice you get. It doesn't pay to turn your ally into an adversary.

Getting off on the wrong foot

With parades, speeches, interviews, and internships, first and last impressions have the most impact. New interns get off on the wrong foot by missing or drifting through their orientation, passing up any chances to orient themselves, and acting like a know-it-all before learning the ropes. Other sure-fire wrong-foot mistakes include setting yourself apart from other interns or trying to organize interns against management without knowing what the issues are. Wrong-foot errors tend to occur when interns fail to use the crucial first days to listen more than they talk, to read, observe, and learn all they can about their new work environment before making decisive moves. Active interns don't sit around and wait for someone else to make something happen. Active interns conscientiously use that critical feeling-out period to learn the policies, procedures, culture, customs, and dynamics of their new workplace, which allows them to be intelligently active later on.

Violating your employer's policies

Violating the employer's policies can also get you into trouble. Being constantly late for work, failing to report absences in advance, and misusing equipment create a reputation of not caring or being unreliable. Violating other policies such as those involving sexual harassment, confidentiality, and safety can result in reprimand or dismissal. And this blot on your record can haunt you when applying for other internships or jobs. Be sure you understand that the phrase "ignorance is bliss" doesn't apply to your situation. Violating an employer's policy from not knowing about the policy or failing to understand it can cause as much trouble as willingly violating that policy. To avoid this trouble, learn what the policies are, make sure you understand them, and follow them. There may be some policies that don't appear necessary, but follow them anyway. There probably is a reason for these policies, and if not a reason, you can be sure there is a consequence for violating them.

Failing to be a good colleague

Good colleagues support each other, listen to other colleagues, and cooperate when necessary. Good colleagues show willingness to share in the mundane tasks and pitch in during a crisis. Good colleagues are generally pleasant, helpful, and trustworthy. Good colleagues attract good colleagues and even help others to be better colleagues. Bad colleagues, on the other hand, tend to be irritable, critical of coworkers, indifferent to their feelings or needs, indiscreet, and missing-in-action when a crisis hits or the unpleasant tasks get shared. Good colleagues tend to be more successful, have more influence, attract more contacts, and generate more opportunities than do bad colleagues. Remember that how you act on the job is part of the job.

Being out of balance with your life

Some interns make the mistake of sloughing off on their internship work to do their schoolwork, improve their social life, or even put in hours in a dead-end job that pays minimum wage. Other interns become so motivated and consumed by their internship that schoolwork, health, family life, social life, and everything else suffers. Either extreme or any other drastic imbalance in your life invites disaster. Something or someone will suffer for this lack of balance — and that someone is usually you! Either your internship performance or school performance will likely suffer or your health or something else will suffer if you go full-tilt at school *and* work. This is one reason many internship and cooperative programs don't require an academic load at the same time as the internship or co-op placement. Because internships usually offer change from studies or from routine jobs, they can frequently add balance and variety to your life. But internships can't provide balance if you go overboard with any part of your life to the neglect of others.

Alienating your on-the-job intern supervisor

Interns generally have the most contact with their on-the-job supervisors. Usually, only one person is assigned to supervise an intern; less frequently, an intern may have more than one. The supervisor usually is the one who gives interns assignments, evaluates their work, and helps them connect with other workers and professionals. If interns get references from their internship, they tend to be from the supervisor. Why would interns want to alienate the very person who has so much control over them? Beats us, but it happens. Interns alienate their supervisors by bothering them too often over trivial issues or the opposite extreme of leaving supervisors in the dark about where the interns are and what they are doing. Other things that bug supervisors include being disrespectful, being untrustworthy, and only thinking about oneself. Don't forget the political ways to alienate a supervisor: trying to go over the supervisor's head or trying to undermine the supervisor's authority. Interns who alienate their supervisors do so at their own risk.

Failing to bridge to the next career opportunity

Some interns do their homework to find a good internship and get a fast start. They may also work competently and get along with colleagues. They risk blowing all this good effort, however, if they don't think about the next link in their career and work toward that opportunity. All internships end. The ending can come when the semester is over, the intern runs out of money and has to go home, when the intern is hired for full-time work, or for some other reason. Passive interns tend to coast through their internships day by day without thinking ahead. When the internship ends, passive interns start thinking about what they will do next. But by then, they are probably doomed to no follow-up opportunities or to poor opportunities because they hadn't built the bridge to other opportunities. Active interns work at outperforming other interns, being good colleagues, building a network, scouting follow-up opportunities, and building sound relationships with people who may hire them or recommend them to other employers.

Acting passively throughout your internship

The biggest mistake interns can make is to be passive interns. Because passive interns fail to take responsibility and initiative for their own internship, they commit many mistakes like the previous nine. The passive approach leads to no real reflection on goals; a minimal, haphazard search for an internship; a tentative start on the job; lackluster day-to-day performance; limited contacts; and no follow-up opportunities or limited opportunities. The biggest gain you can get from *Internships For Dummies* is to learn how to be an active intern and then go ahead and be one.

Chapter 20

Top Ten Habits of Successful Interns

In This Chapter

▶ Doing your job well
▶ Keeping your eyes and ears open

There are two kinds of successful people in life: On one hand, you have the one-hit wonders who through some combination of being in just the right place at just the right time manage to luck into the occasional success. On the other hand, when you look at the people who are successful time after time, in spite of the sporadic failure or bump in the road, you see some patterns. Call them habits, if you will, because they are shared patterns of behavior that hold true time after time. You too can develop this same set of habits in yourself to help you become a successful intern. The fantastic bonus is that this same set of habits that can make you a successful intern can also make you successful in the rest of your life.

Work hard; play hard

Work hard. Play hard. Give it your all. If it's worth doing it's worth doing well. All of these say the same thing. Successful interns are not the passive minimalists who do no more than they are asked to do or must do. Successful interns put in a 110-percent effort most of the time.

Never settle for less than your best

Never become complacent. Successful interns follow the Japanese concept of *Kaizen,* or continuous improvement. When something goes well, don't just bask in the glow; analyze it to see why things went well and how you can do even better the next time. When things do not go well, don't sulk, but again look to see what you need to change to improve.

Carpe diem! Seize the day! Seize the moment!

Successful interns look at situations, analyze options, then they make decisions and keep on going. Don't be sidetracked by what you should or ought to do. Give things your best shot and then move on. Look back only to learn not to worry about failure or blame.

Focus on the here and now, especially with other people

Successful interns stay tuned in to the here and now. When they are with another person they give 100 percent of themselves, not allowing themselves to be distracted by the past or the future. These interns never seem to be dashing madly about from task to task and yet they get so much done. They don't waste their time; they use it, and they focus on and enjoy whatever they are spending their time on at that moment.

Keep things in perspective

Successful interns keep things in perspective. This means that they are able to stay relaxed and focused when times are good and when times are stressful. "Don't panic!" is their motto. Successful interns are the ones we all want to be around because they never lose their sense of humor, patience, or ability to realize that no matter how great the crisis, this too shall pass.

Be active rather than passive

Successful interns function actively, not passively. They get the information they need and act. They don't procrastinate. When something needs doing, they do it. Successful interns are the ones who are flexible, quick to respond to new opportunities and to new problems. In fact, successful interns anticipate problems and try to avoid or minimize problems while anticipating and acting on opportunities.

Tune in to your sense of wonder

Successful interns are tuned into the world and notice new events, new situations, and hence new opportunities. It is this sense that sees a new medicine in a mold spore rather than a failed experiment or sees a major business trend or opportunity in a simple children's game. Strive to see the potential in an opportunity rather than seeing it just as it already is.

Know how to learn

Successful interns know how to learn and how to apply their learning, and they never stop learning. Being successful is more than just learning things by rote and repetition. The real world requires you to be creative and able to develop new answers and new processes to deal with the problems and possibilities that lay before you. Look at the people around you and see who are the ones active in their professional associations, constantly reading new books and journals, attending conferences, and the like. Successful, active interns are active learners.

Join forces with others

Successful interns don't operate in a vacuum. They know that life is a team sport and so they are always networking, but not in a manipulative way. This is not about being the always-on, life-of-the-party person but instead about being the one-you-can-count-on person. Successful interns, because they listen to other people and help other people, are seen as valuing others and hence being of value to others. When a need arises, successful interns know whom to call and they know their calls will be returned. Successful interns know this because they faithfully respond when other people reach out to them.

Strive for synergy

Synergy is the condition where qualities work well together, are in balance, and reinforce each other. Successful interns are synergistic. In simple terms this means that successful interns work hard to strengthen and develop and use each of these abilities in their daily lives until they become ingrained habits, a part of their personality. And in strengthening one habit they strengthen other habits and make them more effective. Successful interns are self-made. They continually work for their success and know it is not a right of birth, nor one of passage. Successful interns actively work to become successful *people* and to stay that way throughout their careers and their lives.

Index

• •

FOR DUMMIES
BOOK REGISTRATION

We want to hear from you!

Visit **dummies.com** to register this book and tell us how you liked it!

✔ Get entered in our monthly prize giveaway.

✔ Give us feedback about this book — tell us what you like best, what you like least, or maybe what you'd like to ask the author and us to change!

✔ Let us know any other *For Dummies* topics that interest you.

Your feedback helps us determine what books to publish, tells us what coverage to add as we revise our books, and lets us know whether we're meeting your needs as a *For Dummies* reader. You're our most valuable resource, and what you have to say is important to us!

Not on the Web yet? It's easy to get started with *Dummies 101: The Internet For Windows 98* or *The Internet For Dummies* at local retailers everywhere.

Or let us know what you think by sending us a letter at the following address:

For Dummies Book Registration
Dummies Press
10475 Crosspoint Blvd.
Indianapolis, IN 46256

™
...FOR DUMMIES

BESTSELLING
BOOK SERIES